A Gift of Blue Water

Memoirs of a Family Sailing Adventure

Danica Cowan

RITZ BOOKS

A Gift of Blue Water: Memoirs of a Family Sailing Adventure
Copyright © 2025 Danica Cowan

Paperback ISBN: 978-1-960460-38-7
Kindle ISBN: 978-1-960460-39-4

All rights reserved. No portion of this book may be reproduced, distributed, transmitted, or utilized in any form, or by any electronic, mechanical, or other means, without the prior written permission from the publisher. This book is for entertainment purposes only. Each person has unique physical, emotional, and spiritual needs; and the content in this book is not intended to replace or interrupt the reader's relationship with a physician or other mental health professional. If medical or legal advice, or other expert assistance is required, the services of a competent professional person should be sought. Although the publisher has made every effort to ensure the information in this book was correct at press time, authors are responsible for their own words. The publisher hereby disclaims any liability for any loss, damage, or disruption caused by this book, and will not be held responsible for any adverse effects resulting from the use of the suggestions outlined in this book.

Published by Ritz Books
Writing coaching, cover design, and interior layout by Steph Ritz

Ritz Books guides authors to create books, courses, stage talks, websites, marketing, and educational materials for professional development, self-improvement, and online learning. We support entrepreneurs, business professionals, and industry leaders to voice their passions – with ghostwriting, editing, graphic design, copywriting, photography, publishing, and more. Do you have a book idea, or have you already written a book manuscript you'd like us to consider publishing?

Please visit www.RITZBOOKS.com to learn more.
Or email Steph@StephRitz.com to get started today.

Dedication

To my parents and to my son. This book is a very long thank you note to my parents, and a love letter to my son. Here's to all the adventures – past, present, and future.

Introduction

This book was a labor of love over two decades in the making.

Memory is imperfect and so is this book. I've done my best to recount these events as accurately as possible, but there are differences of opinion from time to time. But I'm the one who took the effort to write things down, so it's my account you're getting. Do with that what you will.

Despite having one author on the cover, this book has three authors. Kind of. The first half was written by teenage Danica, the second half was written by twenty-something Danica, and thirty-something Danica did all the rest. Twenty and thirty-something Danica are a bit in denial that teenage Danica is in fact the same person. You'll see what I mean.

Some of you may know that thirty-something Danica is now a registered dietitian, and as such tells people what to eat for a living. By and large she does not endorse the recipes in this book. They are to illustrate what it's like cooking and eating at sea. There's a reason sailors are famous for having nutrient deficiencies.

Table of Contents

GLOSSARY OF NAUTICAL TERMINOLOGY 8
- Parts of the Sail 9
- Parts of the Boat 10
- Types of Boats 11
- Navigation 11
- Nautical Actions 12
- Miscellaneous Terms 12

BEFORE 14
- Halcyon Youth 15
- Wooden Sibling 20

FIRST VOYAGE 23
- 1 Raising Sail 24
- 2 Hauling Anchor 31
- 3 Flaking Chain 35
- 4 Seaside Stargazing 40
- 5 Going Offshore 44
- 6 Tropical Showering 52
- 7 Swapping Tales 56
- 8 Precipitous Provisioning 69
- 9 Waxing Poetic 72
- 10 Saltwater Spelunking 79
- 11 Embarrassing Exploits 86
- 12 Living History 93
- 13 Chasing Iguanas 101
- 14 Jungle Hitchhiking 105
- 15 Heading North 112
- 16 Battening the Hatches 115

TEN+ YEARS LATER 125

SECOND VOYAGE 127

17 Sea Fever 128
18 Hauling Out 130
19 Adventure Science 135
20 Leaving Maine 137
21 Drinking Moxie 140
22 Leaking Decks 144
23 Reefing Sail 149
24 Visionary Art 153
25 Knock Down 156
26 Cheesy Chocolate 162
27 Retracing Steps 170
28 Midnight Mooring 178
29 Spectacular Devastation 182
30 Boat Kids 187
31 Bananaquit Smoothie 190
32 French Preservatives 193
33 Unicorn Potluck 197
34 Spice Island 200
35 Turtle Tales 204
36 Boiling Lake 209
37 Classic Regatta 213
38 Airplane Sandstorm 219
39 Living Meditation 223
40 Last Hurrah 228

AFTER 232

Koukla's Continuing Adventures 233
Danica's Reflections (The Journaler) 235
Ted's Reflections (Dad) 237
Bev's Reflections (Mom) 239
Horatio's Reflections (Brother) 241
Molly's Reflections (Sister-in-Law) 244
Isaac's Reflections (Husband) 246

ACKNOWLEDGEMENTS 249
REFERENCES 250
ABOUT THE AUTHOR 252

Glossary of Nautical Terminology

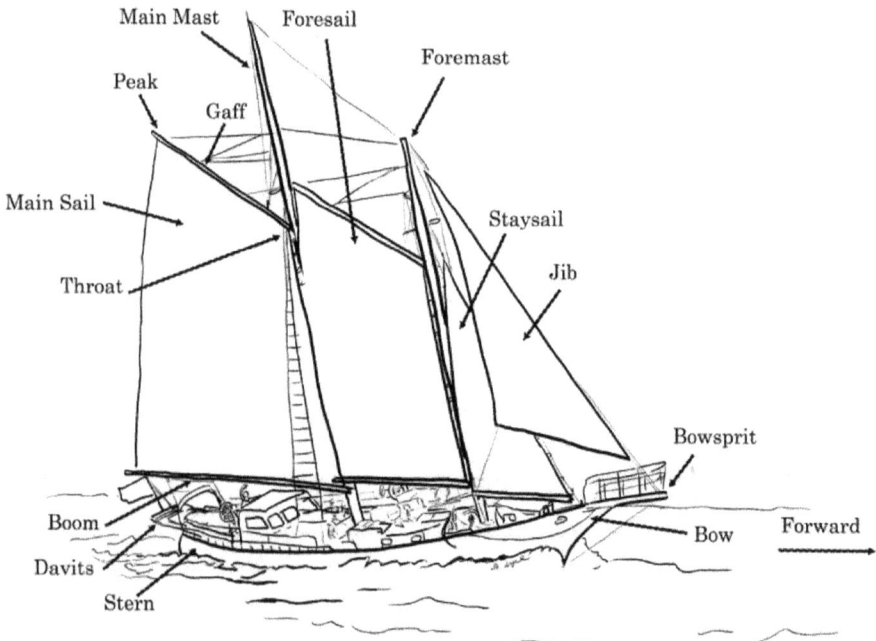

Parts of the Sail

Main: the largest sail on a boat

Foresail/Fore: the second largest sail

Staysail: the second farthest forward sail

Jib: the farthest forward sail

Boom: A pole used to support the bottom of a sail

Gaff: A pole used to support the top of a sail

Staysail club: another name for the boom below the staysail

Peak: the upper back portion of a sail

Throat: the upper front portion of a sail

Bowsprit: A pole extending forward from the bow, used as an attachment point for sails

Stay: A strong rope or metal cable that supports the mast. The stay connects from the top of the mast to the hull of the boat.

Bobstays: A stay that pulls the bowsprit downward, to counteract the upward force of the sail, usually made of wire cable or chain.

Sheet: a rope connected to the corner of a sail, used for controlling the direction of the sail in relation to the wind.

Parrel: a movable loop or collar used to connect a gaff to the mast. The parrel is often fitted with beads to reduce friction (sometimes called parrel balls). The parrel allows a gaff-rigged sail full range of motion.

Winch: a mechanical device used for pulling on a rope, usually a sheet or halyard. A winch can be either hand operated (with a crank) or electrical (Koukla only had mechanical). Winch can be used as either a noun or a verb.

Halyard: a rope used for raising and lowering a sail

Parts of the Boat

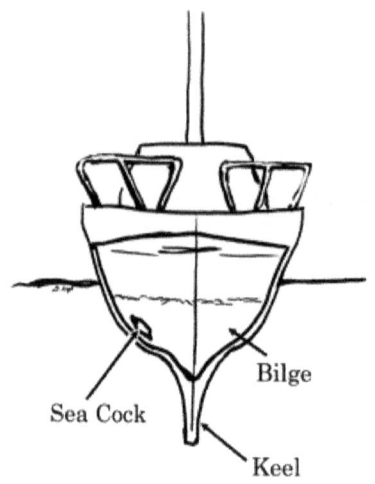

Bow: Front of the boat

Stern: Back of the boat

Davits: A set of poles extending off the side or stern of a boat, connected to a set of pulleys. Davits are used to haul heavy items onto the boat, such as a dinghy or anchor.

Seacock: A valve in the hull of a vessel to allow water in or out. They may be used for taking in seawater for engine cooling or a salt water faucet, or letting out water from a sink or toilet.

Porthole: A water-tight window on a boat, usually round or oval.

Bilge: The bottom compartment in the hull of a boat, where water collects and has to be pumped out. The basement of a boat.

Head: Bathroom on a boat, can refer to both the room or the toilet.

Main saloon: Living room on a boat.

Doghouse: A small cabin, usually aft near the steering wheel to help protect from the elements (we used doghouse and wheelhouse interchangeably).

Wheelhouse: Where the wheel is located (we used interchangeably with doghouse).

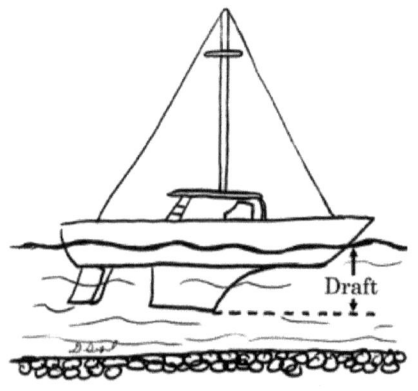

Draft: How far down a boat extends below the waterline. Koukla has a 9 ft draft, so it takes at least 9 feet of water for Koukla to not run aground or hit the bottom.

Keel: The bottom central ridge of the hull, which provides ballast (to prevent sailboats from tipping over).

Lazarette: Storage locker in the back of a boat.

Foc'sle (alternate spelling: forecastle): Forward deck of the ship. Historically on sailing ships this was the crew's quarters. It was a forward storage compartment on Koukla.

Types of Boats

Sloop: A one-masted sailboat.

Schooner: A two or more-masted sailboat where the front mast is shorter than the aft mast. Koukla is a gaff-rigged schooner.

Ketch: A two-masted sailboat where the aft mast is shorter, and the aft (mizzen) mast is ahead of the rudder. Also the name of my cousin.

Lapstrake: A boatbuilding technique where the planks of the hull overlap, kind of like shingles on a roof.

Tender: A small boat, used as transportation from ship to shore (often used interchangeably with dinghy).

Dinghy: Another name for a small boat, usually carried or towed by a larger boat. (Often used interchangeably with tender. Koukla has both a lapstrake tender and an inflatable dinghy.)

Navigation

Nun: A cone shaped navigational buoy. (usually red).

Can: A cylindrical shaped navigational buoy (usually green).

Chart: A map of the ocean and shore. Can be used as a noun or verb.

Nautical Actions

Becalmed: Unable to move due to a lack of wind.

Gunkhole/gunkholing: A type of sailing in shallow water, meandering from place to place, spending the nights in coves.

Tack: A sailing maneuver where a sailboat changes course so that the wind fills the sails from the opposite side. When sailing, or beating, into the wind, tacking back and forth in a zigzag pattern is required. The verb 'tacking' can also be referred to as coming about or going about.

Jibe: A sailing maneuver changing from one tack to the other, with the wind coming from behind.

Bone in her teeth: A phrase describing the look of a vessel making a significant amount of wake at the bow. From a distance, the white churning water looks like a dog carrying a bone.

Sculling: To propel a rowboat with a single oar, using a figure-eight motion, keeping the oar submerged.

Broad reach: When the wind is coming behind a vessel at an angle.

Miscellaneous Terms

Green water: A large amount of water passing over a ship's deck after a wave.

Blue water: Several hundred miles from shore. The open ocean or deep sea.

Knot: Nautical mile per hour, approx. 1.15 mph.

Foul weather gear: Nautical raincoats and rain pants keep you more dry than your average rain coat. Ours also had reflectors.

Slack tide: Between high tide and low tide, when there is no tidal current.

Dock: A fixed structure used for tying up boats. Often used interchangeably with pier or wharf. Can be used as a noun or verb.

Mooring: A fixed anchor. A permanent weight placed on the sea floor, with a rope or chain connecting to a buoy, and a boat can be secured to the buoy. A place to tie up a boat, not connected to a dock.

Gimbal: A device that allows an object (such as a ship's compass, table, or stove) to remain horizontal even as a boat rocks.

Heel: Lean over as a result of the wind's force on the sails.

Before

Halcyon Youth

My dad never bought anything shiny and new, especially boats. Our first, a 20 ft motorboat, had previously sunk. Our second, a 40 ft sloop, had holes clear through the hull when we first bought it. And our third, a 60 ft gaff-rigged schooner, had been trashed and was on the verge of sinking when we found it. My dad likes to call these sorts of boats "cosmetically challenged"—which means they had "good bones" but look like a piece of junk.

My summers were spent in boatyards sanding, scraping, and painting. I hated sanding most of all. I hated how my arms would continue vibrating long after I finished using the orbital sander. I hated how the dust stuck to my sweat-drenched arms and face. I hated the smell of the dust—it would either make me sneeze or I would wear a suffocating facemask that made me sweat even more.

Painting I didn't mind as much. It required skill and finesse rather than brute strength and endurance. However, my father was a perfectionist. Whenever I would finish painting a section of the hull or varnishing part of one of our 60 ft masts my father would inspect every square inch of them for spots I had missed. He called them "holidays." Often these spots would not be larger than the eraser end of a pencil. If I missed more than one spot the size of a dime I would have to go back and redo the whole thing.

One summer I was particularly put off about having to work on the boat. It was the summer the fourth Harry Potter book came out. When I first started reading the series only the first three books had been published, and I'd had to wait over two years for the fourth book. I even went to the midnight release at my local bookstore and dressed up as Hermione. I read until my eyes refused to stay open. I was still expected at work in the boatyard bright and early the next morning. When my parents weren't paying attention I would sneak off and read in our van. When they found me they'd put a paintbrush or sander back in my hand.

Boats and sailing infused every aspect of my childhood, even my very existence. My parents met on, you guessed it, a wooden boat. My father was crew on the three-masted schooner the Victory Chimes, and my mother was a passenger. Although she was hardly the dainty lady this makes her sound like.

When we weren't in the boatyard scraping and painting, we were at a different yard or marina looking at boats in various stages of decay and disrepair. I was frequently bored to tears spending hours on end in marine supply stores, nautical antique purveyors, and junk yards across New England and beyond, my dad in search of the perfect ship's wheel, signal light, or brass trinket to outfit his latest or future vessel.

Each boat we owned had a role to play in our lives. The first was a wooden motorboat we named Boppy, after my great-grandfather. It was relatively inexpensive to fix up, and quickly got us all out on the water for day trips to enjoy Maine's rugged coasts. We learned a valuable lesson on our first outing.

It was early spring in Maine, which meant it was just barely not winter. We packed a cooler with sandwiches and little else and set out to our favorite pine tree lined rocky cove, just a short ride from our home port. It was our first attempt at anchoring. Mom was at the helm, and dad handled the anchor. With the anchor down, dad asked mom to go in reverse to help set the anchor. Well it so happens we forgot about the little lapstrake tender we were towing. When mom put the engine in reverse, the engine stopped suddenly. It didn't take long to realize what had happened. We had wrapped the line towing the tender around the propeller.

My dad had to dive into the frigid Maine waters and cut us loose. Those not from the area may not realize just how ridiculously cold the water is here. This time of year the ocean temperature maybe gets up to the low 40's. From that point on all future vessels were equipped with a wetsuit and goggles.

Our second boat, Halcyon, a 40 ft motor sailer, required a bit more prep work. We had to replace a couple of planks and recaulk the hull. But it was simple for my parents to sail with just the two of them. My brother and I were too little to be more help than hindrance. And there was room for all of us to sleep, so we could spend Maine's short summers sailing to remote islands.

We also learned the challenges of boat cooking on Halcyon. A staple for chilly days out on the ocean was corn chowder, as all the ingredients were shelf stable.

Corn Chowder

1 can evaporated milk

1 can corn

½ onion, chopped

2 potatoes, chopped

2 Tablespoons butter

Don't have those exact amounts? It doesn't matter, use whatever you have. This is the essence of boat cooking. Sauté chopped onion, and combine with remaining ingredients. Simmer until potatoes are soft. Add salt and pepper to taste. Serve in a mug, so it's easier to hold on to.

This also went well with boat bread, a recipe my mom came up with out of necessity. We'd brought a frozen loaf of bread dough in our cooler, and it had thawed and expanded to over twice its size and needed to be cooked immediately. We didn't have a working oven. My mom jury rigged a steam oven with a metal loaf pan and a large skillet with a lid. As kids, we liked the soft edges and lack of crusts from steam cooking so much my mom often made it this way even after we had fixed the oven.

Sailing on Halcyon helped to prepare us for the cruising life. Cruisers are a nomadic subset of sailors who live on their characteristically unpretentious boats and travel the world. These are not the J. Crew wearing yacht club set, but more like #VanLife at sea.

For several of those brief summers my mother, an ultrasound technician, would work in hospitals far from our house in Rockland, so we would live on Halcyon for weeks at a time. We often stayed in the small port of Bucks Harbor. It had a well protected anchorage, and a marina with chilly outdoor showers and laundry access. There was an old-fashioned but well stocked general store a short walk away. My dad, brother, and I would go hiking while my mom worked. But she would get to come "home" to balmy sunsets and weekend trips in Acadia national park. Many summer evenings a steel drum band played next to the general store and we'd listen while we ate our picnic dinner of pizza and blueberry pie. While my brother and I enjoyed the literal Halcyon days of our youth, all the while my dad had been looking for the right boat for a bigger sailing voyage—months, not weeks, at sea.

When I first saw Koukla, I felt nothing. My parents had dragged my brother and me to yet another boatyard, and I was none too thrilled about it. Yet visiting this musty old sailboat on a chilly autumn day in Long Island would be one of the most important events in my young life. And I was completely unaware. Coincidentally, I was also completely oblivious when I first met the love of my life, but we'll get to that later.

As my mother recalls it, when she first saw Koukla at the end of the long pier, it looked like a derelict wreck, and thought "thank god he's not going to want this."

My father said nothing, showed no sign of emotion except for an almost imperceptible twinkle in his eye. He would later tell us that as soon as he saw Koukla he thought "this is it!"

I was less impressed as we got closer. The cockpit was packed full of coolers of half-empty beer cans. Sails lay limp over the cabin top, and uncoiled piles of rigging were scattered over the decks. The galley sink was full of dirty dishes, and the air was so full of dust and mold spores that I couldn't stay down below for more than a few minutes without coughing and sneezing. The electrical panel that controlled the lights and instruments had been cut away, leaving a tangled mass of wires. When my dad started looking at the structural integrity of the boat, examining the hull, deck, and bilges, he realized that the seacocks—openings in the hull to allow waste and other things overboard— were frozen open and had little more than flecks of dirt keeping the boat from sinking. However, the interior woodwork was impressive. Oiled rosewood paneling and jade green marble countertops were visible beneath the clutter and grime. Koukla was begging to be rescued.

My father was probably one of the few people not only crazy enough, but competent enough to rebuild Koukla. A marine engineer by trade, my father is a real-life MacGyver. Seriously. He once fixed a broken windshield wiper in a rainstorm with nothing but the inside of a pen. So we made an offer on Koukla, but to my mom's relief it was rejected. The owner didn't realize how much the value of the boat had deteriorated due to neglect. And that was that. We went back home to Maine and I forgot all about that dilapidated old boat.

Wooden Sibling

Koukla was once a magnificent vessel. The boat was commissioned by a wealthy New York restaurateur who wanted a fishing boat that reminded him of his childhood in Greece. The name Koukla roughly translates to child's toy or baby doll in Greek, and it was indeed his play-thing.

Hundreds of man-hours went into the building of Koukla. The tough-as-steel dragon's eye wood frames were carefully constructed, and it was planked with rot-resistant cypress. She was outfitted with luxurious teak decks, and the rosewood interior was carved by skilled hands and polished till it gleamed. The masts, sails, engine, etc were added, and Koukla was born. She was designed to go anywhere and last a hundred years.

Our acquisition (adoption?) of Koukla is a convoluted and somewhat darkly mystical tale. Over a year after that unassuming yet life-changing day in Long Island, we received a call. It was the owner's widow, and she wanted to know if we were still interested in buying Koukla. The boat had initially been put on the market when the owner was in the hospital and appeared to be dying. The boat had been in such bad shape because he had been in and out of hospitals for ages and unable to maintain her. However, he made a miraculous recovery, went on vacation to his home country and tragically died in a car crash. It was almost as if Koukla had singled out my dad as her savior and willed their connection. It gets rather dark and creepy if I think too hard about it.

My dad did her proud. Our literal blood, sweat, and tears went into restoring Koukla to her former glory. My brother and I joked that Koukla wasn't our boat but our sibling—and our parents' favorite child. Our parents carried around photos of Koukla in their wallets, but not either of us. And like siblings, my brother and I both loved but at times resented Koukla.

Before we set sail my dad made sure his crew was as competent and prepared as possible. My dad had spent his career as an engineer in the merchant marines and knew what to do in just about any disaster scenario, and how to fix pretty much anything onboard. My mom was also prepared for her role in emergency scenarios, and had earned an advanced life support credential, or ALS. As a healthcare professional, she consulted with her doctor and nurse peers to put together an extremely comprehensive medical kit, and knew how to use everything in it. She'd earned her HAM radio license to communicate with others and call for help if needed—and on at least one occasion we really did. And last but not least we had life rafts and emergency beacons that would alert rescuers to our location if the worst were to happen and we had to abandon ship.

This trip had been planned long before I was born. My dad built his life around the plan to go sailing around the world. He chose his career and partner with this in mind. His job as a marine engineer gave him the skills and training for life at sea. And my mom, for the most part, knew what she was getting herself into when she married him. If I could sum up my mother in one word it would be tough. She grew up riding horses in rural New York and owned more tools than my dad when they first got married. My brother and I were raised with the knowledge that we'd go off and have adventures at sea one day. My parents liked to joke they had kids for the free labor. Yeah, they weren't joking.

My parents also made sure the youngest members of their crew were as prepared as possible. We were decent swimmers and crew members and knew how to sail, steer, navigate, and take watch. We knew we were active crew members and not passengers. We knew this was not a vacation—it was an adventure.

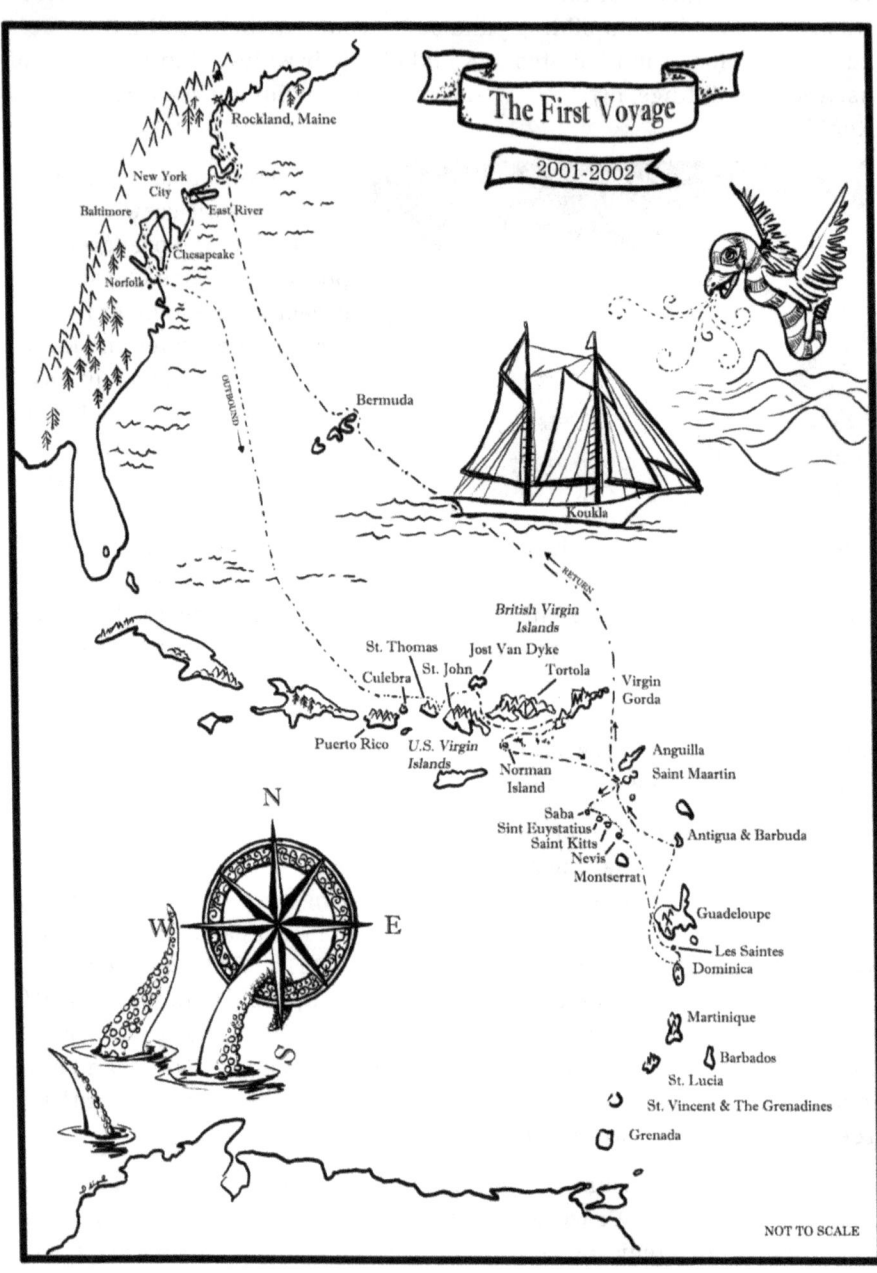

First Voyage

1 Raising Sail

September 27, 2001
Rockland, Maine

After living onboard for a week I thought I had everything all figured out. I was used to sleeping in a tiny bunk, using the ocean as my sink for brushing my teeth, keeping all my clothes in plastic bags to stave off the dampness, and piles of clutter everywhere. I was even used to the annoying anchor taking up valuable space under my bunk and the enormous coil of rope in my cabin. Then we left the dock. It was not the departure, sailing off into the sunset that I had envisioned. The seas and skies were a stormy gray.

After three years of repair work, three months of heightened preparation, and an additional month of delays we finally set sail. My parents knew they were running out of time—my childhood was almost over. I was turning 16 in a few months, and heading off to college in just a few years. It was now or never, so we left before we were truly ready. There was no electricity, no working toilet, no running water, and no refrigeration. Instead we had flashlights and oil lamps, a port-o-potty, a hand pump for water, and coolers. There was no TV, and no internet except for when we went ashore. We had one cell phone, which was next to useless, since I couldn't talk to my friends for more than a few minutes, and was completely useless once we got far enough south. Not to mention the spools of wire, coils of rope, electrical equipment, bolts, batteries, anchors, books, clothes, food stuffs, and more that cluttered the decks and cabins of the boat. In essence, my life had been packed up, boxed, stuffed, and stowed onto this boat.

But then there was one thing, or rather one person, I was leaving behind. It was just my dumb luck I got my first boyfriend a few short months before I would be heading to sea.

His family was into skiing the way my family was into sailing—it wasn't a hobby, it was a way of life. Skiing was a part of his personality, his identity, the way sailing was a part of mine. Was he the cutest guy in my class? Objectively, no. But with his passing resemblance to Harry Potter-messy dark hair, vivid eyes (blue instead of green)—to my nerdy self he was.

We'd wasted months in the awkward teenage dance of does he/she like me, with shared friends as go betweens. By the time we figured out we did, in fact, like each other, we didn't have much time left. On one of our first dates, he attempted to recite as many digits of Pi as he could remember. Yes we were dorks. Yes I was into it.

That first night I called him. We hadn't got very far yet, so our cell phone still worked. The note of sadness in his voice as he told me he missed me cut to the core. My eyes watered and burned as the reality of the situation washed over me—I wouldn't see him again for months on end. I hoped he hadn't heard my voice crack as I said my goodbyes. As I started to feel sorry for myself, I remembered adventure always requires sacrifice.

The next morning, I crawled out of my nice warm bunk to be assaulted by the frigid morning air. I dressed quickly, and went straight out into the even chillier ocean breeze. On the ocean the air is thicker, denser. So full of salt and moisture it almost takes more effort to move through. Salt and moisture clung to my skin and clothes, making it impossible to ever be truly dry. Despite my best efforts I was never totally dry the entire trip. And never totally clean either—at least not for long. After a shower I'd almost immediately be rechristened with salt spray.

We raised the sails with my mother at the helm while my father, brother, and I hauled away. Before long, the seas began to steadily increase—waves went from 6 to 10 to 15 to 20 feet, and occasionally even more. Our rugged vessel pitched violently, making any and all movement about a struggle. On deck our cooler went on its side, strewing its contents about. The meat, vegetables, eggs, and other foodstuffs were rescued from going overboard. The only casualty was a bottle of milk that spilled all over the deck, but was quickly washed away by the sea. The ocean continued to rage, drenching the decks. With each wave, an outboard motor lashed to a railing was caught in a tempest of swirling brine. Often the size of our boat tends to cause problems. In this case we were all very thankful that our boat wasn't a foot shorter or a pound lighter, for any smaller of a boat would have made this day even more miserable than it already was. I had to try very hard not to fear what could happen, but just focus on what had to be done. Looking back, one of the scariest aspects of that day was the threat of falling overboard. Of course, you wouldn't want to fall overboard any other day, but with the waves as monstrous as they were, the result could have been disastrous. With waves nearly four times as tall as I am, staying afloat would have been nearly impossible, and getting back onboard quite difficult. Not to mention hypothermia and other such added dangers. Fortunately, this did not happen, but we didn't come out completely unscathed.

While I was down below trying to further secure things, a jib sheet had become caught around a running light on one of the stays. My brother went up to free it, but just as he let go a wave hit. For the split second that he wasn't holding on, he was tossed back, and the side of his jaw hit a belay pin—a small wooden club used for tying ropes to. As I was coming up from the galley, I gasped when I saw his face dripping with blood. My mother, unphased, put her medical training to good use. Another large wave hit, and she was thrown into the side of the wheelhouse. Fortunately, my brother's wounds were minimal and my mother was virtually unharmed thanks in part to a rather thick collar on her foul weather jacket. My father and I were lucky to be little more than fatigued by the labors of such a long and strenuous journey.

After nearly six hours of being tossed about like a rubber ducky in a splashing child's bathtub, we anchored for the night. Although the boat had stopped rocking, our day had not ended. There was still the matter of cleaning up the huge mess caused by the constant lurching. The biggest inconvenience was a large container of rice that had overturned and spilled all over the marble countertop and into all the nooks and crannies of our propane stove. After raising the sails, tending lines, securing gear, and skipping lunch, the last thing we wanted to do was bend over and scoop rice out of every crevice and disassemble a stove. But that's exactly what we did. While my mother was cool as a cucumber during a crisis, once it had passed the physical and emotional fatigue took its toll. She hid her tears over the mess. After an eternity of picking up the rice with serving spoons, spatulas, and hands, my mother pronounced it good enough. We made a chicken and rice dish that my family descriptively named chicken-on-top-rice-on-the-bottom.

Chicken-on-top-rice-on-the-bottom

Place one cup white rice in the bottom of an oven-safe casserole dish. Mix together one can cream of chicken soup, a can of water, and half a packet of Italian seasoning mix. Place two to four chicken breasts on top. Top chicken with remaining Italian seasoning packet. Bake at 350°F for 45 mins.

We'd had some experience with the challenges of galley cooking aboard Halcyon, but living aboard was another beast. Our main pot was a pressure cooker—an old fashioned stove-top one. We ate a lot of one pot meals that can all be cooked together within a short period of time to save propane. Cleanup was another issue. There was no dishwasher and fresh water needed to be conserved, so we hauled up buckets of sea water from over the side, and used this to do the bulk of the washing. As a last step we rinsed with fresh water we boiled on the stove, as there was no hot water either.

My mom is a pretty good cook, and I wasn't too bad myself, but onboard cooking prioritizes practicality over taste. As my Grandma would say, hunger is the best sauce. After scarfing down our dinner, we all went straight to bed. Even my teenage body felt quite ancient after the physical and mental stress of the day. The following day, we stayed right where we were and licked our wounds.

We spent several days gunkholing our way down the coast of New England, spending the night in one picturesque yet forgettable cove after another. Arriving in Gloucester, Massachusetts was a different experience. As we sailed into the harbor we were greeted with a cannon salute from fellow schooner Thomas E. Lannon. Koukla was designed after the Gloucester fishing schooners. It is not your typical fiberglass production boat and is hard to miss in any harbor today. However, 100 years ago there would have been a fleet of schooners much like Koukla filling the harbor, weighed down with the day's catch.

The coast of New England has a long history of fishing and whaling, which continues to this day in different forms. Fishing schooners are largely a thing of the past, but modern trawlers are found throughout the region. The practice of whaling is long gone, replaced now with whale watching. One morning as we were sailing through Cape Cod Bay, I heard a shout from above deck. I dropped my history text book and ran up to see two mighty columns of water rising out of the ocean, followed by glistening backs and curved dorsal fins a few hundred yards off our starboard bow.

A few hours after we had seen the whales, we attempted to moor at Provincetown, Massachusetts. We had decided to purchase a mooring rather than anchoring as usual in order to take showers. Most marinas will not allow you to use their facilities unless you purchase dock space or a mooring. Unfortunately, the marina had started to put away its moorings for the season. Therefore, we had to tie our own line to the ring on top of the buoy, and it was with a great deal of difficulty that we did so, as it was blowing 25 knots. We did not enjoy the benefits of our hard earned showers for long. Due to the wind and waves on the dinghy ride back, we returned all wet and crusted with salt once again.

Although my brother and I were fully fledged members of Koukla's crew, we were in fact still children and as such still had to go to "school." All of our coursework was reviewed and I was assigned credit by a homeschooling organization, North Atlantic Regional Schools. The ship was our classroom. We had the labors of sailing for physical education. I plotted our course and earned credit in navigational science. I read textbooks on the history of New England and the Caribbean in addition to visiting historical sites instead of learning history behind a desk. I was learning the physics of radio waves and studied for my Ham Radio Technician's license. Instead of an English teacher I had an editor. I wrote articles on the entire trip that were published in my local newspaper—the Rockland Courier-Gazette. Those articles are the basis of the book you are now reading. Well, the first half.

The coast of Massachusetts put my navigational skills to the test. As we were coming into the entrance of Plymouth harbor, we had to watch carefully for lighthouses, channel markers, and other reference points to help indicate where we were. We had to use extreme caution because certain areas had only a few feet of water, and some areas were only submerged at high tide. This is not a good thing for a boat with a 9 foot draft, meaning it takes at least 9 ft of water for us to stay afloat and not hit the bottom.

Once inside we thought we knew exactly where we were. We had matched the #2 nun in sight to the one on the chart, but to our great dismay we sighted another nun with #2 on it, and another, and another, and another. Nuns are cone-shaped buoys that well, look kind of like nuns. After carefully examining the chart, we realized that there were at least five red nuns labeled #2 in various areas of the harbor. As we were no longer able to trust our chart, we carefully picked our way back out of the harbor and anchored in a sheltered cove just outside and prepared for inclement weather.

That night the wind howled like ghouls. Lines violently hit the mast. The anchor chain rattled like an army of skeletons. Waves lashed the hull. Small unidentified noises had an uncanny resemblance to the sound of someone pacing the deck. As if that wasn't enough, the fear that the anchor would drag kept me awake that night.

The heavy winds continued through the next day, so we stayed right where we were. My brother and I caught up on our school work, and my father finally hooked up a few lights. Of course, none of them were close to my cabin. I would have to continue to hold my heavy-duty Maglight flashlight in my armpit while I read at night.

Living onboard Koukla lacked many creature comforts—one of those was pizza. We'd heard there was a particularly good pizza place in Mattapoisett, MA not far from their public landing. A few days later we anchored there and piled into the inflatable to go ashore for dinner. But, those infernal winds did not make it very easy for us. Waves crashed over the bow of our tiny inflatable, water crawled up over the sides, and the salty spray stung our faces. In the middle of the harbor we considered going back, but we pressed on.

By the end we were all drenched. I was somewhat fortunate that only the bottoms and back of my jeans were wet, although it was still quite unpleasant. I was just glad not to have soggy shoes. But I was the only one.

My mother had wisely worn her foul weather pants in addition to the foul weather jacket, but because so much water had accumulated inside the boat, she had wet feet. My father had to kneel in inches of water in order to steer. But that was nothing in comparison to my poor little brother, who had been sitting in the bow. His jeans and sneakers were completely soaked, and in spite of his foul weather jacket, even the front of his sweatshirt was wet.

We were quite a spectacle, all waterlogged and decked out in matching fluorescent yellow. One old lady we passed asked if we were selling something. As we walked by a playground we heard a kid shout, "Hey, are those firemen?" But it was all worth it. I think it was some of the best pizza we'd ever had.

2 Hauling Anchor

*Essex, Connecticut
October 13, 2001*

I was looking forward to our next big stop in Essex, Connecticut to visit my "aunt" Diane. I couldn't wait to stay in her house and use her showers and internet, but I would have to. To get to Essex, we had to go up the Connecticut River and under several bridges. We proceeded with caution as we weren't quite sure that there was enough water for us. We also gritted our teeth as we went under one bridge that was a little too close to the top of our mast. The next was a railroad bridge that had to be raised in order to let us through. About half a mile before we reached the bridge, my father called the bridge on our VHF radio. We waited a few minutes, and there was no reply. My father called again, still no reply. He called a third time. Finally, a man came on and exclaimed rather irately that the radio was on one side of the room and the bridge controls were on the other, so he was unable to talk on the radio while the bridge was in motion. Seems like an extension cord or a portable radio could solve that problem.

As we were settling in that evening we noticed a small motor boat slowly drifting toward us. They hollered over to us that they couldn't control the boat because their anchor line was wrapped around their propeller. My father offered to have them tie up to us so they wouldn't drift away. They agreed, and my father asked if there was anything more we could do to help. The man on the other boat said no, but asked jokingly for a wetsuit. To his surprise, we did in fact have a wet suit. Ever since that infamous incident on the Bartender we've always carried one onboard. He gratefully donned the wetsuit, and dove in to cut the line. As he handed back the suit, mask, and towel we had lent him, he stammered his thanks through chattering teeth.

The following day, we took the boat to the dock, where we met my mother's friend Diane and her family. Diane and her husband Steve were more my aunt and uncle than many of my actual blood relatives. My mom and Diane were wild women each in their own right. While my mom had spent years preparing for our current adventure, Diane was an adrenaline junkie. There's a great painting an artist friend did of her weighed down with climbing ropes, a wild look in her eye, and a frozen scream of excitement on her face.

I slept less than I should have that night, talking to my friends and boyfriend till late at night on AIM (AOL instant messenger). While I enjoyed the luxury of being dry and stationary, my friends caught me up on the latest high school gossip—who was dating who, stupid teenage stuff. My boyfriend and I talked about our lives—my adventures at sea, his classes, soccer, math team, and how he was looking forward to winter and ski season. But mostly we talked about how much we missed each other. His absence felt like a physical weight in my chest. It was a steep price for the adventure of a lifetime, but one I was willing to pay.

We hauled up the anchor and sails at the crack of dawn the next day in order to arrive at Port Jefferson, New York before dark. We would be spending over a week there in order to get running lights and other things hooked up and ready for an overnight sail. Our first night there was not very peaceful on account of the slight gale blowing outside, and conditions did nothing but worsen the next day. We stayed onboard all day in light of this.

While much of the trip was exciting, large swaths of time were boring and monotonous. On days stuck aboard Koukla I'd study, read, or write—either newspaper articles, emails to friends, or in my own private journal. Usually I'd read. I dedicated most of my tiny allotted space to books. At the time I was reading The Hitchhiker's Guide to the Galaxy. Ford Prefect's rule to never leave home without your towel is excellent advice if you live on a boat.

That night, none of us were able to get much sleep. A full gale was blowing outside from the worst possible direction, contrary to the forecast, so that we were not sheltered at all. The howling wind violently shook the halyards and anything else on deck that was not lashed down well enough.

The line tied to the anchor chain groaned so loudly that blasting my walkman hardly drowned out all the noise. Weezer was no match for these winds. Lying down in my bunk I could feel the boat swinging around. I felt us spin in circles around our anchor. I deluded myself into thinking that the 150 pound chunk of metal sitting on the bottom couldn't possibly drag.

Just before midnight, I heard doors opening and closing at the opposite end of the boat. I told myself that it was just someone getting up to use the head (bathrooms on boats are called heads). I heard more rustling then a knock at my cabin door. It was my father telling me to get up and get dressed and be ready to flake chain. Whenever we hauled anchor it was my job to make sure the massive length of heavy duty chain was coiled in nice neat piles so it didn't tangle when we eventually dropped it again.

Swinging around full circle had wrapped the chain around the anchor and pulled it at an odd angle, causing it to drag. So we needed to pull it up and move. I hopped out of bed, threw on some clothes, and shoved my hands into the diving gloves I used for flaking anchor chain. Before long I heard the muffled shouts of my father and brother up above, nearly drowned out by the howling wind. I felt Koukla heave and plunge into each wave. I was acutely aware that I was safe below deck, while the rest of my family was exposed to the elements and the dangers of falling overboard at night. Very thankfully no one went over. But something else did.

We had purchased a solar panel to help keep our batteries topped off so we wouldn't have to use our diesel generator as much. It was very difficult to stow and had to be moved around a lot, but we would not have to do this any longer. It hadn't been tied down properly and the wind hit it just right and took it over the side. It sank to the bottom very quickly, making rescue impossible even if the conditions had been better. Losing this piece of equipment was not only a financial blow, but stung all the more as our attempt to be eco-friendly had basically backfired.

It took us a long time to re-anchor because of the conditions. With the howling wind and pitch black darkness, my mother at the helm could neither hear nor see my father and brother up on the bow. The gale force winds were blowing so that you could not shout over the noise. After what seemed like an eternity of motoring in the rough winds and inky blackness, we finally dropped anchor up wind of our original spot. But I would not be able to rest quite yet. It was far too noisy up in my cabin to even attempt to sleep there, so I had to take all my sheets, blankets, and pillows into my brother's cabin, away from the grinding anchor chain. Neither of us were happy with this arrangement, but we understood the necessity. It was in his own best interest that I slept so I'd be more pleasant the next day, even if that meant invading his personal space.

Koukla is kind of a diva. Wherever we go she tends to attract a certain kind of attention. In Port Jefferson, Long Island the local boating enthusiasts, affectionately referred to as schooner bums, came out to see her. One such person was a faculty member of the nearby Stony Brook School. He was out on a boat with a group of students when he hollered over to us asking about the boat. We told him about our trip from Maine and plans to head south. It turned out that he was a sailor too. He invited us to his house for dinner and for showers, as he knew about the limited facilities open to transients in this port. and even took us to the grocery store. He gifted us a marine biology text book that would later become invaluable. This might sound a bit odd to invite a complete stranger over to your house, often with the main purpose of taking a shower, but this is a common occurrence in the sailing community. I reveled in the experience of not only taking a shower, but a shower in a private bathroom, a shower that was not coin operated like in most marinas, and would not abruptly turn off after a set number of minutes.

Koukla caught the attention of yet another helpful captain in Port Jefferson. SoundWaters is the name of both a boat and an environmental education nonprofit. Soundwaters' captain invited my brother and me onboard for one of their programs. One fact that's stuck with me is that about half the Earth's oxygen comes from the ocean, from phytoplankton. And one species in particular, Prochlorococcus, which is also the smallest photosynthetic organism, produces 20% of the earth's oxygen. That's more than all the tropical rainforests combined!

3 Flaking Chain

October 25, 2001
Port Washington, New York

The day started out pleasant enough. The winds were sufficient and the seas weren't bad. About midday, the winds began to pick up and everything was drenched with salty brine, even below deck. One of the many corners that had been cut in order to leave Maine in a timely fashion had been fixing deck leaks. It just happened to be my luck that I would have the wettest cabin. It wasn't necessarily the leakiest cabin, but was furthest forward, and therefore received the most spray.

On its own my cabin leaked quite a bit. Most of the time things would just magically get wet and I couldn't find where the water was coming from.

To make matters worse, my father had drilled more holes in the deck to run wires for running lights and, unbeknownst to me, hadn't gotten around to making them water tight yet. I also had this nice little spot underneath a step in my cabin where I could put all my shoes and not worry about them getting wet, so I thought. As I soon found out, the holes my father had drilled leaked tremendously and the water ran right into that great little spot I kept my shoes in. So now all my shoes, except the ones on my feet, were soaked.

Seeing as the spray wasn't enough, thunder showers had been predicted and the foreboding, overcast skies added to the threat. I tried to further prepare my cabin and air out my soggy shoes as best as I could. My brother and I put on our foul weather jackets just in case we would be getting wetter. My parents suited up completely, for they would have to be out in the elements in order to steer. We nervously watched the sheets of rain coming down from the gray, ominous clouds. Of course, since we were ready for it we did not get rained on. But something we were not ready for did happen.

It had been very windy that day, and all the sails were under a good amount of strain. It was too much for the old glue joints in the staysail club (the wooden piece under the staysail. The staysail is the one between the jib and the fore) and it split in half. When we found it, there was one half attached to the sail, and the other half somewhere in Long Island Sound. We could still use the sail without it, it just wasn't nearly as efficient.

Finally, after a very rough and unpleasantly eventful sail, we reached Port Washington. We anchored near sunset in heavy winds in a spot that we later decided was too close to a submerged wreck, so we decided to move to a spot with more swinging room. Since it was getting dark and very windy, my father wanted to move as soon as possible, he did not bother to wash off the anchor chain, to my great annoyance. In the semi darkness of the chain locker, I could just barely see the thick, gray, gloppy mud encasing the anchor chain. I could feel the sickening stuff squish between my gloved fingers.

Flaking that chain was a pretty nasty business, but things would only get worse after the job was done. Since my gloves were now encrusted with this gray goop, I had to haul up a bucket of seawater and rinse them off. It was rather fortunate that I was up on deck while my father was dropping the anchor, because the mud that was on the anchor chain splattered all over the chain locker and forward head. These great sticky globs of muck now covered the walls just forward of my cabin.

The weather was not any better the next day. We heavily debated going in to take showers, for it would be a nasty ride in, but we felt so disgusting we decided we were up to a rough ride in order to be clean. We suited up in our rubber boots and foul weather pants and jackets, and piled in our dinghy.

The waves crashed over the tiny inflatable and the water piled up in the boat. The wind howled and the seas rolled, but we all stayed dry under our waterproof mantles. However we all ended up with wind-burned, spray-stung faces. We finally reached shore and went directly to the showers. There is nothing like a nice hot shower after going days without one, and it was definitely worth all the trouble we went through to get it.

Our first overnight sail was coming up. I woke up to a bright and sunny, yet cold and windy, day. We were approaching Hell Gate, so named for its incredibly strong tides. We had heard that a schooner even bigger than ours had been completely turned around by this monstrous current, and almost crashed into a dock. Fortunately, we timed it just right so that we arrived at slack tide and we went through quite easily.

I'd been to New York City a year ago on a school trip, but it was quite strange seeing New York City from such a different perspective. From the water, the buildings looked much smaller and strangely older. Perhaps it appeared this way because of the recent tragedy. Everyone who was past the age of five on September 11, 2001 remembers where they were and what they were doing. I was varnishing a bathtub. Koukla had come equipped with a wooden barrel style bathtub, which we'd refurbished and I was putting on one of a seemingly unending number of coats of varnish when the towers fell. I talked to my boyfriend that night, and he'd told me his soccer coach had insisted on not canceling practice. He felt that if we stopped living life as usual, the terrorists had truly won— and we couldn't let that happen. We were deep into our preparations for setting sail that fateful day, and we briefly discussed canceling our trip. But in our own small way, we couldn't let them win either.

As we passed ground zero, it was even stranger to see nothing but a crane where I so vividly remembered the Twin Towers standing. Since this devastated area was inland and I was on the water, I saw no more than this. But, I could smell an acrid burning odor as we went by Manhattan, a reminder of just how recent that event had been.

I didn't think sailing overnight would be that bad, I'd go to sleep and just wake up and we'd be there. I had no idea how wrong I was. Since it was just one night, my parents would keep watch and let my brother and I sleep through it, or so we thought. It started off not so bad, lying down in my bunk, starting to drift off to sleep. Then suddenly, a gust of wind hit, causing the boat to heel, and I was thrown into the bulkhead next to my bunk.

I tried to wedge myself in and go to sleep. But, at one point I stretched out my legs and felt something cold and wet. I bent over and felt the foot of my bunk, it was soaking wet. I had to pull off my comforter (which I practically had to wring out), blanket, and sheets and hang them up in the main saloon to dry. Since all my bedding was now unusably soaked, I had to take my pillows and spare sheets into my brother's cabin. He was sleeping in my parents' cabin because it was more comfortable, and they would only be taking cat naps in the cockpit that night. I had no other choice than to use his blanket and comforter, which wasn't warm enough for me. There weren't any easily accessible, unused, dry blankets so I had to curl up in a ball to try and keep warm, which worked eventually. At the same time, I had to twist myself into a pretzel because of the heeling. I also stole my brother's pillows and put them next to me because I was basically sleeping on the bulkhead next to me rather than in the bunk. I got precious little sleep that night, but my parents slept even less. Although, they said it wasn't really that bad, and it wouldn't have been bad at all if we had just had inside steering.

By the time the sun was dipping down below the horizon, we were half way up the Delaware River and decided to press on to the entrance of the Chesapeake and Delaware Canal. This would allow us to transit the canal in the morning with the tide in our favor.

Going through the C and D canal the next morning was almost like going by car rather than by boat. The canal was fairly narrow, so when you looked straight out there were fields of tall grass on either side. This looked quite

strange to my eyes that were used to seeing mostly water with only a few specks of land here and there.

Once we were finally out of the canal, there was a noticeable temperature change. It was slowly but surely getting warmer as we headed south. By the time we entered Baltimore Harbor the following afternoon we had shed our layers of jackets and were all in t-shirts. I couldn't believe that it was November 1st and I was in a t-shirt and jeans.

We were all happy to be warm and in civilization again, but my spirits would soon be dampened a bit. We had planned to anchor inside the inner harbor, right near all the big attractions. But we didn't realize it would be that small, as they had decreased the available anchorage area. We started out in one spot and tried to put out a stern anchor to keep us from swinging into the channel. This didn't really work, and my father wasn't happy with the spot we were in, so we had to move. We were in a bit of a hurry because other boats were coming in and we didn't want them to take our spot. So yet again, my father did not wash off the anchor chain. I was extremely thankful for my diving gloves because this black goo that was coming through the deck was some of the nastiest stuff I have ever dealt with. I had to handle it very gingerly because this mud was very watery and could easily splatter all over me. This stuff smelled like rotten eggs. The festering stench wafted about the forward section of the boat, which included my cabin. Yet again it splattered all over the forward head, but this time it crept into my cabin. Without the smell, this ordeal would have been bad enough, but the putrid odor that accompanied this tar-like muck made it unbearable. Very soon after my father installed a washdown pump.

4 Seaside Stargazing

November 15, 2001
Baltimore, MD

The six weeks we spent waiting out hurricane season were not the most exciting, but it was perhaps the most enjoyable thus far. The geography of the bay made for fairly easy sailing and anchoring. We would stay in one place for an extended period of time and make occasional short hops south toward Norfolk, Virginia, our last stop before going offshore.

Baltimore, Maryland was the highlight of the Chesapeake Bay. It was unseasonably yet delightfully warm. We actually got to do normal family vacation stuff—we went to the aquarium, the science museum, and shopping for more than just groceries.

After spending a week in Baltimore, we proceeded south for a few days until we reached our next significant stop, Solomons, Maryland. It was a small yachting community with many marinas and easily accessible facilities, including very nice showers, and, to my delight, internet access.

Internet access meant a lifeline to my friends back home. I was able to email friends and chat on AIM on almost a daily basis for the first time in ages. Because of this my boyfriend asked me to do him a favor.

Not unlike how I had a whole other life at sea separate from my life in

Rockland, he had a whole other life skiing. His family had a condo at Sugarloaf, and lived there basically every weekend there was snow on the ground. This other life included friends—friends I didn't know.

Apparently he'd told them he had a girlfriend who lived on a boat, and logically, they didn't believe him. I mean, can you blame them? It's a bit more creative than the "I have a girlfriend in Canada" line, but also somehow less believable. I'm sure he was teased mercilessly. So he gave me their AIM screen names and shared mine with them. I was eventually able to get a hold of his friends, and they grilled me to prove that I was in fact the girl he had described and not some internet rando. While the teasing from his friends may have stopped, now he got it from me.

Living onboard, our lives were more in sync with the rhythms of nature. Electricity and lights were limited, so we went to bed when the sun set, and rose when the dawn broke. Our movements were dictated by the winds and tides. We were forever at the mercy of the elements. We were also much less connected to modern technology. It had been ages since we'd had access to any sort of TV/movie/video/moving picture of any type. Because of this we were more in awe of the wonders of nature. The Leonid meteor shower was an example of this. All four of us went up on deck in the early morning, during the peak display, and were treated to quite a show. All four of us lay on deck, or stood with our necks craned up towards the heavens until the wee morning hours. Every few seconds a pinprick of light would appear out of nowhere, streak across the sky, and suddenly disappear. It was well worth losing a bit of sleep for.

While we were fairly disconnected from the rhythms of modern life, we weren't totally disconnected from holiday traditions. That Thanksgiving aboard Koukla in Solomons, MD would become one of my all time favorites. We could not have a traditional turkey because it would not fit in our tiny galley oven, so we roasted a chicken instead. Besides, we wouldn't know what to do with the leftovers, having no refrigeration at all. We invited an interesting cruising couple to have Thanksgiving dinner with us, partially because they didn't have a usable stove to

cook on. We had gone over to their boat the previous day, and saw that they were really camping out. They had parts and various not-yet-installed things all over the place, even more so than we did, and that is saying something. You would need to have a sense of humor to live in those sorts of conditions, and the woman had an excellent one. She was constantly making wise cracks, telling jokes, and harmlessly poking fun at her companion and others. With her incredible wit and sense of humor, and his polite acceptance, they made for very enjoyable company.

We all sat around our gimballed table, chowing down on roast chicken, stuffing, canned cranberry sauce, mashed potatoes with gravy, the usual. It was a miniature version of a traditional Thanksgiving dinner. My mom had managed to whip up a feast on limited provisions on our tiny galley stove. She kept us all fed and happy with no refrigeration and unpredictable access to provisions the whole trip, but she'd outdone herself this time. She'd even made a pumpkin pie for dessert, as most of the ingredients are shelf stable. It was challenging to cook and eat as both our stove and table rocked with the waves. The constant oven use and our wood burning soapstone stove kept the galley and main saloon toasty warm. The wall mounted oil lamps—also gimballed—gave the entire room a homey peaceful glow as we ate and chatted into the twilight hours.

My 16th birthday was shortly after Thanksgiving. We were in a secluded cove off the Chesapeake Bay. My milestone birthday came and went with little fanfare—no party, no friends, not even a phone call. My parents did their best to make it a little special with a cake and a few presents. But I missed my friends deeply that day. There were no calls or emails from friends that day—not because they'd forgotten me but because there was no way to reach me.

Norfolk, Virginia would be our last stop before heading offshore. As we were approaching Norfolk we could see battleships, hovercrafts, and fighter jets off in the mist. We passed Norfolk Naval Base, which, to my knowledge, is the largest in the world. The enormity of this place was incredible. We passed dock after dock after dock of battleships, aircraft carriers, destroyers, submarines, cruisers, and amphibious landing crafts. As we were going by, multiple, low-flying, double-ended helicopters were constantly patrolling the area. With all these close, impressive-looking helicopters flying overhead, it felt like being in a James Bond movie.

We stayed in Norfolk for a week, getting more things hooked up, restowing things more securely, provisioning, and doing anything else that needed to be done before heading offshore. In spite of all the running around and having much difficulty finding parts, my father was able to hook up the autopilot and refrigeration, two critical features for an offshore passage.

For the offshore passage, we picked up another crew member. My dad was aware of the dangers of sailing hundreds of miles from shore and wanted another adult on board. My brother and I were competent crew members, but were still in fact children. And my parents didn't want to expose us to any more danger than necessary.

Ray, a friend and colleague of my father's, would be joining us. A fellow engineer and Navy vet, they'd worked together for years and my father knew him to be competent and likable—important when you can never be more than 60 ft away from someone— and kept a cool head in difficult situations. He also found the idea of blue water sailing exciting—he was in.

5 Going Offshore

December 9, 2001
Norfolk, Virginia

We left behind hot showers, grocery stores, and telephones, and headed out into the great blue waters of the Atlantic. From the very beginning, the winds were very strong and the seas were quite large, and that should have been a warning to us.

The conditions were reminiscent of when we first brought Koukla up from Long Island just after purchasing her. We had made it to Portland, Maine, and we were continuing north towards Rockland, but it was so incredibly rough and windy that we turned back.

That is what we should have done now but didn't. The main reason we didn't turn back this time was because the winds were favorable for getting across the Gulf Stream quickly. We flew across the Gulf Stream, but unbeknownst to us, there was a low-pressure system waiting for us on the other side. This caught us by surprise, not because we hadn't prepared and meticulously watched the weather forecast—we had. It was just wrong.

Now I thought we had been in gales before. We have been in twenty-foot seas and forty knot winds before, but not at the same time or for such an extended period of time. With the constant, erratic movement of the boat, after a number of hours we were all beginning to feel nauseous. Everyone is susceptible to motion sickness, it's just a matter of how much motion it will take. For some it's a gently swaying dock, for others it's a hurricane. My dad and I are particularly resistant, but even we have our limits.

Before the end of the day everyone except for me had lost their lunch. I think this was largely because I was able to quickly find a spot on the boat that didn't smell like vomit and hunker down there. But even I felt the chunks beginning to rise in my throat every now and then. My poor father had it the worst because he was constantly going up on deck or on the bow to check, secure, or fix something. An unbelievable amount of critical things were breaking left and right and he had to go fix them. The first day, the parrel balls and the rope they go on, for the foresail, and the fore gaff jaws broke, and without these the fore was useless. Together the parrel balls and gaff jaws wrap around the mast, allowing the gaff and the sail to slide up and down the mast.

The second day out everyone was at their sickest, or at least I was. I came very close to needing the bucket, but I fought it somehow. Within that 24-hour period, the fore and main lazy jacks came loose and had to be taken off to save them, and the stitching came out of the jib and staysail. The jib could eventually be repaired under way, but the staysail was in ribbons, only connected by the wire running down the side. Fortunately, we were able to replace it with the storm jib.

To make an already horrendous situation infinitely worse, by now, absolutely everything above and below deck was completely and utterly soaked. We had been taking large amounts of water over the bow, which alone would have been bad enough, but we were in torrential rains for over 48 hours, so finding a dry spot on the boat was nearly impossible with our numerous openings and leaks around the boat.

Water swirled like miniature whirlpools on the various parts of the deck when we hit the trough of a wave. With this action, the copious amounts of rope all over the boat would uncoil and slosh around in enormous matted heaps. A few were even washed overboard, so someone—almost always my dad—would regularly have to go up on deck and coil lines to prevent them from snagging the propeller.

The main congregating place on the boat, the cockpit, was a foul smelling swamp, with the fragrance of wet dog and vomit permeating throughout the small enclosed area. This odiferous bog was also the bedroom for most of us because the motion was too bad in our own bunks, or they were too wet, or both. The motion was so horrible that you couldn't stand to be up forward, above or below deck, for more than a few minutes without tossing your cookies. Down below, the only usable parts of the boat were the two aft cabins, the chart table, and the head. Being a bit more sensitive to the motion than I am, my brother couldn't stand to be down below at all, and couldn't use his cabin, so I did. Unfortunately, his cabin leaked tremendously in numerous places. The upper bunk was covered with a multitude of soggy things that I tried in vain to keep dry. The bottom bunk, which I slept on for a while, had at least three leaks over it. I slept in sort of an S shape to avoid the wet spots, but as the days went on, the wet spots grew so that they were unavoidable. I eventually ended up on the floor, which is about a 3 by 3 square of hard wood, a bit oddly shaped because of the contours of the boat. I somehow contorted myself to fit on that small square and use my comforter as both cushion and blanket.

I rode out the majority of the storm essentially curled up in the fetal position on this spare bit of dry hard floor. There wasn't anything else I could do but wait it out. To try to keep myself from wallowing in a pit of despair, I thought about the only bright spot on the horizon that had nothing to do with this stupid boat or my present predicament. I thought about my boyfriend. I pictured his nervous smile, his vivid blue eyes, and messy dark hair. I thought about playing tennis, going rock climbing, and watching movies together. I lived out entire dates in my head. I wanted it to be over—the motion, the storm, the fear and anxiety. Even the whole trip itself. I just wanted it to end. Escaping into my imagination, dissociating from my present condition, imagining happier times not on the ocean, it helped.

As miserable as these conditions were, and miserable they certainly were, mine were probably the best. Everyone else was crammed into the dank, smelly cockpit, but eventually some of them ventured out to find bits and pieces of dry floor, and once a spot was found it was usually fought over. Fortunately for me, no one else could fit in my spot, so I had no competition.

The adults onboard were usually quite thankful to have even a small bit of hard floor to sleep on because most of the time they functioned on very little sleep. Although sleep was not the only thing we were deprived of. With the terrible lurching of the boat, there was no way my mother could have cooked anything, but that was just as well because no one felt like eating. On the rare occasion that someone did eat anything, our diet consisted of salted crackers and ginger ale. (Fun fact: while ginger is known to have anti-nausea properties, most ginger ale does not contain any ginger at all.)

But it didn't work very well for most of us.

The third day out wasn't quite as bad, just because nothing broke. My father had almost completely run out of dry clothes from going out on deck and getting completely drenched so frequently. But for one dangerous task even foul weather gear wouldn't have kept him dry.

Because of the constant violent movement of the boat, the stays for the masts and bobstays for the bowsprit kept loosening up and he would have to go tighten them. These aptly named stays are very important, as they make the mast and the bowsprit stay in place. Tightening the bobstays on the bowsprit was a particularly difficult and miserable job. The bowsprit would frequently become completely submerged because of the enormous waves, and several times my father was unfortunate enough to be on it at the time. One time, he was lying down on it tightening the bobstays and holding on for dear life. (Of course, he had a safety harness on and was tied off, as anyone up on deck had to be.) As a wave approached, the bowsprit went down with my father on it and water flooded the forward end of the boat. The bow came back up and his head came up a bit further and issued a spurt of water, like a whale.

The bilges were incredibly full by now, from all the water that had leaked through the decks, and seeped up through the floorboards when we heeled. I could hear the water sloshing around with the motion of the boat very clearly from my position on the floor.

Those first three days out to sea were a blur of misery, each day melding imperceptibly into the next. After being beaten up for three days straight we were ready to turn back. None of us had eaten more than a few crackers since we left the protection of land, and most of the time those came back up. Just moving became an Olympic event. After not eating and barely sleeping for three days, I think my father had had enough. And this was HIS dream. My parents made the difficult decision to head to the closest landfall, back to the US. After being turned around for a few hours my mother called for weather advice on our HAM radio.

We had heard from other cruisers about a man in Canada who frequently gave weather advice to cruisers in just the sort of predicament that we were in. He was a former cruiser himself and had become a skilled amateur meteorologist after he and his family had been through a storm at sea even more dangerous than the one we were currently in. (Note from the future: I didn't realize it at the time, but Herb Hilgenberg, the amateur meteorologist, is world famous among the sailing/cruising community. He has a Wikipedia page and everything. He's helped countless sailors in similar situations, and saved the lives and property of many. He very well may have saved ours too. At the very least he saved us from days of suffering. However, someone sued him back in 2012 and he's stopped providing this (free!) service.

My mother braved the vomit-inducing motion of the boat down below to use our ham radio, for she was the only licensed radio operator onboard.

She interrupted his regular program with our urgent situation, and he stopped what he was doing to help us. We were advised to go as far east as quickly as possible to get out of the system. We turned on the motor and steered a compass course as close to 90 degrees as we could keep. Although our boat is an excellent one for offshore sailing and the like, it doesn't have very good fuel capacity, so we had to watch that very carefully. We were headed back towards our destination in the Caribbean now, and hopefully would be out of the storm soon.

Once we were clear of the system, we were becalmed for a week. For the most part, this was a rather pleasant change, but we didn't have the fuel capacity to motor the whole way. So our wonderful weather resource told us which way to go to find some wind. Who knows what we would have done without him. But once we did find some wind it was rather light, and it takes at least 15 knots to start moving this 33 ton tank, but it was certainly better than nothing.

If it hadn't been so incredibly rough and so long, overall I think I would have a much more positive opinion of offshore sailing. By the 5th day out we were able to stay down below and cook, and everyone was starving after eating next to nothing for days. It was quite an experience to simply sit down and eat a meal. Our gimballed table rocking back and forth made it impossible to eat off, but it did a good job of keeping everything from going everywhere, so we ate off our laps.

By now the motion was such that I could sleep in my own cabin. I was quite surprised to see that it had stayed relatively dry in comparison to the rest of the boat. It was still fairly wet, and my cushions needed to be dried out for a while. After they were dry enough to sleep on, the salt in them and my sheets attracted more moisture, so they were always kind of damp, but it was a big improvement over a tiny piece of hard floor.

For a few days we were in an area of the Atlantic known as the Sargasso Sea, due to the large patches of Sargasso seaweed floating around in the cobalt blue waters. I was amazed by the incredible shade of blue of the water in the middle of the ocean. It is unlike any other shade of blue I have ever seen. I loved watching the water swirl around in the portholes in my cabin when a large wave hit. It was like a swirling blue raspberry creamsicle slushie.

My favorite part about offshore sailing was stargazing. Out in the middle of the ocean, the only unnatural source of light at night was our own running lights, or the occasional pinprick of light from a passing vessel. The night sky was more incredible than any planetarium I have ever been to. I could identify all sorts of constellations, planets, clusters, the Andromeda galaxy, and even our own galaxy, the Milky Way. I can't imagine seeing the

Milky Way any more clearly with the unaided eye than we did out there. It was incredible. The most amazing natural phenomenon we saw was a meteor, or at least we think it was a meteor. It was at least ten times as bright and impressive as any we saw in the Leonid meteor shower. I've never actually seen a comet, but I think this meteor looked somewhat similar. It even had a tail. It was about 1/10 of the size of a full moon and just as bright. It slowly streaked across the sky in a large arc, leaving a small trail of light behind it. We all stood with our eyes and mouths as wide as they could go, completely in awe of the workings of nature and our universe.

Flying fish are yet another of nature's marvels. They look a bit like a small mackerel, except for their spiny little wings, which are really large, elongated pectoral fins. We had quite a few wander onto the boat, but unfortunately only one made it back into the water alive.

It came aboard at night. I was steering well after sunset, and all of a sudden I heard what sounded like a candy wrapper flapping around in the wind. I looked over to where the noise was coming from, but it was very dark so all I could see was a dark mass much bigger than a candy wrapper. I told my mother, who was half-asleep in the cockpit, to come see what it was, and she unceremoniously tossed the little guy back in.

As strange as they look up close, they are even stranger to see from afar. Gliding over the water in schools, from a distance they look like swarms of insects hovering over the waves. It's amazing to see how long they stay out of the water, it's quite a bit longer than seems possible.

My brother and I had felt like deadweight through the storm—our parents hadn't let us do anything, not that there really was much we could have done. But once the storm passed we were promoted back to full crew members—whether we liked it or not. And that included standing watch.

I quickly got used to the routine of daily life in the middle of the ocean. Steering became one of my favorite chores. I would sit at the helm, listen to one of the few CD's I'd brought in heavy rotation. Gorillaz became my favorite. The tempo and mood somehow fit well with the rhythms of the ocean, especially at twilight—my usual time to steer. (They only had one album out in 2001, so it was that one. To this day, I have such a strong association with that album and being on a boat, that I feel like I'm swaying when I listen to it.)

On the 8th day out, we had a bit of unpleasant excitement. A piece of the rigging that keeps the main sail up broke (the throat, which keeps up the part of the sail closest to the mast). The sail had slid down the mast, so we had to make the repair and haul it back up. Putting up the sails on a gaff-rigged schooner isn't exactly easy in the best of conditions, and it's especially difficult when you're rolling around. You have to pull and somehow keep your balance at the same time. As annoying as that was, that same day, something even more critical and difficult to fix broke.

An unexpected wind shift caused an uncontrolled jibe (the sail suddenly swung from one side of the boat to the other), which broke the port cross tree spreader tip (an important bit way at the top of the mast.) At the time, we were rolling around quite a bit, and the masts were going back and forth at unnerving angles. In spite of this, my father had to go up and fix it.

Back home in Rockland Harbor, I had been up the masts oiling the batons when a ferryboat went by, and the boat rocked a bit and the ratlines shook with me on them, and that was a bit nerve-wracking. I can only imagine that going aloft in rolling seas must have been a million times worse. With the masts swinging like a pendulum, my father went up. Of course he clipped on once he was in reach of the spreaders, and somehow was able to fix it, and we could continue south.

After a few more days of going discouragingly slow, worrying about fuel consumption, and trying to head towards a sufficient amount of wind and the Caribbean, we sighted land on December 22nd, after 13 days out to sea.

Those tall, dark green, volcanic islands shrouded in mist were sure a sight for sore eyes.

As we approached, some of the islands looked like moss-covered rocks that had been placed in a pool of water. Once we were between the various islands, we had to go through a very narrow passage. After not even seeing the stuff for over two weeks, it was a bit awkward navigating around the land. The fact that we could see the bottom was also a bit disturbing, even though it was deep enough.

The sun was beginning to set as we reached the entrance of Charlotte Amalie Harbor, St. Thomas, in the U.S. Virgin Islands. Just as we were about to enter the harbor, an enormous cruise ship was on its way out. We figured we'd wait for it to go by, but just as it was clear, another one was on its way out. Since it was now fairly dark, we announced on the VHF that we were going to sneak by while the ship was turning the corner. And it was a good thing we did because a third one was just behind.

We had finally made it. We anchored by the light of civilization, and went to bed soon after. I think we all had the best night's sleep we'd had in weeks. Tomorrow brought the promise of showers. After over two weeks without one we were all unbearably disgusting. We had exhausted our fresh food supplies and had been eating nothing but canned food for days. So restaurants and grocery stores were also going to be a luxury. The list of all the little things that we had been deprived of for those two weeks goes on and on, but the important thing was that we had made it. We had all worked very hard to get where we were, and there had been many obstacles along the way, but we had beaten them all. We finally made it to the golden Caribbean and we were ready for some serious recreation. But we were already dreading the trip home.

You might be wondering where my dad's friend Ray was this whole time. He did help my parents steer and take watches as they'd hoped, but that was mostly after the storm had passed. To be honest, he just blended into the background for me. But as soon as we sighted land, he wanted off. He joked that he'd had it with the ocean—with all bodies of water. He was selling his boat and moving inland. I couldn't tell if he was joking or not.

After the ordeal of the offshore passage, I felt different somehow—changed. I was worn out, mildly traumatized, but I'd been to hell and back and survived and I felt powerful because of it. I'd done it—I'd crossed an ocean, weathered a storm at sea, and spent 14 days no more than 60 ft from my little brother without throwing him overboard. At just 16, I was a bona fide blue water sailor.

The ordeal made me understand why sailors get tattoos—after emotional and physical trauma at sea you feel like you need to commemorate it—the experience becomes a part of your essence, lives in your very skin. I felt like a badass. I did not get a tattoo.

I felt more disconnected from my friends back home than ever. They simply could not relate to the ordeal I'd just survived. I could tell my boyfriend tried to empathize, but what frame of reference could he possibly have? I used the phrase "you just don't even know" far too often in my emails, and I know it bugged him. But he didn't and he couldn't. Nobody else but a fellow sailor could. If I ever did this again my partner was coming with me.

I had an understanding of how beautiful, precious, and fragile life is, of the majesty and fury of nature, far greater than my number of years typically allow.

Those three days in the gale would become the yardstick to which I measured all other difficult events in my life. School stressors, tests, friendship drama—nothing else would measure up for a very long time.

6 Tropical Showering

December 22, 2001
St. Thomas, USVI

The U.S. Virgin Islands: the American paradise. That was the notion I first had as we were sailing in amongst the emerald-like islands sprinkled over a sea of turquoise. But my dreams of lush green rainforests, coconuts, palm trees, and white sandy beaches were in for a serious reality check. Charlotte Amalie, St. Thomas was not what I expected the Caribbean to be like. It was hot, crowded, touristy, dirty, over-populated, and commercialized. It was not the exotic tropical paradise I had hoped for. In many ways it was much like the cities we had left back in the states. Other than the intense heat there was one very noticeable difference: the rain. From the day we arrived it rained. And it rained, and it rained, and it rained. But we much preferred these rain showers to the grotesque showers we had on first arriving, which is a story in itself.

 After spending two weeks in the middle of the ocean without one, we were all in dire need of a shower. Because we were so desperate, we went to the first place we could find and paid whatever they asked. They were part of a run down, hurricane damaged old hotel that had been mostly condemned. The showers were in the locker room near the covered-up pool. There was no electricity in the place, so we had to leave the bathroom doors open in order to see. Fortunately we were the only people there, and it was quite obvious why. The linoleum floor was so crusted with dirt I half expected to see plants growing out of them. Bugs scuttled across the disintegrating walls. At least two of the five toilets had "out of order" signs on them, and the sinks sprayed water all over you when you turned on the faucet. Thank goodness we were all smart enough to wear sandals in any public shower, or else I'm sure we would have contracted some rare tropical type of foot fungus. There was absolutely no water pressure in the showers, and the little water that the pipes managed to squeeze out was freezing cold. It was literally like taking a shower under a dribbling hose. As disgusting as these showers were, we were all incredibly grateful to finally be clean again.

Once we were all finished taking showers, we couldn't wait to get out of there and explore. But, we would be forced to stay there much longer than we would have liked because of a sudden downpour. Eventually the rain stopped, for a few minutes anyway, and we set out into this unknown land. The city was far too crowded for our taste. Sidewalks were sparse in parts of the city and so overcrowded that you get pushed into the bushes, street, or stores. All the shops that lined the bustling streets of Charlotte Amalie had the same cheap t-shirts, glossy postcards, and plastic souvenirs.

I was surprised to see how Americanized this island was. Sure, this was the U.S. Virgin Islands, but I didn't expect to see KFC, Wendy's, McDonald's, Pizza Hut, Subway, Burger King, and K-Mart in such a small radius.

One benefit of the industrialized nature of St. Thomas—internet cafes. To save time I would write emails on our laptop on the boat and save them to a floppy disk. Then I would copy all my emails from my friends onto the disk to read (and reread) later.

I was happy that almost every time I had the opportunity to check my inbox there was an email from my boyfriend. He described his excitement about the latest snowfall, and annoyance with school, complaining he still had to take the English final even though he already had an A. And a song he heard on the radio that reminded him of me. It was Wish You Were Here by Incubus. It became our song.

In addition to the internet cafes, we soon had even more access to technology. It all started out with the four of us lugging enormous sacks of laundry down to the local laundromat, a hole-in-the-wall sort of place crammed chock-a-block full of washers, dryers, and people. When we first arrived we had to wait a while to get a few washing machines. After we had filled all the machines we could find until we ran out of clothes to fill them with, we sat in the coolest spot we could find, considering it was half full of machines whose main purpose was to produce heat.

It was then that we met our email savior. She was a fellow cruiser from Canada, who had been traveling for many years. From just looking at us she realized that we too were cruisers. The heaps of laundry gave us away. She and her partner and their two visiting teenage grandsons were stuck in Charlotte Amalie because of a broken generator. She asked, semi jokingly, if we knew anything about generators. My father, a marine engineer, knew quite a lot about generators. My mother asked if she knew anything about pactors and ham radio email. We had purchased a pactor—a magical device that allows you to send and receive email via ham radio—but had yet to figure out how to get it to work. As it turned out, she had the highest possible ham radio license and had almost exactly the same ham radio and pactor we did. Except she actually knew how to use them. So we swapped expertise. My father went to their boat to see if he could help with their generator, and she came over to our boat to help with our pactor.

I think I may have been the most excited of all to have our ham radio email up and working, as it meant I could email with my friends almost every day, as long as the weather conditions allowed.

Not far from St. Thomas there was a place on our chart named Christmas Cove, off Great St. James Island. So on December 24th we felt we kind of had to go there. The golden Caribbean sun dipped below the horizon, leaving behind it a spectrum of color, bespeckled with fluffy white clouds. A large fish jumped clear out of the water and showed us his strange body, while prehistoric-looking birds soared overhead, and large graceful manta rays played around our anchor chain. These were our gifts that year, as well as this poem I wrote for my parents.

Christmas Poem

Merry Christmas Mom and Dad
I hope that you are not too sad
Because of the lack of presents this year
But you should know I still hold you dear
It's not that I have not tried or thought
But a meaningful present I have not
And with all the tough times we've been through
We should try and remember too
That the spirit of this holiday is not
Of gifts and money, something that the Grinch forgot
Now you may think me full of beans
But think about what this poem means
Though our stockings may be empty and presents few
We're doing something most people only dream to do
We are down here having the adventure of a lifetime
So I hope you realize that this card and rhyme
Took much more effort and thought
Than anything I could have bought.

7 Swapping Tales

December 28, 2001
St. John, USVI

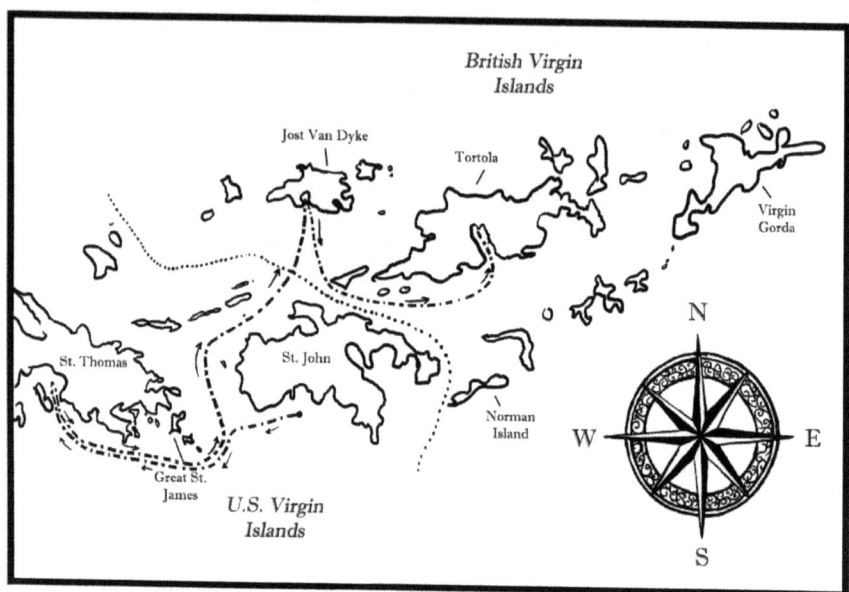

Between a rock and a hard place. That is where we found ourselves after leaving beautiful Christmas Cove, off Great St. James Island. We had set out that day for Jost Van Dyke in the BVIs (British Virgin Islands) to attend the legendary New Year's party at Foxy's. Foxy's bar and restaurant is an institution to sailors worldwide. It is particularly known for its New Year's parties, which fill the tiny harbor with wall to wall boats. But it was not meant to be.

Just as we were approaching a rather narrow passage between St. John and a large mass of jagged, unfriendly looking rock, we decided to turn on our engine to pass through. So my father turned the key, pushed the button, it started up as usual, and we carefully approached the tight space. Meanwhile, I was midship looking at the pretty green islands and the beautiful turquoise water that had now become almost alarmingly clear as we entered the somewhat shallow passage. All of a sudden, the engine sped up to a disturbing roar, then fell lamentably silent. My father flew down below to see why the engine had decided to quit at such an inopportune time, and tried to restart it to get us out from between the rocks. He restarted it, but it just sped up and died again. In his rush to try to purge the fuel system and restart the engine yet again, the starter motor broke when the engine raced with it still engaged. Now the chances that it will start up again are slim to none. So we were stuck between a large island and some menacing rocks with no motor. We frantically tacked back and forth between the rocks and tried desperately not to come in contact with them.

Up ahead a little ways I could see a small sailboat perched upon a jagged rock. Not really what you want to see at a time like this. All I could do was hope that we would not suffer the same fate and assist in switching over the jib sheet and duck to avoid the booms when we tack. Fortunately that was enough. We somehow made it out of the passage unscathed. There was still the nagging little problem that we did not have a usable engine. So we ducked into the closest anchorage, which just happened to be Caneel Bay, off St. John. As we were dropping the anchor we all crossed our fingers and muttered to ourselves, "please don't drag, please don't drag."

After determining that he could not repair it, my father had no other choice but to take the starter motor ashore to see if he could get it fixed. So he, the 80-lb starter motor, and my little brother all headed into Cruz Bay, which was a long, wet dinghy ride away. There was no one on St. John who could fix our starter motor, so my father and brother took the ferry back to St. Thomas. After lugging around the starter motor a great deal and a number of phone calls, they found a guy who would be able to fix it. He was

all the way on the other side of the island and ready to close up, but willing to wait for them. So they hailed a taxi to trek over to the other side of the island. Before they got in the taxi my father realized he didn't have enough cash on him to pay for the cab fare and the starter motor repair. So he ran to the nearest bank, where the security guard practically had the key in the lock, burst into the bank and was able to get the money just in time. The repair guy was able to fix the starter motor without any problem, and my father had the engine running that evening. That still didn't completely solve our engine problem. The engine would run now, but my father would have to spend the next week completely redoing the fuel system so we wouldn't get any more air bubbles in the fuel line, which is what had caused the engine to die earlier. So we were stuck in Caneel Bay. But it was a pretty good place to be stuck.

Caneel Bay is surrounded by lush green hills, a picturesque white sandy beach in front, and an interesting city nearby. Cruz Bay, one of the larger settlements of St. John, was just around the corner. It was such an enormous and pleasant change from Charlotte Amalie. It was much cleaner, less touristy, more low key, and more like what I had originally expected the Caribbean to be like.

One of the first things I noticed was the wild chickens running around the streets. It was rather odd, they were like pigeons or sea gulls would be in most cities, but most people don't eat pigeons or sea gulls. (Although we used to eat pigeons, and still do in some parts of the world.) There were lots of interesting little shops, most of which were in this beautiful labyrinth-like stone mall. Brightly colored bushes of hibiscus, bougainvillea, and other tropical flowers were all over the place.

The beach in front of us was absolutely perfect in my mind. Unfortunately, lots of other people shared this opinion and it was often a bit crowded, but that was really the only drawback. We would put all our beach stuff in the dinghy, pull it up on shore and go swimming, snorkeling, or just lie around on the soft white sand. The water there was so warm it was almost like bathwater, and it was so clear you could see the tiny fish playing around your ankles, but if you moved they would be lost in a cloud of sand. To either side of the beach were coral reefs with all kinds of different sea creatures in them. There was a piece of brain coral the size of a large boulder and some Elkhorn and Staghorn coral the size of small bushes. Sea fans swayed lazily back and forth with the motion of the gentle sea. A school of French grunts would swim by and I would get lost amongst them. Multi-colored parrotfish would nibble at the coral. At the same time we heard a strange clicking sound that we later learned was the same parrotfish chomping away on the coral. We had this fish to thank for the beautiful sandy beach. The pieces of coral went through its digestive tract and were excreted as sand.

In addition to the parrotfish, we also had the Rockefellers to thank for this beautiful beach. Much of St. John had been donated by the Rockefellers to the National Park Service, which is why it is today the same pristine natural wonderland it was hundreds of years ago. Although today there are many nature trails weaving throughout the island.

One day we decided to hike one such trail that went from the beach to Cruz Bay. I was surprised and a little disappointed that it wasn't a rainforest. It was more like a cross between desert scrubland and deciduous forest, not exactly what I had expected in the Caribbean. There were various types of cacti, birch-like trees with camouflage bark, tiny lizards crawling through the undergrowth, hermit crabs scuttling along the path, and various birds singing from their perches. I was fascinated by the giant succulents. There were enormous plants that looked a little like aloe vera, but were roughly the size of a refrigerator. I believe they were called century plants. They reminded me of "Little Shop of Horrors." Whenever I walked by one I half expected it to reach out and try to eat me. But I had problems with something much smaller eating me.

It had been a long rainy season this year and there were lots of mosquitoes. We all had a bit of a problem with them, but I think I had it the worst. I don't know what it is, but I have always been one of those people that mosquitoes just love. I had so many itchy mosquito bites it was like having chicken pox. I was constantly covering myself with bug spray to try to keep the tiny vampires at bay. I even put on bug spray before bed, but every morning I would wake up with even more bug bites. Fortunately, we met some pharmacists who recommended some industrial strength bug spray and anti-itch cream and I haven't had a problem since.

Wherever we go, we're used to attracting a fair amount of attention. We're usually the only classic wooden boat in most harbors. Not so in Caneel Bay. The Lynx, a brand new sail training/charter vessel designed after the Baltimore clippers, came in just a little while after we did. It was built in Rockport, just around the corner from our hometown. One of the guys who worked on its construction had made our wheel box and davits. As they were coming into the harbor we called them on VHF to inform them of our current situation, because it looked like they were going to anchor near us. At the time, our engine didn't work, so if we dragged anchor there wouldn't be a whole lot we could do. They ended up anchoring quite a ways away.

We went over to say hi, and they invited us over for cocktails and gave us a tour. It was made to look very traditional and old, yet I knew it had just been launched that year. We sat around that big beautiful boat with cold drinks in hand, and talked with the crew about how lucky we all were to be in this beautiful place doing what we were doing.

The Canadians who had helped us with our ham radio email on St. Thomas had also arrived in Caneel Bay. We went over to visit them on their boat, and were soaked from both above and below on the dinghy ride over. The waves crawled over the sides of our too small dinghy. The clouds must have thought we were now too salty and wanted to wash us off, because it started raining when we were less than 100 yards away from our destination. So we four drowned rats scurried aboard our friends' boat to avoid further saturation. We dried off quickly in the tropic heat. While we were there, our hosts entertained us with a few more sea stories that we hadn't yet heard. Some of them they had just heard from others and some had happened to them first hand, and some of them were about hurricanes, tsunamis, and other nasty things of that sort. My favorite of their tales was of a much lighter nature.

It happened when they were out in the middle of the Atlantic. They were sailing along out there, absolutely nothing in sight, no land, not even another boat off in the distance. But in the water, they saw a person swimming out there with nothing around him. There was no sign of a boat, not even a piece of a boat, nothing. It looked to them like he was just out for a leisurely swim. So being courteous, concerned citizens they sailed over to him and asked if he wanted a ride. He replied very nonchalantly, "Oh, sure", and climbed aboard. They offered him a towel and a drink, both of which he accepted, and he asked to use the head. They tried to ask him why he was there, but hadn't received a definite answer. They were completely flabbergasted when out of nowhere, he said, "Well, it's getting kind of late. I'd better be going now. Thanks for the drink." And he just jumped overboard. They watched him swim away with their jaws on the deck. Moments later a periscope broke the surface of the ocean. The submarine had been trailing them the whole time. Our new friends had been the butt of a very good prank.

It was the warmest, sunniest, most beautiful January 8th I had ever known, far from the snow and cold of Maine winters. My world was now full of warm, gentle breezes, swaying palms, and splashing fish. Koukla's fuel system had been completely redone, and we could now explore the Caribbean without the fear of the engine quitting on us at an inopportune time.

For the moment we'd decided not to venture too far, seeing as one of the world's most beautiful beaches was just around the corner. The blessedly short sail over was just an hour or two between weighing and setting anchor. With its sparkling white sandy beaches, translucent turquoise water, and lively coral reefs, it was quite obvious why Trunk Bay was considered one of the nicest beaches in the world.

Under the bright yellow sun, my family and I dinghied over to the beach for an afternoon of snorkeling. A v-shaped trail of ripples across the water followed behind us, and we turned off the outboard motor moments before the propeller would start churning up sand.

We all jumped out into the knee-deep water and pulled the dinghy ashore. Our feet sank into the loose submerged sand. As we trudged along, we dragged the inflatable across the beach and left it high and dry. We all grabbed our flippers, masks, and snorkels and headed back towards the water. Our snorkeling gear transformed us into undersea fish people, with the power to stay under water for long periods of time and cut easily through the waves.

The briny bathwater flowed over us like silk as we all got a first-hand lesson in marine biology. Trunk Bay, in addition to its incredible beauty, also boasts a self-guided snorkeling tour, explaining all the marine life you see on underwater plaques built into the reef. One of the most interesting fish that we came across was the cowfish. As its name implies, it actually looks a bit like a cow. It has little horn-like projections on its head, and it is black with white spots. It has a peculiar method of hunting. It squirts a jet of water into the sand to scare up whatever might be hiding there and gobbles it up.

After our legs ached from propelling ourselves through the water, we headed back to Koukla and hauled anchor. We had to leave palm tree-lined Trunk Bay for a spot with better anchorage. Francis Bay was our location of choice for the night. Vibrantly green, undulating hills enclosed the inviting bay. Large schools of fish no bigger than my pinky toe would all jump at once to escape predators. Their fleeing sounded like a handful of sand being thrown into the water.

After only a short time of sailing that day, I guess my parents hadn't had enough, so we rigged up our sailing dinghy for the first time. For cruisers your boat is your house, so your dinghy—or little boat—is your car. A dinghy can be propelled either by oar, motor, or sail, or some combination thereof. Up until now, this little boat had just sat on deck filled with all the junk we couldn't fit down below. So we first had to take everything out and spread it all over the already cluttered deck. It turned out to be worth the hassle. There is an enormous difference between sailing a 60 ft. schooner and a 14 ft. lapstrake tender. With the big boat, it takes quite a bit of time and effort just to get the sails up. And Koukla isn't exactly fast or maneuverable. The little boat, on the other hand, just has the one sail that is relatively easy to put up, it goes fast even in a small breeze, and it's infinitely more maneuverable. But you wouldn't want to sail a small boat like that all the way from Maine to the Caribbean.

The next morning, we made a miraculous discovery. Just around the corner were actual showers that we were free to use. They were cold water showers with no roof, and you had to pull a chain for the water to come out, but we thought they were wonderful. To be able to use as much water as you wanted and completely get all the soap out of your hair was an absolute luxury.

These showers were part of an eco-resort that was welcoming to cruisers. That night we went there to explore. It was a complex maze of wooden walkways built into the mountain and blended in with the forest. At one point I set out to explore this labyrinth on my own in search of a pay phone. My boyfriend's mom answered. He wasn't home. He was at a soccer game or something. I hadn't thought about what day or time it was there. I usually didn't know what day it was. It didn't really matter here, until you actually wanted to talk to a normal person, living a normal life, following a normal weekly schedule.

Walking back from the pay phone, I got a bit lost. It was dark and my flashlight decided to die on me right when there were no sources of light nearby. The nighttime sounds of the jungle made the hairs on the back of my neck stand up. The dark jungle activated some primitive part of my brain that had once worried about becoming someone else's dinner, and I half expected something with sharp teeth and claws to jump out at me at any moment. I came across no such prehistoric animals and eventually found my way back.

The resplendent sun rose in the clear blue sky as we raised Koukla's sails. Rubbing my sleepy eyes, I looked at our course on the chart, and was quite happy to see it was relatively short. At least it was in theory. My drowsy eyes had missed the fact that we would be going through The Narrows, a very windy passage between St. John, of the U.S. Virgin Islands, and Tortola, of the British Virgin Islands. The wind and current funneled down through the passage between the islands, making it very difficult to beat against. Motoring, we would barely creep along at less than one knot. Under full sail tacking back and forth through the slowly widening passage we gradually made enough headway to ease the sheets and glide around the eastern end of St. John. Tacking, a rather exasperating ordeal already, was made more difficult because our jib sheets were too short. During the offshore passage our aforementioned jib sheets had each worn through in a spot, leaving them barely three-quarters their former length. This meant that when we tacked we would have to fight with the billowing sail, and muscle the too-short line onto the winch.

After a four-hour-long slugfest through the narrows we finally made it to Coral Bay, St. John. As we entered the bay we observed many dilapidated boats of all shapes and sizes that were anchored, tied up to the mangrove trees, stuck in the mud, or beached. This was a place where it appeared that many hopeful cruisers' dreams had died. It was also a place where others, unwilling to let go of the Caribbean lifestyle, had settled. Many of the derelicts we saw may have belonged to cruisers whose sailing fantasies had not met their expectations, so the boats appeared to be abandoned. Perhaps others simply ran out of money. The rest, unable to return to the daily grind of the real world, made Coral Bay their home. Many of Coral Bay's occupants made their livelihood through carpentry, marine repair, and the like. Their decorative workbenches dotted the beach. A few had more empty beer bottles than tools on them.

After roaming the town for a while, we wandered into the local hangout/bar/restaurant, Skinny Legs. The place was packed with cruisers and former cruisers turned locals. The ambiance of the town was magnified in this restaurant that was little more than a hut on the beach. From the walls and ceiling hung ancient beer and soda signs, nautical paraphernalia, and a small sign that said "lost soles" on it with a bunch of mismatched shoes that someone must have found on the beach dangling from it. After squinting at the menu, a surfboard in the corner with the items listed on it,

I decided on a hamburger. I don't know if it had just been a while since I'd had a decent burger, but it was possibly the single best hamburger I've ever eaten. Even the fries were exceptionally tasty.

After lunch, we had to go back to the boat and move to a better anchorage because Coral Bay was exposed to the building winds. Our spot of choice was Hurricane Hole. For centuries, Hurricane Hole has been one of the safest places in the Caribbean during a hurricane, hence the name.

Hurricane Hole was just a few minutes away, but I still had to flake anchor chain. This proved to be even more irksome than usual because the padlock to the forward hatch had corroded to the point where it would not open today. With the hatch closed it felt like it was about 110 degrees down there. Later, my father had to take a hack saw to that lock, and the next one we bought was marine grade.

From fellow cruisers, we had heard about a bus that went across the island of St. John, from Coral Bay to Cruz Bay. We had been told that there was a certain spot we had to wait at, that the bus would come by, that it cost a dollar per person one way, and that taking this ride was a must. So we all woke up bright and early one morning and made the long dinghy ride from our anchorage, climbed onto the wobbly dock at Coral Bay, walked a short way to the stop, and waited.

After about 15 minutes the bus stopped right where we and a few other people were standing. We piled in, paid the bus driver, and took our seats. From the outside as well as inside we could tell this was not meant for tourists. It was sort of old looking and the interior and exterior were subdued colors. The tourist buses, on the other hand, had fluorescent parrots and hibiscuses painted on them and they typically cost five times as much. The only people on the bus who weren't, or at least didn't appear to be locals, were other adventurous cruising types.

This ride was not for the faint at heart. In the U.S. Virgin Islands, people drive on the wrong side of the road. Here the right side is really the left. Since we were not used to this scenario, whenever a car would pass us we all got a little agitated. Since the other car would be on the right side of the road, our befuddled brains convinced us that we were going to crash. This fear was even more plausible because the roads were quite narrow, and the bus wasn't exactly small. But neither of these factors were the most unnerving aspect of this bus ride. What disturbed us the most was the incredible speed at which we were going, and the fact that the roads were very twisty-turney and winding didn't help our already frazzled nerves.

Off we sped through the lush interior of the island. Half the time we were only a few feet from the edge of a cliff, but the dense vegetation deceived us. The wildlife we observed wasn't exactly what you'd expect in a tropical forest. We passed herds of goats, chickens, cows, a few pigs, and an old abandoned rusty stove. At the top of the mountain, I caught a glimpse of the breathtaking panorama of the verdant, green islands and aquamarine sea.

After about an hour or so of this roller coaster ride, we got off in Cruz Bay, where we had been about a week before. It was amazing to see the difference between one side of the island and the other. In comparison, Cruz Bay was more polished and touristy, and Coral Bay was much more laid-back and relaxed.

Following another hour or so of zooming down the curvy mountain roads at break-neck speed, we arrived back at Coral Bay. But the day's excitement wasn't over yet; we still had to get back to our boat. The bay looked quite choppy from land, as the wind had significantly picked up over the course of the day. But crammed into our little inflatable it was much, much worse. We were heading into the wind and waves all the way back to Koukla. My mother, brother, and I huddled underneath a piece of plastic we stuck in the boat for just such an occasion. My father had to steer, so he wasn't able to protect himself from the stinging salty spray. The sea swells tossed our little inflatable to and fro. The water crawled up the sides of the boat and under the plastic, and the heavy spray fell upon us like rocks. After an eternity of put-putting from one side of the bay to the other, we made it back to Koukla with our boat half full of water.

As we were less than thrilled with the anchorage in Coral Bay, we continued in search of a more comfortable anchorage. Sailing into Great Lamisure Bay, St. John, it looked like we had left the Caribbean and were back sailing off the coast of Maine. The rugged coast, gravelly beaches, and comparatively flatter terrain set Great Lamisure Bay apart from the rest of the Caribbean. But we hadn't come here to be reminded of home. We were here for the petroglyphs. Starting at Great Lamisure Bay, there was a 2.5 mile hike inland to a seasonal waterfall that the Taino, one of the indigenous people of the Caribbean, had visited hundreds of years ago. We know they had frequented this spot because they etched drawings and symbols into the rock face.

One morning, my father, brother, and I set out to see them. My mother had injured her foot the day before and wasn't up to the long hike. My mother dropped the three of us off at the dock of a deserted ranger station, and we began our expedition. Early on, we passed this strange swampy place full of dead, blackened, skeleton-like trees standing eerily to the side of the path. We passed them quickly. Onward we marched in the searing Caribbean sun. If we stopped for too long the mosquitoes would find us, especially in the shade. Part of the trail was through an open field with nowhere to hide from the sweltering rays. On we pressed for what may not have been, but certainly felt like hours. Towards the end, the trees hunched over the trail, forming a thin, yet dazzling green canopy. The sun shone through it and tinted everything green.

After an exhausting, sweaty hike we had reached our destination. In the rainy season, there would have been an impressive waterfall plunging into a small pool. Since it was the dry season it wasn't much more than a glorified puddle, but a neat one at that. Dragonflies flitted over the brownish pond, and small freshwater fish swam lazily below. The spot was fairly sheltered from the sun, and the dragonflies kept the mosquitoes at bay, making it a very pleasant resting place. These petroglyphs were done by Taino, who once inhabited much of the Caribbean. Some archaeologists believe one of these petroglyphs (the swirly one) represents the nose of a bat, an important symbol linking the natural and spiritual worlds. At night bats can be found eating insects out of the pool. Some petroglyphs are just faces. Humans like faces. The glyphs are at a height where they are reflected by the pool, but never submerged. (Notes from the future: I was oblivious to the history and symbolism of them at the time, I just thought they were cool squiggles. I did wonder where the original artist would have stood. Did they squat down from above, or did they stand in the water with their tools?)

When we were done with our hike, we called my mother on our portable VHF radio, and she came and picked us up. Once on Koukla, the three of us quickly threw on our bathing suits and jumped overboard to cool off.

8 Precipitous Provisioning

January 19, 2002
St. Thomas, USVI

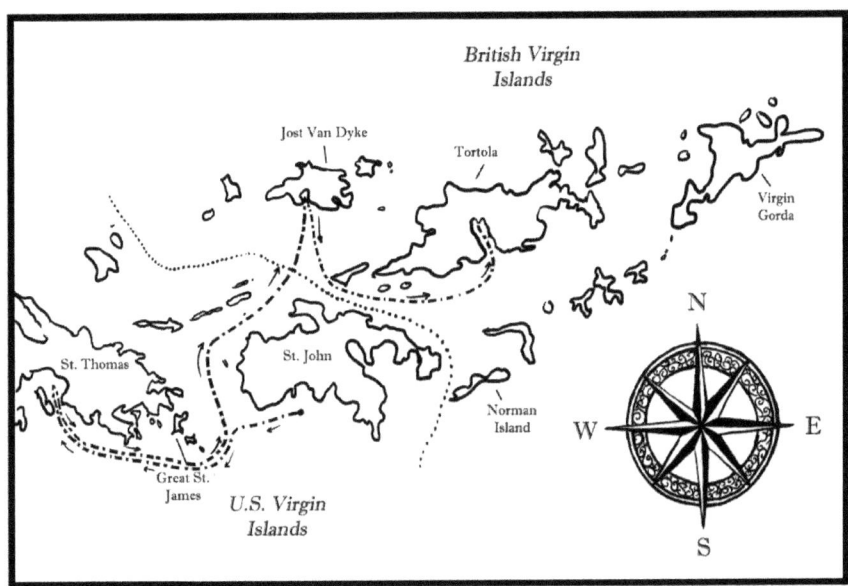

Before leaving the USVI's we went back to Charlotte Amalie to stock up before continuing south. Once we were there, we didn't waste any time idling. We were there to provision, and we wanted to do so as quickly as possible and move on to new and more interesting places. Unfortunately, with lots of groceries to buy, tons of laundry to do, and all the odds and ends that needed to be taken care of, we ended up staying there a whole week.

Grocery shopping when you are traveling and living on a boat is quite an ordeal. After making our purchases, we had to stuff everything into all the bags of various shapes and sizes that we had scrounged up from around the boat. Paper towels, milk, two liter bottles of soda (for my dad this was a necessity), meats, cereal, canned goods, etc, all had to be packed up and carried to the waterfront. With only the four of us and tons of stuff to carry, we were all heavily weighed down. The walk back seemed four times as long as the walk there. Back at the boat, we had to stuff everything into every nook and cranny we could find. Over the course of the week we must have made at least three or four trips to the grocery store. By the third trip, all the usual spots to store things in were used up and we had to get creative. Anything that could go in the bilge went in the bilge.

There was even a Kmart in Charlotte Amalie. We all bought a few more items of clothing, as our limited wardrobes were getting a bit worn by the elements. I bought a few new CDs, as I'd been listening to my very limited options on repeat. I bought Weezer's The Green Album, and Incubus' Morning View.

As much as we wanted to escape from Charlotte Amalie, it seemed that the weather gods wanted to keep us there. It rained for at least a few minutes a day every day we were there, but usually for longer. When it rained we had to close up the boat to keep the water out, which also meant keeping the fresh air out, so we melted below deck. The worst thing about the rain was that it prevented us from doing our errands, and therefore delayed our departure. Keep in mind, this was not the standard rainfall of New England, these were intermittent torrential downpours.

One day, after we had been cooped up for most of the day because of a number of consecutive showers of varying lengths, my mother and I wanted to make a break for it in between the rainstorms. My father had agreed to take us ashore as long as we went quickly so he could get back to the boat before it started coming down too hard. So off we went with the dark, ominous clouds chasing us ashore. When we were a few hundred yards away from the dock it started to sprinkle. We were puttering along nicely, so I was sure we'd be able to get to shelter before the precipitation truly set in. It would just be my luck that our piece of junk outboard motor would die just as the rain was really picking up. My mother and I scrambled to the oars and attempted to row while my father fiddled with the engine. Anyone who has ever rowed an inflatable will know it's not easy. It's like rowing a bathtub.

As the rain intensified, I could see the people on land were quite amused with our situation. Within minutes it was absolutely pouring, and I was soaked. Trying to row was now an exercise in futility, so I gave up and just let the rain fall upon me. There was nothing left to do but laugh at our ill luck. I'm sure that's what everyone watching us was doing. The fact that my father fixed the engine just as the rain subsided made the whole situation that much more hilarious. Oh well, that was probably the best shower the three of us had all week.

Later on that week a much less jovial incident occurred. My father and brother had to take the inflatable a few miles around the corner to the industrial part of Charlotte Amalie to refill our propane bottles. They had been gone for quite a while, so I was looking to see if they were on their way back yet. After searching for a little while, I spotted our little inflatable, but that wasn't all. They were being tailed by a local police boat and what looked almost like a Navy SEAL boat. My only thought at that moment was that whatever this meant could not be good. When my father and brother came back to Koukla, the police boat also came alongside, while the camouflage-clad SWAT team boat sat a few yards off.

Apparently, the police boat had come up to them in the inflatable and interrogated them, asking what boat they were with, how many people were on board, our nationality, how long we had been there, and finally, if we had a weapon. And thus was the root of this soon to be nerve-wracking ordeal. Because of the fear of pirates, not the swashbuckling, parrot-clad kind, but the type with machine guns that drive high speed cigarette boats, and because we had heard horror stories about them, my parents had made the difficult decision to carry a firearm on board. This was a particularly difficult decision to make because one must be absolutely meticulous about documenting and declaring it. Some countries even confiscate it during your stay.

Flash back to one month earlier, when we first arrived in St. Thomas. My father was heading into customs to check in. He tried to check in at customs, but he was basically turned away because we are all American citizens. When the firearm was mentioned, the officer told my father that so long as it stayed locked up on board our boat there was no problem. My father adamantly requested some form of verification, but the customs official insisted that since we were U.S. citizens in U.S. territory there was nothing to give. Unsatisfied with this, my father figured he should at least write down the name of the official that had refused him any paperwork, and he did so, and left with that name as his only form of verification.

Now, one month later, we have a big problem because we have no paperwork for our firearm. The police officer authoritatively demanded paperwork while my parents frantically pleaded that we had asked for paperwork, but none was given to us. Also, what I found quite rude on the part of the police officer was that he would only speak to my father because he was the captain, and basically disregarded every word my mother had to say because she was not. Meanwhile, my brother and I sat quietly by in fear of what this could all mean. When the haughty police officer said, "we had a big problem here," the image of my father sitting in a dank, dirt-floored jail cell flashed through my mind.

After much frantic pleading on my parents' part and much authoritative insistence on the part of the officer, the officer seemed to be getting frustrated and asked to see the ship's papers. My father went and fetched the papers, with the name of the customs official included. As he went down below for the papers, he noticed that the police officer looked familiar, and it soon dawned upon him that this was the exact same police officer that he had encountered before. As soon as my father said something, the officer quickly recognized him as well and left. We too left Charlotte Amalie shortly after.

9 Waxing Poetic

January 28, 2002
Jost Van Dyke, BVIs

Wispy white clouds galloped across the powder blue sky, blown by a strong but hardly blustery wind. These clouds were headed for Jost Van Dyke, in the British Virgin Islands, as were we. As we headed out on the morning of January 28, 2002, the four of us were astounded to find that the wind was blowing in the best possible direction for where we wanted to go.

For most boats, 25 knots of wind is a bit much, but not for Koukla. We passed numerous smaller reefed vessels. We even soared past a heavily reefed Hinckley. For those who aren't familiar, Hinckleys are very fast and very expensive sailboats. We flew towards Jost Van Dyke on a beam reach the whole way, which is the fastest point of sail for a schooner. Very, very quickly the island of Jost Van Dyke went from just a dot on the horizon to a green, looming hulk.

Just when we were starting to enjoy the one really good sail we'd had so far we had to come to a screeching halt, literally. Great Bay, Jost Van Dyke may have been pretty great aesthetically, but great in size it was not. It was a dead end harbor with coral reefs on either side, and we were screaming towards this veritable brick wall at 8 knots. But the four of us were undaunted. We knew our places and set about lowering the sails, readying the anchor and such like a highly trained racing pit crew. Even with the sails down we were still moving a bit too quickly. So my mother had to kick it into reverse to prevent what would have been our eventual collision with a coconut palm. We very quickly dropped the anchor, and we were still drifting backwards a bit when it caught.

It should be noted at this point that this harbor is known historically to have bad holding ground, and most everyone who tries to anchor here drags at least once. But not us. We were well equipped in the anchor department, perhaps a bit too well. All of them, except for our one dinghy anchor, are very big and very heavy. Most people would have one or two anchors, but no, that wasn't good enough. We had to have 6 anchors. Or, I think there were at least six, I kind of lost track. If you lose track of just how many anchors you have you probably have too many anchors. Each of our six or so anchors was intended for a slightly different bottom condition—rocks, sand, or mud. You name it, we were prepared. I think it gave us all some guilty pleasure watching other boats come into the harbor, try to anchor three or four times and still drag a bit.

Now that Koukla wasn't going anywhere, there was just the matter of checking in to customs. I was kind of excited because this was the first time I had officially been out of the country. At this point in my life I had never even been to Canada, despite the fact that my home state borders it. At the same time, I think we were all a bit leery of public officials because of our recent close call with the law back in Charlotte Amalie. We knew we would have to turn over our firearm and we hoped that that wouldn't bring about any problems. Fortunately, we cleared customs without any trouble, and the British officials were reasonable, polite, and professional. The worst part about it was that I had to sit in this room in the customs building that strangely reminded me of my old elementary school for far longer than I would have liked. Perhaps it was the pastel color walls and the small, uncomfortable chairs. There was a whole island right there waiting to be explored and it was killing me that I had to wait so long to see it. Finally, my father had finished all the paperwork, our passports were stamped, and we were free to go.

When we left Customs and Immigration we just picked a road and started walking to see what there was to see. The road that we picked was an unpaved path along the beach. Every hundred yards or so we would pass a brightly painted plywood shack plastered with beer posters with a sign that said "bar" somewhere in the vicinity. After we passed about five of these we tried a different direction. The opposite direction led us past many small sun-baked houses, some with cloth doors, goat pens, or chicken coops. As we plodded on, the houses became fewer and farther between, and the road gradually got steeper and steeper. The incline was so gradual, in fact, that our legs noticed long before our brains did, until suddenly a small mountain/large hill sprang up before us. The road went up, so up we went, straight up in fact. The dirt road was practically vertical and often crumbled underfoot, making only every other step count. Every now and then a goat would stroll by the side of the road and I would become quite jealous of the ease with which it scampered about the steep terrain.

Slightly less than half way up we realized that we should have brought water with us. We had not anticipated such a hike so we were unprepared and thirsty. My mouth felt like a desert and each step in the blazing sun was more difficult than the last. Finally, we reached the end of the road and were rewarded with a panoramic view of the harbor.

Thanks to gravity, the hike down was immensely easier than the hike up. Down the mountain we trailed a herd of goats. My father attempted to converse with them, but they just rudely bleated and ran away. On our way back into town, we stopped at a convenience store of sorts that was essentially just a few sparse shelves and a refrigerator in someone's basement. But they had cold drinks so we didn't really care much. I bought a Ting, a beverage found only in the Caribbean, to my knowledge and dismay. It's not quite a soda, not quite juice, and made from Jamaican grapefruit. I became quite fond of it.

My Ting was gone in no time and daylight was slowly fading, so we headed to where we had planned to eat that evening, Foxy's. Foxy's Bar and Restaurant is a legendary hangout among the cruising community. It is most famous for its world-renowned New Year's parties. We had planned to go, but, as you may recall, our engine quit on our way there. It was probably just as well because even from a few islands back we could see the mass of toothpicks sticking out of Great Bay. We had heard that the rather small harbor was so chock-a-block full that you could literally walk from one end of the harbor to the other by hopping from boat to boat. I don't think any of us were terribly disappointed to have missed that. The important thing was that we had made it to Foxy's, a major stop on our itinerary.

What made Foxy's so illustrious was the owner, Foxy himself. He was a man of African descent somewhere between my parents' and grandparent's age. Salt-and-pepper dreadlocks emerged from beneath a worn baseball cap. He was dressed very casually for a wealthy business owner, for Foxy's had been very successful for much longer than I have been alive. A genial smile never ceased to grace his weathered features. My family and I spoke but a few strained words to him, but I overheard him say something rather profound. When asked how he was doing by some random person I remember him emphatically reply, "I am doing fantastic, but tomorrow I'll do better." I thought that was a great philosophy, if only it were possible to live by. That sort of philosophy must be a lot easier to live by if you live on Jost Van Dyke.

We whiled away the time before dinner listening to Foxy play the guitar and sing and tell jokes, sipping soft drinks, and watching a few silly tourists make fools of themselves dancing. The sun went down and flickering candles were placed on all the tables in the open air restaurant. The place was practically an extension of the beach with a roof; the floor was even purposely all sand. Every square inch of the ceiling, posts, and walls were covered in business cards, signatures, flags, even articles of clothing, all left there by their former owners to prove that they had been to Foxy's. One drawback to the restaurant being completely open to the night air was that its patrons were at the mercy of the mosquitoes. They were so bad that my father and I had to run back to the boat for some bug spray so that we could enjoy our dinner without being dinner ourselves.

We ate in the velvety evening air while the savory smell of West Indian cuisine wafted across the island. The stars twinkled in the heavens and the moon spilled beams of light over the water. Today had been wonderful, but tomorrow, perhaps, I will do better.

Back and forth like a pendulum swung the masts of Koukla, while simultaneously the bow bobbed up and down. This was the anchorage we had gone to because we had found the one at Jost Van Dyke a tad rolly. We knowingly subjected ourselves to this monotonous motion for nearly a week.

When we first arrived in Road Town, Tortola, we immediately looked for a sail maker to make a new staysail and salvage our frayed jib–both of which had been heavily abused offshore. Tortola would be our best bet to have the job done, and the next possible island was an overnight sail away. We found someone whom we thought would do a good job for a reasonable price, and hired them immediately, for the job would take several days. Unfortunately, it was just after that we realized what a truly abominable anchorage Road Town harbor really was.

Ashore, the town wasn't bad, but it was a long, extremely wet dinghy ride away. Road Town, Tortola, was almost comparable to Charlotte Amalie, St. Thomas, but the former was quite a bit nicer, friendlier, and slower paced. As with many other places in the Caribbean, flocks of chickens ran wild. Apparently in Tortola you could capture a chicken off the street, take it home, and eat it. One restaurant we frequented had outside tables and a mother hen and her chicks would flitter and peep beneath the tables looking for breadcrumbs, while a proud-looking rooster strutted a few yards away.

Unfortunately, we were unable to go into town often and see the sights, sounds, and chickens. We did not want to get drenched on our way into town, which is exactly what happened every single time we left the boat. One day, my mother and I decided to risk getting soaked rather than continue to suffer from cabin fever. My father ferried us ashore, and we had a pleasant afternoon exploring the town. When we went to the dock to signal for a ride back to the boat we saw that our dinghy was gone. We scanned the harbor, but there was no sign of my father, brother, or our dinghy. After waiting for nearly half an hour we were quite concerned. Then we saw our little inflatable with the two of them in it coming around the bend from outside the harbor and bouncing quite violently. My mother and I watched them swing by Koukla, signal to us, and my father left to fetch us a minute or two later. When he came to pick us up he had quite a tale to tell.

That afternoon, my father and brother had been working on installing some gadget or other, and they had left our VHF radio on. Out of nowhere a man came on the radio and frantically called "Mayday" and said that he was alone, a line was caught around his propeller, he had no control over the boat, and he was headed toward the rocks. The two of them dropped what they were doing to listen, assuming the Coast Guard or the Tortolan equivalent to it would respond. They listened for a few minutes and were surprised that no one said anything to the vessel in distress. My father, in good conscience, could not just listen to this man's pleas for help and do nothing, so he responded. He told the man he would only be able to come out in a small inflatable, but that he would go out and assist however possible. The man, now absolutely panic-stricken, replied in a quavering voice that he'll take any help he can get, for he was close to going on the rocks. So my father asked for his location, and my brother and he set out with a chart in a water-proof case and our portable VHF radio. The man had said he was just outside the harbor, but when they arrived, there was no boat in sight. Even before they left the harbor they were soaked to the bone, but outside was even worse. The strong wind lashed about them and the spray stung and blurred visibility. They searched for over twenty minutes but found nothing. The whole time they were in contact with the man, but that was of little good to them, for the man was now fear-stricken to the point of incoherence. Before they could reach him he was on the rocks and they lost contact.

Their rescue attempt now futile, and there being nothing else they could do, they headed back in. My father asked anyone we met for news about the unfortunate sailor. One person my father talked to nonchalantly replied he had heard the man's call for help, but it didn't even seem to faze him that another human being's life and property were in danger. This was not the only person with this attitude. My father was the only person who had heard the "Mayday" and was willing to help. We eventually learned that some marina had heard his call and pulled the boat off the rocks the next day. Apparently, on many islands there is no Coast Guard or equivalent, and if there is, it is often of little use to a boat in trouble. This was a rather unsettling piece of information to have gained, but we tried not to let it worry us too much.

We were now down to our final day in Tortola, since our sails were almost done, and we decided to rent a car and see the whole island. We dinghyed ashore and walked to the car rental place just as it was opening. We rented an open, airy, old jeep-like thing and aimlessly set off down the road. In the B.V.I.'s they drive on the left side of the road, as you might expect for a British territory, and my father did a pretty good job of staying in the proper lane, but every now and then my mother would have to remind him what country we were in. The steep, winding road and multiple hairpin turns also made me thankful that I wasn't the one behind the wheel. Most of the roads we took had the ocean on one side and palm trees on the other. We drove by the Narrows, the windy passage with a strong current that we had gone against a while ago, and were thankful that we weren't out on the water today, as it looked exceptionally windy. It was so choppy out there the caps of the waves looked almost sharp. On land it was a beautiful day. The warm tropical air whipped through my hair and the smell of exotic flowers and fresh cut grass followed us wherever we went.

After we had been up and down just about every road on Tortola we decided to ascend Mt. Sage in our vehicle. Mt. Sage is the highest peak on the island and there was a tropical rainforest at the very top. We penetrated a shroud of mist as we went up until we reached a small dirt parking lot at the very top. We dodged muddy spots and hopped over puddles as we climbed out of the car and continued to do so as we set off down the path into the rainforest. Moss-covered trees and giant ferns loomed on either side of the path. While we were tip-toeing around the mud and water we were startled by a rustling from just off the path. We looked around and saw a field just beyond the forest and the heads of two cows peering between two trees. The presence of farm animals kind of ruined the whole mysterious tropical rainforest atmosphere.

Shortly after we passed the cows we decided we'd seen enough and headed back. On our way back we passed the curious sight of a man in a hard hat and rubber boots riding a donkey. Wishing we too had rubber boots or a donkey to ride, we continued down the muddy trail to the parking lot. We left Mt. Sage and had the car back to the rental place before the sun had even thought about setting.

10 Saltwater Spelunking

February 7, 2002
Virgin Gorda, BVIs

On a bed of rippling turquoise sheets lay a large, green, curvy woman. This was Virgin Gorda, named thus by Christopher Columbus because of the island's resemblance to a woman lying on her back. Or so I'd been told. As we approached, I sort of had to unfocus my eyes before I saw the verdant lady, like looking at a Magic Eye.

We would be spending a few days in well-protected Gorda Sound, which was an extremely welcome change from rocky Road Town harbor, Tortola. Going into Gorda Sound was a bit treacherous because of the abundance of coral reefs jutting out into the entrance. We all had to look carefully for a change in water color, for it could be a sign of a reef below. Inside Gorda Sound there was hardly a ripple over the water, except for the few we made slowly plodding along. Once the anchor was down and we were completely stationary, the water turned to glass.

Virgin Gorda was mainly a resort island, with many hotels and, obviously, resorts, and few other settlements as far as we could tell. There were two main resorts in the vicinity of where we were staying. The first was a very posh establishment that was home to the Bitter End Yacht Club. For a hefty price, one could participate in a number of water-related activities such as windsurfing, snorkeling, and sailing by either renting a small Laser sailboat or going for a cruise on the Lynx, the vessel we'd met on St. John.

There was an elaborate boardwalk heading to a rock swimming platform with good snorkeling nearby. There was also a semi-artificial beach; it being semi-artificial because extra sand had been added to the natural stuff so you could walk out in the water farther. On the beach, there were luxurious covered beach chairs that we took advantage of at one point of our stay. We half expected to see some famous face lean forward to adjust their awning. Instead we saw iguanas roaming freely along the beach. Iguanas are pretty docile, plant-eating creatures, but there is something a bit unsettling about strolling along the beach beside a 3 ft. long lizard. This was a get-away for the well-to-do and we felt out of place here. The fact that a box of cereal in the resort convenience store was over $9 alone showed the type of people this place catered to, and it wasn't us.

The second resort was in a rather strange location. It had been built right on top of a large, mostly dead, coral head named Saba Rock. The resort on Saba Rock was separated from the rest of Virgin Gorda and only accessible by boat. There were numerous hammocks on the premises for lounging that we tested out. Both of these places were very nice, but they were both practically deserted. They had been hit hard by the after effects of September 11th.

For four days we lounged around sunning ourselves on resort beach chairs or hammocks, or went snorkeling or swimming. Swimming off our boat in the warm motionless water was like floating through air. The lively fish-filled mangrove tree roots lining the shore made for interesting snorkeling. But it would soon be time for us to be moving on. Our last day would be the grand finale.

The Baths on Virgin Gorda are world famous rock formations, so of course we could not leave without seeing them. We had waited till the last day because they were notoriously difficult to get to. We had to leave Gorda Sound and go around the corner to an unprotected cove before we were a reasonable dinghy ride away. Our guidebook had said there would be a dock visitors could use to tie up their dinghies, but when we arrived we didn't see anything that remotely resembled a dock. So we landed our inflatable on the beach, which wasn't an easy task, considering the huge rollers pounding the shore. The first thing we saw on shore was a sign authoritatively stating in bold letters, "Do Not Beach Dinghies." Not knowing what to do, we asked some random person what one was supposed to do with one's dinghy if it could not be beached. He pointed out towards the water, and sure enough there were a few inflatables all tied to a buoy. Our guidebook had used the word "dock" in the very loosest sense of the word. We would have to push the little boat back into the water, and my father would have to go out and tie it to the buoy and swim ashore. We had known there would be a chance that we would be getting wet since this was a beach, so fortunately my father had worn his bathing suit. Swimming ashore wouldn't be terribly difficult since the waves were rolling towards the beach, but swimming back would be an entirely different matter. But we'd deal with that later.

The rocky shoreline had been carved by the elements into moderately interesting configurations, but it wasn't close to impressive enough to warrant international notoriety. We wandered the beach looking for friendlier signs than the ones we had met earlier, and hoped that this was not all there was to see. We eventually stumbled upon a picnic area carpeted with coarse grass, with a few open-air vendors with their wares lying out on blankets, and, low and behold, an information booth. Apparently there was much more to see, we had just gone in the wrong direction. The person in the booth pointed us in the direction of the trail that went through The Baths, and off we went.

We had only gone a few hundred feet or so before the "oohs" and "aahs" started. Sadly, we did not take any photos as we'd forgotten our camera that day. The first thing we saw was a bunch of boulders about the size of elephants that looked like a giant had molded them with his bare hands. These were interspersed with desert-like vegetation along the sandy path. The trail gradually led upwards and in between a decent sized opening between two cliffs. Inside the crevice were wooden stairs and a rope handrail for easier access. The crevice suddenly widened and bloomed into a lofty cavern. In the back of the cave was a very narrow crack that allowed water in, for we were right on the ocean. A few columns of light squeezed in between a couple of rocks, yet the remainder of the beach-cave stayed dimly lit. A few people were swimming in the small pool, for it was four or five feet deep in places. We could even make out a few lethargic fish in the murky water. The spelunking continued as we exited this cave by climbing up a slanted rock face with the aid of a rope. The trail continued to go up and down ladders and through the maze of gargantuan rocks. Eventually the labyrinth led into an open beach. Right outside the opening was a mammoth windswept cavern. You could see the lines on the walls where it had been carved out by wind and sea for eons. A little way down the beach we saw a sign naming this spot "Devil's Bay", along with a bunch of warnings, mainly because of undertow. Just by looking out over the water it was easy to see how this spot had earned its name. Enormous rollers violently crashed upon the sand in an explosion of white foam. Just wading out to your ankles you could start to feel the strong tug of the undertow.

After a short rest far above the high water mark at Devil's Bay, we headed back into the maze of rock sculptures that Father Time's steady hand had chiseled into the breathtaking formations before us. As we left the Baths on Virgin Gorda we were humbled by nature's power and beauty.

That night, the weather conditions were amenable to sending emails via the radio waves. I sat in our log desk—a modified closet cubby hole by the main saloon hatch, and wrote emails to my boyfriend and my other friends about my water-filled cave exploration adventures, bouncing my messages off the ionosphere. There were none waiting for me.

"Sixteen men on a dead man's chest, yo ho ho and a bottle of rum." This pretty much summed up Norman Island in the British Virgin Islands. Supposedly, this island had been the inspiration for Robert Louis Stevenson's Treasure Island. A relative of his had been a sea captain, and Stevenson had come up with the idea from reading his old letters. While possibly erroneous, this tale was quite believable. Looking at the craggy shoreline dotted with short strips of white sand, you could almost see Long John Silver lumbering through the forest.

As we came into a small cove, called The Bight to anchor, the wind was unsettled and the sky was a metallic blue-gray. I amused myself by scanning the shore looking for anything that remotely resembled an X, but disappointedly found nothing. Lying in my bunk that night, the sound of the rigging banging against the mast, in my mind, turned into the eerie din of rattling bones.

The following morning, we hopped in our dinghy and set out to explore the fictitious pirate's hangout. We were going to see the locally well known sea-caves. The poorly protected cove was rather choppy that morning. Hoping to go snorkeling, we all donned our bathing suits and brought our gear. Unfortunately the chilly wind discouraged us from such aquatic activities. It may be difficult to believe that the Caribbean could ever be chilly, but sitting exposed to the elements, soaked with spray that day, it indeed was. While we were heading towards the black spot on the side of the cliff that was the mouth of the cave, our outboard motor began to spitter and sputter. It coughed and groaned while we all crossed our fingers. If our motor should quit our next landfall would be Mexico. Fortunately, the old girl made it to the mouth of the cave.

Inside the cave, I was quite disappointed to find that there wasn't much to see. I had envisioned a lofty, cavernous space, somewhat like the Pirate's of the Caribbean ride at Disney World, complete with pirate bones and buried treasure. I was disappointed to find there were no animatronics skeletons, not even a measly bat. I suppose in retrospect it was sort of neat, but it wasn't even close to being worth the trouble we went through to get there and back.

Norman Island had little else to offer, so we left the following afternoon. We would soon be making the next substantial leg of our journey, to Sint Maarten. First we had to check out of the B.V.I.s and retrieve our firearm. When we checked in at Jost Van Dyke, we had told the officials that we would be clearing out in Tortola, for there are a few different locations in the B.V.I.'s to clear customs. We assumed our firearm would be there waiting for us when we returned, as we had been told it would be. But it is never that easy.

My father walked the distance inland to the police station where we were told the firearm had been kept. When we asked for the weapon to be returned, the officials proceeded to put on a Monty Python-esque performance. My father would have found them looking in such odd places as what appeared to be someone's lunch bag—rather amusing if he had not been worried that they had actually lost the gun. The Three Stooges-like searching continued for quite some time until the firearm was discovered in a closet with a broken light. It took them so long to find it that my father thought they may have been hoping that he would lose patience and leave assuming it was lost. The officials made my father take a cab back, but it was a reasonable request he acquiescently complied with.

This winter had been particularly rough and windy in the Caribbean, and the Anagada passage, the expanse of water between the B.V.I.s and Sint Maarten, was notoriously rough and windy. Throughout our stay in the B.V.I.s we had been carefully listening for a weather window, and it sounded as if the predicted relative calm for the next few days was the opportunity we had been looking for. As soon as we heard this we made sure we would be ready to leave at sunrise, and hopefully make it to Sint Maarten sometime in the late afternoon the following day.

On the morning of February 12th, I begrudgingly awoke from a peaceful slumber while most of the sun was still comfortably resting below the horizon. It was a bit blustery and choppy when we weighed anchor, but we figured it was just because it was so early, and we expected the winds and seas to drop at any moment. Well, they never did. The weather guessers had fouled it up again, and now we had to suffer for our ignorant, optimistic, blind faith. In fact, if anything the winds and seas had increased as we slowly snailed along. And, of course, the wind was coming directly out of the direction we were going.

Trying to carry out simple daily tasks in the lurching vessel gave me an unpleasantly acute case of déjà vu. The fact that it couldn't possibly be much over two days total was something of a comfort. But cooking was impossible. Just trying to boil water was incredibly dangerous, but none of us had much of an appetite anyway. A comfortable spot to sleep in was as elusive as Brigadoon. I just sat in a corner in a dazed state and hoped that slumber would overtake me and thus shorten this miserable voyage. I never got so much as a cat nap until well after midnight when I stumbled into my rolling cabin. At that time, the seas had dropped an infinitesimal amount and I was quite tired, so I thought I'd see if it was any better up forward. It wasn't really, and I hadn't honestly expected it would be, but I fell asleep in spite of this.

I was quite sound asleep, in fact, because late the next morning I did not awake to hear the enthusiastic shouts of my family. They had spotted dolphins. When I eventually stumbled astern I was quite perturbed that they had not made more of an effort to wake me. A large pod of dolphins had come up alongside and swam in the wake of our bow. I was even more disgruntled as they described the dolphins' amusing antics. They said it was better than any aquarium  show any of them had ever been to, and that it was especially impressive how they jumped clear out of the water and flopped backward. It just figures that I would be unconscious for the one good part of the passage.

Later on, I was awake for an event almost as exciting, but exciting in a bad way. Out of nowhere, a freak wave reached up 7 or 8 feet above our deck and hit our side light, breaking the three-quarter inch teak board, leaving it dangling by a wire. We had to go up on the bouncing deck and take it down. It wasn't a huge deal, but it struck us odd that a wave could reach up so high and hit with such force.

Around noon that day, it was obvious that at the rate we were going, we would not make it to Sint Maarten until sometime the following day. So, we turned on our motor in hope of avoiding another night out in this inclement weather. We slugged it out and somehow made it into Simpson Bay on the Dutch side of Sint Maarten before sunset.

In the days to come, we would find out that we were not the only ones who'd had a rough passage and were ticked off at the same weatherman. Half the boats that left at the same time we did turned back in frustration. The best evidence of this frustration with grossly inaccurate weather forecasts was told to us by soon-to-be friends of ours, a professional yacht captain and his wife. She took out her aggression by making pizza dough and violently slamming the dough on the counter and cursing the egregiously inaccurate meteorologist. Unfortunately, this would not be the last time we would need an outlet for our anger at weathermen.

Cathy's Pizza Dough

1 egg
1/2 tsp salt
1/4 tsp sugar
2/3 cup water
1 tbsp yeast
2 1/4 cups flour

Add the egg together with warm water, sugar, 3/4 cup flour, mix until pancake batter consistency. Wait for the dough to sponge (get full of bubbles and look like a sponge), then add the rest of the flour. Knead until your anger dissipates, then top with sauce, cheese, and toppings.

11 Embarrassing Exploits

February 16, 2002
Sint Maarten/Saint Martin

One island, two countries. Sint Maarten/St. Martin is composed of two separate halves— the French side (Saint Martin) and the Dutch side (Sint Maarten). There was an old tale on the island that the French and the Dutch had been so civil to each other that rather than fight over the island they each sent a man to opposite ends of the island, the French man with a bottle of wine, and the Dutch man with a bottle of rum. They walked towards the center of the island and where they met a line would be drawn to divide the island. The story goes that the French side was a little bit bigger because the rum was stronger. However this island came to be split like this, each side added their own unique flavor to the experience of Sint Maarten/Saint Martin.

The Dutch side was further divided into the Simpson Bay area, which was extremely cruiser-friendly, and the Philipsburg area where the cruise ships came in and thus was tourist-oriented. In Philipsburg, there were many stores selling the same old souvenirs we'd seen on past islands. It also had a few Dutch stores such as the Delft-Blue pottery store specializing in expensive fine blue and white Dutch pottery, and a Dutch linen store with just about anything for the home that could be made of lace.

We were anchored in Simpson Bay. From the smallest simple sloop to the massive mega yacht, just about anything those living and working on them could want could be found here. And if you still couldn't find what you were looking for, it could always be shipped here.

With this in mind, we were contemplating replacing our frustratingly wet, tiny inflatable, with a slightly longer one with bigger tubes. From fellow cruisers we had learned that larger tubes were crucial to staying dry. We took about a day going to the various marine stores and comparison shopping, then took an additional day to mull it over, and the following day we had a new 14 foot dinghy with a 25 horsepower motor. What a difference! It was such a luxury to leave our boat dry and arrive at our destination in the same state.

It was very fortunate that we had this new dinghy here, because of a heavily polluted, sorry excuse for a body of water called Simpson Bay lagoon. Before I arrived at St. Maarten and first heard that there was a lagoon, the scene from "The Little Mermaid" where they are rowing through a glittering tree-covered lagoon with various singing marine life came to mind. I was sorely disappointed. It resembled a cesspool more than a lagoon. Hundreds of boats were huddled inside, and most of them pumped their heads overboard and turned the lagoon water into toxic waste. (Legally, boaters should be 12 nautical miles from shore to pump out their waste tanks. We always made sure to do this or use a pump-out service, but like many laws they are not always followed. A few years later, pump out services became a little easier to access in the lagoon.) This water was so disgusting you would not want to even stick your big toe in. This was also just about the only place in the Caribbean that we had been to where you could not see the bottom at all.

The lagoon was split in half along with the rest of the island. The French side was a bit less polluted because the current brought fresh water in from that side, or so I'd been told. Zipping across the scummy lagoon water to the French side, we passed a locally well known landmark called the Witch's Tit. This uncompromising mountain was aptly named by some filthy-minded Frenchman no doubt. Past this sordid hill the water began to clear up minimally, and the boats we passed were decidedly more colorful. We later learned that the French are somewhat known for painting their boats vibrant hues. The channel led us into a small cove in the middle of downtown Marigot, the main city of the French side. The dinghy dock, which was basically a bunch of rings along the sea wall, was jam-packed with an assortment of dinghies of all shapes and sizes.

The city surrounding us was impressive at first glance. It was unequivocally French and well kept. Tidy boutiques and charming little cafés lined the waterfront and surrounding streets. Outside the restaurants, the menus were displayed in at least two languages: French and English. All the signs and just about everything else was written in French. This was the first time in our trip that we had really encountered a foreign language. I had taken a semester of French, so I could understand a few words here and there. I could say bonjour in a reasonably convincing accent, but not much else. Fortunately nearly everyone could speak English.

In addition to all the wonderful stores, there was an open air market three times a week. Many locals would come and set up shop selling everything from tacky plastic trinkets to locally handmade wood carvings and jewelry. The most interesting thing there were tiny statuettes that looked like they were made of ivory. Upon further investigation, we found that they were actually made from the pit of a tropical fruit called a tagua nut. After being extracted from the fruit, the pit was dried and would harden to a consistency comparable to that of ivory. Thus it was sometimes referred to as vegetable ivory. It could then be carved into just about any shape imaginable. Laid out on a cloth covered table were tagua nuts carved into tiny tropical fish, monkeys, birds, boats, manta rays, etc. All were intricately carved and each was a work of art unto itself. I bought a parrot for myself and a manta ray for my boyfriend.

The best thing of all on the French side was definitely the food. There were bakeries and restaurants galore. Most were reasonably priced and a bad one was difficult to find. While we were in St. Martin, we had fresh, buttery croissants almost every day for breakfast. A simple salad and lemonade for lunch at one of these French restaurants was exquisite.

Going to the local grocery store here was a treat. The shelves were filled with strange and exotic things. There were tons of foreign cookies and candies and other sweets. My personal favorite was chocolate mousse. It was in the yogurt section in small pudding size containers. Each container held a serving of rich, velvety chocolate mousse. All the non-junk food was very good too. There was a multitude of fresh fruits and vegetables, and good meats and cheeses.

There was only one thing I did not enjoy about the French grocery store. Since I knew some French and my mother knew none at all, she would often ask me what various unfamiliar words meant. In the meat section one day, my mother inspected a strange looking package labeled "lapin." Not even attempting a French accent, she asked me what "lapin" meant. Recalling that lapin was French for rabbit, I glanced down at the saran-wrapped package and was horrified to see an intact yet mangled skinless rabbit, with one glassy eye staring back at me. My mother had not noticed the eye, and once she did she immediately put it back. We bought some nice pork tenderloin instead.

Of all the interesting people we met on our trip, some of the most interesting we met here in St. Maarten. I could go on and on about the professional captain and his wife, the family of four from Washington state taking the winter off, or the Canadian couple who built their boat and everything on it right down to the cleats, steering wheel, and anchor windlass, just to name a few. But most astoundingly, there was the couple we had met a few years earlier when they were cruising up north and stopped in our home town of Rockland. They actually lived on the island of St. Maarten and owned a marine repair business and had since sold their boat and become landlubbers. They had been up just after we had purchased Koukla and we told them of our dreams of cruising the Caribbean. When they saw the sorry state of our vessel they didn't think we'd ever make it. When we dropped by their business one day, they were astounded yet delighted to see us. They were fairly prominent citizens on the island, and particularly prominent in the renowned Sint Maarten Heineken Regatta. They were among the top organizers of this big event, and they immediately volunteered us to help out.

A common meeting place for all these cruisers is the Simpson Bay Yacht Club. The term yacht club conjures images of the meticulously dressed sipping martinis in overstuffed leather chairs next to the ocean. Not so with this one. Made out of two old shipping containers, with picnic tables scattered about the premises, the yacht club is conveniently located near the Simpson Bay Bridge. At 9 am and 5 pm the bridge is raised to let boats in and out of the lagoon. At 5 pm many cruisers and a few locals flock to the Simpson Bay yacht club for drinks and to watch the boats come and go. Everyone is friendly and talkative and has a million stories to tell. Probably the most fascinating person we encountered here was Captain Fatty Goodlander. He has written many articles for various cruising magazines as well as a few books, and is something of a celebrity amongst the cruising community. He had come to Sint Maarten to write about the Sint Maarten Heineken Regatta. He had been flown by regatta officials to Sint Maarten from some remote location on the other side of the planet where he was in the middle of circumnavigating the globe. He exuded an almost Santa Clause-like joviality, although despite his name he really wasn't that fat. We spent many a balmy evening at the yacht club sipping soft drinks, chatting with fellow cruisers, and watching the boats come and go from this epicenter of cruising in the Caribbean known as Sint Maarten.

After traveling in our slow moving vessel for months, we'd nearly forgotten faster modes of travel existed. We were reminded of this in the St. Martin airport, waiting for my mom's friend Diane and her husband Steve to arrive. Although we were excited to see our friends, it felt like cheating getting here in a matter of hours rather than months.

Diane and her family had come up to Maine to visit us each summer for a number of years, and we always went sailing, so they knew a bit more about boats than your average landlubber. Being the adventurous, outdoorsy sort, they weren't afraid of roughing it. They would be staying on board with us and getting a taste of the cruising lifestyle.

Sailboats of all shapes and sizes were flocking to Sint Maarten for the upcoming Heineken regatta. We'd been volunteered for the regatta, and as temporary crewmembers aboard Koukla, Diane and Steve had automatically been volunteered as well.

One "perk" to being a volunteer in this regatta was that we had been invited to an exclusive volunteers'/officials' pre-regatta bash. When we arrived, the party was just beginning. There was a free bar serving a number of adult and non-adult beverages. Trays of various hors d'oeuvres and other savories circulated through the crowd. After about an hour the band started blaring soca music. Soca is a type of loud, fast-paced, thumping, and in my opinion rather annoying, type of music found almost exclusively in the Caribbean. The crowd began to throb to the music. I even spotted Captain Fatty bouncing to the music. Everyone around me seemed to be enjoying themselves immensely. I was not. Perhaps it was because there was no one else close to my age. Perhaps it was because most everyone over the age of 21 had lost count of the number of free rum punches and Heinekens they had consumed. There was a sea of people, but I felt utterly alone. I missed my friends, especially my boyfriend.

After three or four hours of trying to tolerate the atrocious music and pretending not to know anyone, I was finally able to leave. After my long night of teenage torture, I was rewarded with an incredible sight. As we entered Simpson Bay from the lagoon, a million points of light sprang up before us. It was pitch black out, and we could see no farther than the distance of the rays of our flashlight. We quickly realized that each pinprick was the mast light of a boat. The bay had been peppered with a plethora of artificial stars.

The next day, we decided to rent a car and show Diane and Steve the island. The day started off innocently enough. We drove along the hillside overlooking the ocean, and passed the lagoon and salt marshes. But soon this merry ride would take a turn for the worst. An event more terrifying than an ocean gale, more mentally scarring than the saran-wrapped skinless rabbit incident at the French grocery store was about to occur. We were headed for a beach by the unsuspecting name of Orient Bay, a famous nude beach.

As we walked along the beach we noticed that people were progressively wearing less and less until they were wearing nothing at all. Of course, nearly all of the people who were wearing nothing were the people who really shouldn't have been. I tried to look straight ahead and down, limiting my peripheral vision as much as possible. At one point we passed a man leaning up against a large boulder. I could tell from behind he was wearing nothing but a hat, even though his behind was covered by the boulder. I walked by him still looking straight ahead and down, but I had annoyingly good peripheral vision. At which point I did a cartoon worthy double-take. I only saw him for a split second before I looked away, but it was long enough to leave me very confused. Now at this point I hadn't even seen pictures of male genitalia outside of health class. But I was pretty sure they weren't supposed to be as big around as other extremities, or nearly as long as them. I emailed my girlfriends (and not my boyfriend) describing this encounter. I believe I used the phrase "by his knees!" I think I gave them a good laugh as well as some of the same questions I had. (To this day, 30-something Danica, who has a biology degree and a kid, is still a little confused about what she saw that day. Did he have a disease? Surgery? Prosthetic? Optical illusion? I honestly don't know.)

After this experience, we treated ourselves to a fantastic dinner on the French side. We went over early to look at all the different menus displayed. By the time we had chosen a restaurant overlooking the harbor, the sun had turned into a blazing orange ball barely above the horizon. Daylight was dwindling as the waiter took our orders. As we were waiting for our food, we were entertained with a number of unusual sights. The six of us were pleasantly chatting away when two burly men came running from the nearby dock each carrying an enormous gutted fish, nearly as big as me. They made a couple of trips from the dock to the kitchen, and in mid-run a woman passing by asked to take a picture. The man stopped and smiled widely, waited for the flash, then ran off.

Festive lights and candles emerged from the twilight, giving the place a carnival-like atmosphere, complete with sideshow acts. A human statue stood just a few feet from our table. Her skin was painted shimmering white and she wore metallic gray clothes. We watched her set up as our food was brought out, so the effect was somewhat spoiled for us. As we savored our scrumptious meals we watched passers by stop and put money in a slot in a box the motionless woman was standing on. When they put in money she would move robotically.

At 8 am the following morning, we were standing on the dock outside the Simpson Bay Yacht Club waiting to be ferried out to the start boat. We would be signaling the start of the races and aiding the officials in watching for foul play. On the start boat, we were given a course in flag raising and horn blowing, and each assigned specific tasks. Diane, Steve, my father, and I were to raise and lower flags, my brother blew the horn, and my mother manned a special warning flag. There was a complicated array of different flags that had to be raised and lowered in a certain manner to get them up and down as quickly as possible. There was also an exact sequence of horn blasts that needed to be blown to signal various warnings and the starts of races.

The regatta was a two day event, consisting of a multitude of individual races of all different types of boats. It was amazing to see all the boats jockeying for position at the starting line, with their sails flapping wildly. On the start boat, we had the best spot to watch all the action. There were many near misses and a few paint-scraping collisions. It was all very exciting, and we were right in the middle of it. We could watch it very safely too, because they had used a rugged salvage vessel for the start boat. We had talked to a few people who had done a lot of these sorts of races, and they said it can be very nerve wracking being on a smaller boat with all the close, zooming sailboats. My favorite part was watching the big high-tech racing boats with gleaming silver carbon fiber sails. It was a tiny bit depressing watching these stealthy vessels zip along at ten times as fast as we could ever hope for Koukla to go. Helping out at this regatta was an unexpected task we fell into that turned out to be a highlight of our trip.

12 Living History

March 8, 2002
Saba

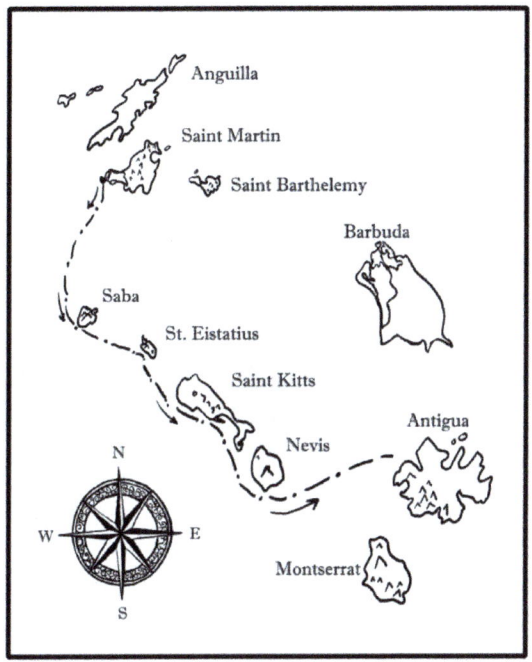

Small but mighty Saba rose sharply out of the depths, with rugged rock faces on nearly all sides of the island. There weren't any decent anchorages, in fact there is no place to anchor at all as most of Saba's coastline is protected marine sanctuary. There was one spot on the west side of the island with about six moorings for visiting yachts. From our vantage point, we could see a winding rock staircase etched into the side of the cliff. Our guide book had told us that these stairs were one of only two ways onto the island. And at one time, this was the only way. Any people or goods entering the island had to go up these stairs, known as The Ladder. This famously included a piano. That must have been one dedicated pianist.

At first, we tried to beach our dinghy at the bottom of the stairs, but when we approached we saw that there really was no beach to beach our dinghy on. Plus, we were getting swamped from the gathering surf. So, we turned back, dried off a bit, and went to the other spot on the southern end of the island to clear customs.

The next morning, we set off for a whirlwind tour of Saba. We were only able to stay for two days, as the weather was deteriorating. Fortunately for us, Saba was a pretty small island and it would be possible to see it all in one day. We dinghied into the miniscule harbor lined with dive shop after dive shop and little else. On shore, the only way to go was up, so up we went until a taxi spotted us struggling against gravity. Once we were in the car, we noticed we were driving on an odd sort of road. It looked like we were driving on the Great Wall of China, for there were stone walls on either side. The road wound all around the island, flowing almost naturally with the mountain itself, for Saba was basically a mountain sticking out of the water.

We later learned the story behind these strange roads. The people of Saba had wanted roads practically since the island had first been populated. They had consulted numerous civil engineers, and each time they were met with no avail. They had been told that it would be impossible to build roads on Saba because of its extraordinarily steep and rugged terrain. Yet the people of Saba were adamant. In the mid 1900's, they finally found their savior in Joseph Lambert Hassell, who took a correspondence course in road building. He and all the farmers and craftsmen of Saba built these magnificent roads with only the blood, sweat, and tears of the islanders, and a few donkeys as well. It became known as "the road that could not be built."

Once we entered a small town, one of only a handful on the entire island, our attention was drawn away from the roads and towards the quaint uniformity of the village. Every single building on the island was white with a red roof. We had not noticed this at first, but as we went up and up we could see more of the settlements. They looked like sparse red dots on a background of green.

We were going up to hike the trail to Mt. Scenery, composed of a series of

1,764 steps with a panoramic view of the Caribbean at the very top. Our taxi let us off at the bottom of the trail, and off we went into the forest. As we climbed, we could see that the jungle had attempted to swallow up the path, but it had been well maintained and the plants had been cut back recently. As we trudged up step after step in the searing sun I thought about how all the cement and stones in each step had been carried up by wheelbarrow or donkey. Going up all those steps in the blazing heat was extremely exhausting and we therefore had to stop to rest and hydrate every few minutes or so. There were very few trees along the way and thus precious little shade to be found. Fortunately, as we climbed higher and higher we would occasionally be caressed by a cool breeze.

After what seemed like hours but was actually just one, we finally reached the top. At the top there were quite a few more trees than there had been along the way, so we had to search for a clearing in order to see the view we had worked so hard for. We were now so high up that we were literally in the clouds. We had to wait for them to clear before we saw anything. The clouds slowly parted and we were gradually able to see the red roofed town nestled in amongst the forest. It felt almost godlike looking down at the world through the clouds from above. The majestic turquoise sea spread out like a carpet and sparse dots of green could be witnessed here and there. We sat there amidst the clouds while the cooling zephyr refreshed us.

Our renewed energy was soon depleted as we made our way back down the mountain. Once we were very near the bottom we passed a few people on their way up. We knew they hadn't gone far at all and they looked more than a bit out of shape and already quite fatigued. They asked us how much farther it was, and we hesitated to respond, but uncomfortably replied that they still had a little ways to go.

Once we reached the bottom, we spent the remainder of the day meandering through the villages. It was a bit strange to think that tomorrow we would be on a new island. Tomorrow we would be exploring a new place and continuing the adventure.

The island of St. Eustatius, commonly called Stacia, was like a derelict mansion, still somewhat magnificent in its faded way, yet only a shadow of its former self. In the heyday of the Caribbean, when all the different European powers were trying to gobble up as much of the verdant land and azure sea as possible, Dutch-owned St. Eustatius had been the epicenter of trade and commerce of the Caribbean. The most profitable yet most heinous of goods kept and traded on this island were fellow humans. After making the infamous Middle Passage from Africa, these poor souls were marched up a steep cobblestone street to their meager dwellings where they would await auction. I could almost feel the pain and suffering radiating from the stones beneath my feet.

To this day that road is still referred to as "the slave road." It was strange walking up the gruelingly steep stone road and imagining the hundreds of chained men, women, and children that must have walked up this very same road that I had tread upon. At the end of the road were the still existent and occupied slave quarters, which were now private homes. They had doubtlessly been rebuilt many times over the centuries, yet they still appeared to be in a rather sorry state. The tiny yards were ill-kempt, and the paint on the houses had faded and flaked away to reveal the dusty gray wood underneath. Adjoining a few houses were goat pens, and others had one or two tethered goats in the backyard. But more often, as we walked down the littered streets, we'd pass a small herd of wild goats bleating agitatedly.

In front of the slave quarters was once mighty Fort Orange which had doubtlessly seen a lot of action in its day, yet now looked like ancient ruins. A branch of the fort on the water had been washed away after centuries of erosion. Hundreds of years ago, musket and cannon fire filled the air in a display of deadly fireworks, for St. Eustatius had been highly fought over because of its fertile soil and convenient location. Subsequently, St. Eustatius had changed hands an unprecedented 22 times, yet the Dutch remained the primary force controlling the island.

The once fire and brimstone spewing volcano, named The Quill, now rests quietly overlooking the island. Early one morning, we set out to hike up The Quill and into its crater. This crater is home to one of the oldest rainforests in the world, for it is protected from hurricanes and other disasters by the mountain itself. In order to get to the start of the trail, we had to first walk a good mile or so inland. At the start of the trail was a billboard telling of a few species found only on this island, including a species of purple-clawed hermit crab and a type of small non-poisonous snake. We only saw the hermit crab, and I think my mother was quite all right with that.

As we marched deeper and deeper into the forest we didn't quite feel like we were hiking up a volcano and towards a rainforest, but more like we were strolling through some common deciduous forest back home. The only thing reminding us we were even in the Caribbean was the sweltering heat. Thankfully the trail was fairly well shaded. Because we had just hiked up an even larger mountain, Mount Scenery on Saba, the hike didn't seem quite as strenuous as it might have otherwise. We trekked through the unimpressive forest for a couple of hours, but at the top of the mountain we were met with an extraordinary view. We decided to venture into the crater itself, for how many people can say they've been inside a volcano and lived to tell about it?

There was a long piece of old sodden rope leading into the steep crater to be used as a handrail of sorts. The squishy terrain gave way under foot, and we all would have fallen repeatedly if not for the scraggly rope. We had been told that this rainforest was among the oldest on the planet, yet I hadn't expected the forest to actually look old. Gnarled trees intertwined with each other and bedraggled vegetation crept into the sparse path. Here and there an uncommon, vibrant flower interrupted the tangled mass of vegetation. Once we reached the pit of the crater we went back out rather quickly, for it is slightly unnerving standing in a volcano, even a supposedly extinct one.

Shaped like a mangled frying pan, the island of St. Kitts, more formally known as St. Christopher, was next on our island itinerary. From a ways off we could see vast expanses of steady green that took up most of the island. Closer we could see people toiling away in the sugarcane fields under the hot noonday sun. Sugarcane was once a major export for the island, it still is in fact, but after the discovery/development of the sugar beet, the sugarcane industry suffered, which was apparent as soon as we set foot ashore. We walked along sodden streets with sparse sidewalks to the dilapidated town. Walls that one could only assume were once painted vibrant tropical colors were now faded and flaked to the point that there was more bare wood or concrete than paint on most of the buildings. Despite the rest of the town, the one meager grocery store we did go in was fairly well stocked and reasonably well priced, although it had the feel of a warehouse.

But we had not come here to shop. We were here to visit Brimstone Hill Fort just outside of the city. Of course, being cruisers we could not take the tourist bus right up to the fort, oh no, we were going to take the local bus to the bottom of the steep hill and walk to the top. We flagged down the most inconspicuous bus we could find, for that would be the local one, and squished in. The bus was filled with an assortment of humanity—sweaty, slightly smelly sugarcane field workers, fellow cruisers, coconut peddlers, and schoolchildren in drab uniform. It was strangely invigorating to ride on that packed bus though the sugarcane fields and shabby villages, pass by goats and children riding bicycles, and feel the pleasant breeze across my face.

Soon enough we came to our stop and we began our ascent. Brimstone Hill was named thus because it is a sulfur vent to a large volcano on the island. I could feel the sulfur heavy in my lungs more than I could smell it. This combined with the stifling heat made the hike up this incredibly steep hill all the more unpleasant. The sickly, strangulating heat rose up out of the asphalt and wrapped around us like boa constrictors. By the time we reached the top of the hill we were practically dripping with sweat and our legs were screaming from exertion.

Brimstone Hill Fort is spread out over 38 acres, and after hiking so far none of us felt all that enthused about exploring the place. Yet the areas we did see had an air of mystery, like ancient Celtic ruins. In the cool, dark, spooky areas a specter of a fallen soldier would have been all but expected. On the way back down the hill, I envisioned a line of neatly dressed soldiers in traditional woolen uniforms marching up the hill in this searing heat with muskets slung over their shoulders. Imagining this, I somehow felt a tiny bit cooler. After nearly falling down the steep hill, we waited for our bus out in the hot sun. The bits of cool air that jumped in as the bus rushed by were most welcome.

The night sky was a sheet of black silk enveloping our vessel. As we made our way toward Antigua the heavens were uninterrupted by stars, for they were obstructed by clouds. Below, we were being thrashed about by the uncaring sea. Occasionally a wave would pull our bow down as if our boat was a seesaw, and green water would cover the forward half.

We had been underway since dawn, yet our next destination felt desperately distant, and the weather conditions were exasperating. We had heavy, rolling seas without the wind. And without wind, our underpowered engine often slogged along at under one knot.

It was not until dusk the following night that we made landfall. The shadowy, amorphous boats that welcomed us into the harbor could just have easily been motionless sea serpents, and the buildings on shore sleeping trolls. But the bright sun of the following morning dispelled these notions. The island was incredibly arid, and the only vegetation was a few sparse palm trees. As we stumbled along the parched dirt road we kicked up clouds of dust-smoke.

The formerly English-owned island of Antigua was in competition with St. Maarten to be the yachting center of the Caribbean, and was losing. Everything was grossly overpriced and the yachting community was met with disdain from the locals. Antigua tended to cater more to the wealthy mega yachts than the humble cruiser.

Despite our immediate dislike of deserty, expensive Antigua, the island did have quite a bit of interesting history. The famous British war hero Horatio Nelson had been based here in Antigua, much to his own dismay. In fact, he quite hated the place, due to the bugs and heat. I can only imagine the discomfort of having to wear a formal woolen uniform in 90 plus degree weather. Nonetheless, much of Nelson's Dockyard was still intact and well maintained.

I enjoyed seeing all the different parts of the dockyard, from where sails had been sewn and anchors forged, to officer's quarters, to where ships were "hauled out." I thought it was particularly interesting how they had to clean the bottoms of their boats. Since back then there was no way of completely pulling a huge ship clear out of the water, they had to use other methods. They would have to lean the ship on its side, clean the bottom, and then lean it over on the other side. They would do this with the aid of giant winches with large spokes sticking out that a dozen or so men would have to power. It must have been quite a sight to see a mighty tall ship leaning over on its side, a veritable fish out of water.

The colonial charm of Nelson's dockyard did not make up for the arid landscape or expensive and pretentious atmosphere of the island, and we were not alone in our opinions. We had met a couple who were a professional captain and his wife. They had to stay in Antigua for long periods of time to maintain the boat they were taking care of, and they weren't terribly happy about it. After just a few days we were bored with Antigua, yet weather kept us from leaving, so we could see how they would be unhappy staying here for a few weeks at a stretch. Our week and a half stay would have been a bit more unpleasant if they had not been there. One night we all made pizza together, and it was the best any of us had had in ages, thanks to their wonderful pizza dough recipe. We made three huge pizzas, one just pepperoni; one pepperoni, red pepper, mushroom, and onion; and the third had everything that was fit to put on a pizza. We playfully dubbed the pepperoni pizza the "kid's" pizza, the moderately topped pizza the "teen" pizza, and the garbage pizza the "adult" pizza. I don't think any of us had had that much fun cooking in a long time.

We had dinner together a few more times, but we were also treated to movies at their boat, for they had a TV and DVD player onboard and a limited assortment of movies. This was a real treat for us since we had been without a TV for many months now. Aside from their good cooking and being able to take advantage of their TV, they were also very interesting people. They had been living and working on boats for decades, had traveled all over the world, and had a number of great sea stories to tell.

In the midst of our forced stay on Antigua, we were incredibly bored, so we asked our friends what on earth there was to do around here. They suggested we take a bus ride to St. John, on the other side of the island. We had nothing better to do, so we figured, why not? One morning we arrived at the local bus stop with shoes and ankles brown from churned up dust. The bus we loaded onto was much like the buses we had taken on past islands: plain, old, and inconspicuous. We rode past dry grass fields, British colonial ruins, and humble villages.

In the city, we arrived at an actual bus station, which I hadn't quite expected. Next to us was a large concrete building that remotely resembled a mall or shopping plaza. Inside a large cavernous room was a produce market with all types of fruits and vegetables imaginable. A little further down the road we came across a questionable looking open air meat market. Men in white aprons hacked away at dead animal corpses and the place had a distinctively pungent aroma of disinfectant and blood. We didn't stick around for long. As we walked away, the scenery transformed from something out of the past to touristy shops and high end boutiques almost seamlessly. Here we encountered Hawaiian shirt clad, camera-wielding tourists off the cruise ships. It was strange to think that most of these people would leave this island having never seen the real Antigua.

13 Chasing Iguanas

March 31, 2002
Guadeloupe, French Caribbean

When Koukla dropped anchor in the small port of Deshaies on the island of Guadeloupe, there was a palpable sense of foreboding. Here on this French island we would be up against an obstacle we had never come across before—a language barrier. My father and I both knew a little French, but it was very little, not even enough to communicate really, so this should be interesting.

At first glance, Deshaies was an outwardly charming little fishing village, with cute little shops and a bakery with a multitude of scrumptious looking things. But we were unable to enjoy them because we first had to exchange currency, as US dollars were not accepted here. Up until now, we had never had this sort of problem. Everyone had been more than happy to take our green money, but not here. They would only accept francs and euros, as it is fully a part of France. Think of it kind of like a French Hawaii. It was a bit disheartening seeing all the neat things in Deshaies and knowing I could buy nothing, for there was nowhere to exchange our money. The quaint village was not set up for this sort of thing.

We were forced to move on to Basse Terre, which was a much larger city. But we didn't want to go all that way today, so we tucked in for the night off a small island called Pigeon Island.

The next morning we woke up to a customs boat puttering around, and wouldn't you know that we were the first boat they decided to board. Next to all the other little fiberglass boats we were quite conspicuous, and a lot of times that has worked out to our disadvantage. But fortunately the French officials were quite cordial in their heavily accented English, and caused us no problems. Although when they left, they had a bit of a problem. They seemed to think their 15-plus foot flybridge would fit nicely under our bowsprit, which has fewer than 8 feet of clearance above the water, so they rammed right into us. It would have been quite comical if we hadn't been a bit worried about them damaging our stays, but it appeared that they had done more damage to themselves than to us. When they moved away we spotted a thin, blackish green scrape across their gleaming white hull.

After breakfast we continued on to Basse Terre. It was still a bit dreary in the early afternoon when we came into the unprotected harbor. While we were dropping anchor we rolled to and fro with the heavy ocean swells, which never stopped. When we were getting into our dinghy to go ashore we had to time it just right so that the side we were getting off was down next to the boat, for if we didn't we'd be way up in the air and it would have been a long way down into the dinghy.

Once we were ashore, the very first thing we did was look for a bank. We found one fairly quickly, waited in line, and when it was our turn we were told that they did not change money there, and they sent us to another bank. And then they sent us to another bank, who sent us to another bank, who sent us back to where we started. We ended up changing our money at a rather seedy looking place that also sold lottery tickets and developed film.

Now that we had money we were free to roam Guadeloupe and do as we pleased. For a place that rejected our American money, it looked pretty Americanized. There were many American chain stores with a few French specialty shops here and there. It was a rather interesting experience ordering food in a French McDonald's. My father and I stared at the menu for a good while attempting to translate it with the help of my mini English-French dictionary. The only problem was we first had to guess what the word meant in English, then look it up to confirm that that was what it meant in French. Fortunately, one thing I knew fairly well were my French numbers, so we were able to somehow order, pay, and get our food using broken, atrocious French and a bit of gesticulation. It felt like an accomplishment.

We had hoped to see the island more extensively, for the rainforests inland were supposed to be beautiful, but we didn't think our extremely limited French could handle finding a bus or hailing a taxi and coming back. Although, there was a bigger reason: we were running out of time before we would have to start heading north, and there were still a few more islands we wanted to see.

A small group of islands called Les Saintes, (The Saints), were also owned by France. These islands were positively enchanting. They had an air of French-countryside-meets-tropical paradise. The gently rolling green hills were dotted with red, orange, and yellow roofed houses. We anchored off the largest and most populated of these islands, Bourg des Saintes, which was still pretty small. The town square looked like something out of a fairy tale, with clock tower, steepled church, and narrow streets radiating in all directions. Most shops were filled with interesting items, but there were also your typical, touristy trinkets. I think our favorite was an adorable ice cream shop with the most delectable crème glace we had ever tasted. We walked along the tidy streets, past boutiques and patisseries, and into quaint villages. For the most part, the houses were small and simple yet neat.

As we walked farther inland we came across a pen of bleating goats. They were beneath the shade of a large tree that was raining pink petals. Inside the pen there wasn't a flower to be seen, yet outside the ground was littered with them. Whenever a flower fell inside the pen the goats would all scramble for it, and it was usually the largest and fastest that ate it. We stood there a few minutes watching them, and while we were standing there a baby goat came right up to the fence to look at us. We had noticed that he had been too small and slow to get many flowers, so we fed a few right to him and he gobbled them up.

On our second and, unfortunately, last day in Les Saintes, we hiked up to Fort Napoleon on top of the highest hill on the island. Fortunately for us, the highest hill on the island wasn't that high compared to what we had hiked in the past. As we went up, we passed a tree with a skull and crossbones sign on it, and it had nothing to do with pirates. It was a manchineel tree, sort of like poison ivy in tree form, but worse. The manchineel is also known as the manzanilla de la muerte in Spanish, or little apple of death. It is one of the most toxic trees in the world. Every part of it is toxic—bark, leaves, and fruit, which is potentially lethal if eaten. You would not want to stand under it in a rainstorm. Even one drop containing a bit of the manchineel's milky sap can cause painful blistering. Needless to say, we steered clear of it.

At the top of the mountain stood moat-ringed Fort Napoleon. When I first heard that Fort Napoleon had a moat I had envisioned sharks, crocodiles, and piranha, yet the moat didn't even have water in it. I wasn't exactly disappointed that there were no vicious aquatic animals, and even without them Fort Napoleon was pretty neat. We marched across the drawbridge and into the stone fortress, and explored the labyrinth of narrow passageways. I was surprised and delighted by the botanical garden with iguanas everywhere. The botanical garden was mostly cacti, succulents, and other desert plants, but the fauna of the place more than made up for the flora. You could almost call it an infestation of iguanas, as they ran the place. One of them was near the path we were walking on. My mother, who isn't too fond of reptiles, wanted it to move. So she sprayed it with a bit of water hoping it would go away. Well, it moved all right, but not in the direction that she had wanted. It quickly came towards her and she ran away.

After our legs had grown tired from exploring, we headed back down the mountain and back to the boat. In the glorious sun of the late afternoon I floated around in the warm, still water. As I looked out over the glittering turquoise water at the red-dotted, rolling green hills I thought to myself, what could be better than this?

14 Jungle Hitchhiking

April 6, 2002
Commonwealth of Dominica

Have you ever read a fairy tale that almost seemed more fact than fiction, or a fantasy story that you just wished was real? Well, on Dominica that line between myth and reality is delightfully blurred. On our approach, the vividly green island wore a thin veil of tropical haze. Out of the misty bay shot a single boat that looked like an overgrown dinghy. This boat came out to meet us offering a tour up the Indian River, a must-see attraction on Dominica, while we were still at least a mile out. This was the first sign of the almost cut-throat competition for the almighty dollar on Dominica.

The second came immediately after dropping anchor. The sand on the bottom had not even settled before a second boat of the same style and similar once bright, now faded coloring came out. This man introduced himself as Sugar Daddy. We would eventually find that most people on this island had similarly eclectic names, although whether these titles were self-styled or actually appeared on their birth certificates was unknown. And of them, Sugar Daddy was the most common; there being no fewer than four others that we had come across. He basically came out offering to do our grocery shopping, and deliver it right to our boat. We accepted because we were not able to go ashore today because it was too late to clear customs, and we thought it was pretty neat having fresh fruits and vegetables brought right out to us. And this was only the first such occurrence.

Early the next morning a man paddled out to our boat on a surfboard peddling what he called mango apples, a rare type of mango. At first, we didn't think we were interested, but then he offered us a free sample. I can honestly say that they were probably the best fruit I had ever tasted. They were unbelievably sweet, fleshy, and juicy but very messy. The pale orangey juice covers your entire face and drips down your elbows in a gloriously sticky mess. We bought over a dozen for just a few dollars and a small package of Oreos. Apparently both American dollars and cookies were legal tender in Dominica. The mangoes  did not last long. When we had only a few left we tried to save them for a special occasion, but we waited too long and were devastated to find they were rotten and gathering flies. We never saw the mango apple peddler again, nor did we ever find them elsewhere.

From our vantage point, the island appeared to be a massive blob of green and more green. But the unparalleled beauty of the rainforests contrasted deeply with the impoverished cities. The villages here were more destitute than any we had seen before. The streets were either unpaved or full of potholes, and the sidewalks had been chiseled away. I thought I had seen poverty before, but this was different. The sight of this city caused a strange pang, for I could not quite pity the inhabitants because everywhere it was allowed, life bloomed. Yes, the town was poor and unkempt, but in a charming sort of way. Every available square inch of dirt was occupied with some sort of plant life, including breadfruit, hibiscus, palms, grapefruit, and more. It was almost as if the forest was trying to reclaim the land.

Something I have learned on this trip is that spontaneous occurrences are generally more fun than planned events. The next day we found ourselves taking a bus ride around the entire island. It was something we had not planned on doing, but ended up being one of the best days of our entire trip. It was not your average tourist bus tour. There were eleven of us in something similar to a Volkswagen hippie bus. There were the four of us, a young Canadian couple, and a handsome French family with three cute little children. Because of a bit of a misunderstanding, the tour guide spoke mostly French, though English was his first language, and the French couple could speak English quite well. Half way through the trip the tour guide either gave up speaking French, or figured out that the French speaking people could speak English but the English speaking people could not speak French.

Moments after we exited the city we were surrounded by jungle. Whenever we passed something interesting the tour guide, who was also driving the bus, would either slow down or stop to tell us about it, and it was generally some type of plant. Tree-like banana plants were weighed down by enormous bunches of ripe yellow or immature green bananas, some of which still had the large purple, almond-shaped remains of the pollinated flower dangling weirdly below. Familiar coconut palms and spindly sugarcane were also present in abundance. But the strangest and most interesting plants we saw on the ride were the cashew tree and pineapple plant. The pineapple plant was particularly interesting because it was simply a pineapple sitting on a bed of leaves. It was just so peculiar seeing it innocently sitting on the side of the road. Even more fascinating was the cashew tree. The cashew "nut" that many of us are familiar with is actually the stem of a fruit. Our guide picked a red apple-like cashew fruit for us to look at with the curved "nut" perched on top.

We stopped to stretch our legs in a grapefruit orchard, where dew-laden grass tickled our bare ankles as we stood back while our guide climbed up and shook the tree. Plump, pale yellow-pink grapefruits a-plenty rained down. These Dominican grapefruits have spoiled me for life, because nowhere else are there any sweeter than these.

Up next was a coconut roasting factory, where the workers toiled at husking the coconuts, stoking the fires, and roasting the white flesh till it was left toasty brown with a distinct smokey, nutty flavor. Our bus waded through a very shallow river to a mock Carib Indian village. The infamous,

cannibalistic Carib once thrived throughout the Caribbean, which was named after them. Some never left Dominica. The descendants of the Carib Indians now live on reservations in the forest, and we saw how they lived in pre-Columbian times and who they are today. Just outside the mock village full of small dried grass huts, the descendants sold wonderful hand-made trinkets of impeccable quality. Nearby, they also danced in traditional regalia, like something out of the pages of National Geographic.

Our final official stop was at Emerald Pool waterfall. It was a five minute hike through the rainforest from the parking lot to the waterfall. From the moment I stepped into the forest I was caught under its seductive spell. Sweet floral and cut grass scents wafted through the humid air so thick you could take a bite out of it. The air was positively electric, trees had moss skins and tiny green and brown lizards scurried on tendril vines. I glided through the glimmering, throbbing green forest. Everything glittered with dew, and I could have sworn I caught sight of a fairy out of the corner of my eye. It was magic. The waterfall gushed from the recent rain into the aptly named Emerald Pool. The ever present mist from the falls covered everything nearby, including myself, with dew drops that glittered like diamonds. As soon as I left the forest I could not wait to go back again.

In the parking lot there were stands selling handmade souvenirs and fresh fruits. We sampled guava, sugarcane, fresh pineapple, and coconut candy made from the smoky, nutty stuff we had seen roasted. The fresh pineapple was my favorite and I ate it till my mouth went numb.

On the enchanted island of Dominica there is a magical river heavily guarded by a people known as River Guides. They voraciously guard the mouth of this river and ward off all who might wander up it on their own. But, they do not keep this treasure all for themselves. They will share it for a price.

We wished to see this magical river, so we enlisted the help of a river guide. As he propelled his clumsy vessel with heavy oars, he proceeded to tell us the secrets of the Indian River. As we headed inland the river was quickly swallowed up on all sides by the forest. The titanic trees leaned over us in an almost protective manner, listening to our every word. The mighty roots of the trees dug into the earth and intertwined with each other like writhing snakes. In these gnarled, wriggling roots half falling into the river, crabs nervously scuttled to and fro. Compared to the crystal clear water throughout the Caribbean the brown river looked especially murky, but we could still occasionally see a fish lazily swimming beneath.

The river steadily narrowed and we were well into the forest. Strange chattering and chirping noises were all around us. In a clear patch of sky unobstructed by tree tops, our guide pointed out two parrots soaring high about us, one red as the setting sun and the other blue as the sky they flew in.

We continued on through the eye-popping scenery until the river was so narrow we could go no further. We followed our guide into the jungle. Enormous bunches of bananas and plantains hung from the tall plants. A small rather inconspicuous tree with little round, green fruits was pointed out to us as guava. Our guide also showed us a cayenne pepper plant, something I knew previously as that ground up red stuff on my mom's spice rack. But the most fascinating plant we saw was the sensitive plant. At first glance this tiny weed-like plant did not look very interesting, but at the slightest touch, the leaves all folded up. It was an alien, almost robotic motion the way it recoiled.

Throughout our entire Caribbean cruise we had done an ungodly amount of hiking, and often I was less than enthused about traipsing off into the forest. This time I could not wait to go. Because this time we would be hiking in the rainforest. We had only briefly gone into the rainforest a few days before, but I had been entranced ever since.

We had become friends with the young Canadian couple whom we had met on our bus tour around the island, and they were accompanying us on our hike. Apparently there are so many waterfalls on Dominica that even the locals have lost track of them all. We decided to hike to Middlehelm Falls because it sounded like it wouldn't be that long or difficult a hike compared to many others. After an hour-plus bus ride, a long time of walking down a searing asphalt road, and a bit of hitchhiking, we made it to the start of the trail. Here on Dominica, hitchhiking is a (reasonably) safe, regularly practiced, common institution, and if we had not accepted the ride we would have been too exhausted to hike very far.

After a short while I began to feel the energy of the forest flow through me. Senses utterly overwhelmed, I wished I had at least three more eyes, my two just weren't enough. Everything was a million shades of green with bright flowers carelessly splattered here and there. An aroma not unlike that of cut grass wafted amongst the trees. Tropical birds conversed with one another in the distance. I was light as a feather as I glided over fallen logs and across trickling streams. After a while we heard the rumble of  falling water in the distance. But before we could see or even hear the fall we started to notice the increased amount of moisture on the plants and the trail was a bit more slippery and muddy. The terrain also was steeper and a bit more treacherous as we neared the falls. From high above, a stream fell over a cliff that appeared to have a mass of green plants pasted on, and plunged into a gleaming pool. Cooling mist sprayed everywhere and covered everything with dew drops. I looked down at my arms and saw that they were covered with glistening translucent pearls. Eternal rainbows were caught in a web of mist near the base of the falls. Light captured in water droplets shone brightly and the trees became gem-encrusted. I stood by the fall in wonder, fully in awe of nature.

On the hike out, I slipped on an algae-covered rock and soaked one of my sneakers. Crossing a different stream I slipped on another rock and got my other foot wet. I had to slosh along for the remainder of the hike, which turned out to be a lot longer than any of us had anticipated. Perhaps it was just the adventurous spirit in all of us, but for some odd reason we took a different road out than we did in. The six of us walked that searing, unshaded asphalt road for hours without passing a single vehicle. We did come across a tethered donkey, but that hardly counts. Sensitive plants grew like weeds on the side of the road, and I walked along tapping every one I spotted and watched it recoil. After hours and hours of hiking we were out of food and water, but the island provided for us. Many grapefruit trees grew along the side of the road, and we helped ourselves. Those grapefruits tasted wonderful to our parched lips and rumbling tummies.

At last, in the early evening, a pickup truck finally drove by and offered us a ride. There were even a few other hitchhikers in the back as well. If it hadn't been for that lift we would have been hiking well into the night. By the time we arrived back at the bay we were anchored off, the sun had already set. And we still had a short walk back to our dinghies.

All of a sudden we heard a lot of shouting and screaming and unintelligible exclamations from up the road. It sounded like a riot. We were all quite alarmed at this point, and were thankful that we were all in a group. We did not linger, and hurried back to our respective boats. It was not until the next day that we found out what all the commotion was about. It turned out it was a friendly game of dominoes. Apparently the game is quite popular on the island and is taken very seriously.

Well, this is the end of the line. Our voyage south had ended, and our next stop would be somewhere we'd already been. Heading home wouldn't have been quite so difficult if Dominica hadn't been so wonderful. It was hard to leave behind that island of breath-taking rainforest, eye-popping waterfalls, and mouth-watering fruit. But I had a feeling this would not be my last time on the island.

As much as I hated the thought of leaving, I was excited about the prospect of returning home. I was looking forward to all the comforts of civilization that I had been missing out on for the past few months as well as seeing all my friends and boyfriend once again. Yet home was still a long ways away.

15 Heading North

April 15, 2002
Sint Maarten/Saint Martin

Somehow the wind must have known we did not really want to leave Dominica because we did not pull away very quickly. From here it was straight back to St. Martin to wait for a window to head offshore. Of course, our autopilot was on the fritz, so we'd have to take turns steering all night long.

Late that night, in the enveloping darkness, I stared at the glowing compass with heavy eyelids. I made small, sharp adjustments and the wheel replied with a soft creak. Every now and then steps creaked and a red light was switched on down below, for it was also my brother's watch, and he had to check the radar every now and then for invisible vessels. The lapping of water, the flapping of sails, and the groaning of wood enticed me to sleep, but that wasn't an option. While part of me yearned for sleep, part was also awake and empowered. For the moment, I alone was in control—it was my duty to keep a steady course. My arms grew weary from the repetitive back and forth motion. Finally, my father came up to relieve me. My brother and I headed down below to sleep for a few hours until we had to do it all again. It was four in the morning when we arrived at Simpson Bay, St. Maarten. It was convenient that we already knew the bay pretty well, so all we had to do was drop the anchor and sleep till daylight.

Originally, we had planned to stay in St. Maarten three or four days to restock before heading offshore, but we ended up staying two weeks for various reasons. The most pressing was that we had a broken autopilot. For us, an autopilot is an absolute necessity for offshore sailing. It's basically like having an extra crewmember. While the autopilot is steering, it's much easier for half the crew to go on watch while the other half sleep. It was bad enough having to go without it for just one overnight sail let alone a week and a half in the open ocean. The second reason was the weather. There was a lingering front just hanging off of Cape Hatteras waiting to bash us the minute we left St. Martin. Many other cruisers found themselves in a similar predicament, but that worked out to our advantage.

Every other day it seemed we were over at someone's boat or they were over at ours. Often the host's boat would be full of multiple crews. I remember distinctly the four of us going over to the vessel Solstice Moon, crewed by an older Canadian couple, and the Canadian friends we had met in Dominica, the crew of Spartina, were also there.

Solstice Moon was a one-of-a-kind vessel, and the owners of it were even more unique. They owned and ran a special effects company, and had made absolutely everything on their boat from the hull and anchor windlass to the wheel, cleats, and portholes. He was a true tinkerer and do-it-yourselfer, and in him my father found a kindred spirit. My father referred to him as "Yoda". He questioned him endlessly about every little thing and he would always reply enthusiastically, his eyes a-twinkle with excitement.

At dinner that night, the eight of us squished around the main saloon table, but the homey style of the boat almost made me forget I was on a boat at all. They even had cats. Sitting on the sofa-like benches watching the two cats rubbing up against the small idle woodstove, I felt like I was in a quaint little cabin in the woods rather than the cabin of a boat. The conversation bounced from international affairs, to religion, exotic destinations, sociology, and at one point, to our broken autopilot. When my father asked "Yoda: if he had any ideas how to fix our autopilot, the light bulb in his mind clicked on and shone out of his eyes. He said he had seen a part lying in the dirt on the side of the road that might do the trick.

A few days later, they went and found it. My father cleaned it up and modified it, but it still didn't work. We had to order a new part from England and wait for it to be shipped here, significantly lengthening our stay.

After over a week and a half of waiting for our part, half a dozen trips to the grocery store with our dinghy piled high with food stuffs, and some last minute souvenir shopping, we were ready. Herb, the weather guru of cruisers and our personal savior, had given us the all clear. We were actually leaving the Caribbean. But, there was still one last exotic stop: Bermuda.

16 Battening the Hatches

May 5, 2002
The Atlantic Ocean

It had not completely sunk in yet, in just a few short weeks I would be home. I would be able to take a hot shower every day, sleep on a bed that does not move, and I would not have to pump water or manually flush the toilet. I would get to see my friends and boyfriend again. Unfortunately, I could not begin dreaming of such things just yet.

Four days out of St. Maarten, we still were not completely sure if we were stopping in Bermuda or not. The weather was very fickle, much as it had been our whole trip, and it was difficult to find the shortest and safest route. The first few days had not been bad, just dull and monotonous, but from past experience we had learned that dull and monotonous was a good thing, especially when it came to offshore sailing. We had fallen into our daily routines of eating, sleeping, going on watch, and for my brother and I, doing schoolwork.

Eventually it started getting rough and all the unpleasant memories of our last offshore passage came flooding back. But things were different this time. We were able to cope better. We'd had many weeks to prepare, and things were stowed away properly, for the most part, so all our gear did not go flying every time a wave hit. We knew what meals were easy to cook given the conditions, and when it was entirely too rough we had an ample supply of easy to eat snacks in reach. Most importantly, we were now a much more experienced and able crew.

There was one specific event where we worked so well together we surprised even ourselves. We were five days out, almost six since it was late at night, and my brother and I were just finishing our watch. My father peeked up to tell us he'd be ready to start his watch shortly, when we heard the clatter of something falling on the deck from high above. We whipped our heads around to see the throat of the main gaff slide all the way down the mast. Imagine the throat and peak like suspenders holding up a very loose pair of pants. If one of the suspenders breaks the pants would fall halfway off. In either case, you have to repair and reattach the broken bit before you can continue on your way.

My mother quickly came up to see what all the commotion was about, and we all automatically set to work. In under fifteen minutes we lowered the gaff, fixed the throat halyard, and had the sail back up. All this was in the middle of the night, under the spreader lights, on a pitching vessel in the middle of the ocean. We barely spoke a word to each other, as we all knew what to do.

I both despised and adored those nights out in the middle of the ocean. I loved to look up at the stars, each one a sparkling gem placed on a backdrop of black velvet. I enjoyed trying to spot the different constellations as well as finding my own patterns in the sky. What I hated was trying to sleep. Most of the time on that voyage we were heeling drastically, and if we tacked I would have to switch bunks from one side of the main saloon to the other (the motion in my forward cabin was a bit too bouncy for me to sleep). I felt like an accordion the way I was squished up against the hull and released with the motion of the boat. I had to curl my toes around the edge of the cushion to stay in place.

On our 6th day out, my father made the popular decision to stop at Bermuda. If he hadn't he might have had a mutiny on his hands. We were just under two days away, and we were all very excited to have one last stamp in our passports. The last leg of our trip to Bermuda was beautiful. The winds were agreeable, as well as the seas. The only problem was it was starting to get cold as we headed north. For the first time in months I had to put on long pants. It felt weird having fabric touching the lower part of my legs all the time.

As we neared Bermuda, we kept seeing what we thought at first were clear water bottles floating on the surface of the water. Curiosity got the better of us and we decided to try and pick one up in a bucket, whatever it was. When we pulled out my brother's marine science book to try and figure out what it was, we realized it probably hadn't been such a good idea to catch it. It was a deadly Portuguese man-of-war. A Portuguese man-of-war isn't just one animal, but a number of different types of microscopic animals all living together in harmony. On the top is a clear air sac that floats on the surface and supports a mass of tentacles that can be up to 165 feet long! One type of microscopic animal creates a highly poisonous substance. After we dumped the creature back in the water, my father accidentally touched the bucket we had caught it in, and some of the residue got on his skin. That miniscule amount made his hand numb and tingly for hours.

Later that same day, when we were all just sitting around in the cockpit reading and whatnot, we heard a splash up forward. We all ran up to see what it was, afraid something might have fallen overboard. Off our starboard bow was a whole pod of dolphins welcoming us to Bermuda. I climbed up on the bowsprit and sat with my legs dangling over the side. I looked down between my feet and saw the gray speckled backs of no fewer than three dolphins skimming the surface with their dorsal fins, and off to the side there were many more. A mother with a baby half her size raced along with us. A small group of about five or more dolphins arched their backs out of the water in perfect synchronization with one another. A few even made daring leaps clear out of the water. This was all going on no more than 10 yards away from us. The dolphins below me splashed up water with their blowholes and tickled my feet.

After a long week out on the unpredictable Atlantic, Bermuda's craggy shores were a glorious sight to behold. The island enveloped us as we wound around coral heads and miniature islands with single trees upon them. This maze led us from the raging ocean swells to the calm, smooth-as-glass bay of St. George harbor. From the moment I laid eyes upon it, I noticed Bermuda was an eclectic blend of the two places I knew and loved; Maine and the Caribbean. Stately Bermuda cedars and majestic palms mingled harmoniously. Even the water was a mix of the two. Caribbean turquoise combined with the steely blue-gray of Maine to make a shade of bright teal. The architecture was the only thing that was purely tropical in style. Every house was painted a pastel hue with neatly manicured lawns.

The island exuded an old-world charm unlike anything I had seen before. Just beyond the dinghy dock in St. George was a traditional town courtyard, complete with a beautiful old church and even stocks. Stocks are basically a large board one puts their neck, arms, and occasionally legs through to hold them in place. This was once a form of punishment that is now used for tourist photo-ops.

One of the many attractions of Bermuda is that it pulls visitors right into the past. A few times a week sightseers can watch, or even take part in, a public dunking put on by the Town Crier and the Town Gossip. Both in period dress, the town crier clangs his bell and yells the traditional "Hear Ye, Hear Ye," and people instinctively flock to him. The Crier picks people randomly out of the crowd and accuses them of such crimes as being drunk and disorderly or dressing in more colorful attire than the Town Crier. He even has signs to hang around the people's necks, labeling them "drunk", "nag", or "public nuisance", and on-looking relatives generally take advantage of this photo-op. After he's done good-naturedly humiliating a few tourists he moves on to the Town Gossip. In colonial times, gossiping and nagging was a punishable offense, and a public dunking was one of the milder punishments used back then. The two of them banter back and forth and spit out clever lines at each other. It all ends with the woman getting dunked into the harbor on the dunking stool, which is basically a long board with a seat on the end. While this is all fun and games to us now, it was strange to think that criminals, or victims depending upon how you look at it, actually took part in such dunkings, or were sentenced to stand in the stocks for any number of days, depending upon the crime.

Another link to Bermuda's past we experienced was Fort St. Catherine. Bermuda's first settlers had actually been shipwrecked sailors, and the site of this fort was where they first made landfall. Unlike the Caribbean, and really most of the islands settled during the age of exploration and colonial era, Bermuda did not have a native population, making its colonization much less problematic.

Bermuda was beautiful both above and below ground. The entire island is a honeycomb of glittering caves, and we had the chance to visit them. As we descended into the earth we began to hear the soft ping ping sound of dripping water echoing throughout the cavern. Each droplet had seeped through the earth and picked up various minerals from the soil. When the minerals from the droplets accumulate for thousands of years stalactites and stalagmites form. Light shimmered off of the stalactites dangling from the roof of the cave and stalagmites jutting up from the ground, ranging in size from those no wider than a pencil to those as fat as a baby elephant. Some caves even have underground lakes. One had an expansive body of water 55 feet deep with massive stalagmites looming in the motionless water like the skeletons of ships, creating an otherworldly effect.

Originally we had only planned on staying in Bermuda for a couple of days, but we ended up staying much longer because of the weather. This had been an all too frequent predicament throughout our entire trip. Bermuda was great, but by now we were all rather anxious to get back to Maine. Home was only a week away, but we kept experiencing delay after delay. As soon as one nasty front had cleared another one would come up right behind it. So here we were, stuck in Bermuda. Our friends and relatives were incredibly unsympathetic. The weather was often nasty and we were unable to leave the boat for days. All we could do was wait for the weather, and wait and wait and wait.

If we were stuck here, we figured we'd better make the most of it. The island of Bermuda is so small and the roads are so narrow that the renting of cars is not permitted, but renting mopeds is very popular. The high-pitched whine of speeding mopeds that resonated throughout the island had been slightly annoying, but when we decided to splurge and rent two of our own, that noise went from obnoxious to sounding quite pleasant.

Off we sped past neatly manicured lawns and pastel houses, by palm and evergreen trees, majestic forts and sandy coves. The temperate air whizzing past whipped stray strands of hair in my eyes, and tickled my cheeks. This was our one chance to freely roam the island, and we did not want to miss anything. We zipped over to Hamilton, which by bus seemed far away, but by moped took no time at all. Compared to colonial style St. George, Hamilton had a very metropolitan feel. The streets were lined with boutiques and fancy department stores. The fort that once protected the city, Fort Hamilton, was now a park. With its vibrantly green lawns and exquisite gardens, you would never imagine this place had been used for the purpose of warfare. The moat that was once used to keep out undesirables was now a beautiful walking path with vines and other jungle plants crawling into the moat and narrowing the path.

Up next was Spittal Pond Nature Reserve. The sweet pine scent of Bermuda cedars mingled with the soft chirping of tiny tree frogs. We spotted one of these one-centimeter long crooners hopping along the mossy forest floor. This reserve also has unusual geological formations. There was one area of black and white checkered rock, crisscrossed with cracks, forming a near perfect grid. It would have made a half decent chessboard.

From the outside, the Bermuda Perfumery looked like a cottage nestled among fields of exotic flowers. On the inside, with the large vats and squishing and extracting machines, it looked more like something out of Willy Wonka's Chocolate Factory. We learned all about how perfume is made today, and also how long ago it was made from whale fat. After the tour, we ambled through fields of hibiscus, Easter lily, oleander, and passion flower. The passion flower was my favorite. It was an odd yet beautiful combination of purple, white, and green. I had been told that flower gets its name from Christ's Passion: the 10 petals represent the apostles present at the crucifixion; the 72 filaments represent the number of thorns in Christ's crown; the 5 anthers represent Christ's wounds, and the 3 styles with rounded stigmas represent the three nails.

As much fun as Bermuda had been, we were getting a bit antsy to leave. And we were not the only ones. All over Bermuda, harbors were crowded with boats of all shapes and sizes, just itching to be moving on. Recently the weather had been horrible, with one nasty storm right after another. It was as if they had been moving along a conveyor belt. A few boats that had tried to leave ended up coming right back. Everyone, from the tall ship Picton Castle to the numerous small sloops, was waiting for good weather. Being stuck on Bermuda together, we made quite a few new friends and solidified bonds with others we had met elsewhere. We met a man who also happened to be from Maine, and owned a beautiful sloop named Alice. We even met a few kids close to our own age, who were from Canada, and were also anxious to get home to their friends, and spend some quality time with their televisions. But most of all we enjoyed spending time with the crew of Spartina, whom we had met in Dominica.

We felt the time crunch in a number of ways. My dad had to be back at his ship to resume work as a marine engineer. Come hell or high water he had to be on that ship. Another date loomed for me. My boyfriend was going off on his own adventure. He was leaving for ski camp in Canada just a few days after we were planning to get back. As we sat there the number of days we'd have together quickly shrank.

While waiting for weather in Bermuda, I made heavy use of our pactor radio to email with my friends and boyfriend. It was great to be in regular contact, but as much as we were looking forward to getting home and the comforts of civilization, my boyfriend reminded me of some of the downsides. Despite being a fully-fledged crew member and bonafide blue water sailor, I was in fact still a 16-year-old girl. He confided in me how he was picked on, bullied, and excluded. Right, teenagers did stuff like that. I had also been picked on, bullied, and excluded not that long ago. But honestly? Once you've been through an ocean gale, hiked through rainforests and into volcanic craters, all that teenage drama felt a lot less meaningful. It was just dawning on me what an immense gift I'd been given.

In late May we finally left Bermuda. Which day? Who knows. We didn't know what day it was most of the time. We were lucky if we knew the month. Actually, maybe it was early June. In the wee morning hours, while the island of Bermuda slept soundly in their tidy pastel houses, the harbors were all astir. The harbor echoed with the clinking sound of dozens of rising anchor chains. All those boats that had been waiting for weeks for decent weather to leave had finally been given the all-clear. Everyone was ready to bolt.

The water beside our hull boiled from the frenetic jumping of hundreds of small fish as we slowly wound our way out of the labyrinthine harbor. The tiny ocean oasis of Bermuda quickly sunk into the waves like a sea turtle, and we immediately found ourselves in the gray open ocean. The ambiguous heavens looked as if at any moment the skies would clear to streaming bright sun or they would band together to form an ugly thunderhead.

As we pulled away from the speck of land we spotted a fellow escapee headed for home. The crew of the yacht, Alice, had also been held hostage on Bermuda by the nefarious weathermen, and was also headed to Maine. The captain was a professional photographer, and offered to take some pictures of us under sail if we would do the same for them. Being the more maneuverable vessel, they made a parallel course to ours, we both snapped away, then they pulled ahead and were soon a dot on the horizon.

The first two ponderous days we hoped would be a sign of things to come, for we had learned the hard way that excitement and adventure are quite undesirable out on the open ocean. Each subsequent day the seas increased and the winds decreased, in accordance with Murphy's Law.

We had but one heartening sight during those days of progressively worsening weather. For three days straight a pod of dolphins would frolic in the wake of our bow, yet they would scamper off in a fright when our bow crashed deep into the waves. The last time we spotted them one particular dolphin repeatedly slapped its glimmering gray tail upon the surface of the water, either in warning or mirth. Following one final slap upon the writhing sea, the dolphins were gone.

After contacting our weather guru via ham radio we found we were in for another rough ride, and embraced the cliché to "batten down the hatches." With every nerve-wracking plunge into the waves, green water churned and gurgled on deck and poured down through our leaky main saloon skylight. It literally looked like it was raining down below. The way our bowsprit rose up into the air and plunged into the waves almost rhythmically with the evenly-spaced, gargantuan swells reminded me of the dunking stool we had seen in Bermuda. My father, who had to go up on the bow to replace our torn jib with the storm jib said it was more like riding a bucking bronco.

After a week of being tossed about and not getting much closer to home very quickly, we altered course towards Cape Cod to avoid being set down on Nantucket Shoals. That following morning we sighted land, and by that evening we passed through the placid Cape Cod Canal. The following evening we anchored in Gloucester, Massachusetts to make some much needed repairs before we would finally be able to return home. We spent a few days in Gloucester mending torn sails and recuperating from the offshore passage before our final leg home.

We weighed anchor the evening after our final preparations. We left on the heels of one gale hoping to get in before the next arrived. Ordinarily we would wait for better weather, but my father was due back at work in a matter of days. My father, being a marine engineer, could not simply put off his return, for if we were late he would miss his ship. We sailed all that night through the gale and then motor sailed the following day trying to beat the weather. It was so rough that we would have liked to turn back, but that wasn't really an option. We had to press on.

On the fateful morning of June 14, 2002 I was roused at the ungodly hour of 4:00 am. The previous night had been so rough I couldn't reach my pajamas all the way up in my cabin in the violently bouncing bow. Thus, I had to sleep in my clothes. Now this was quite convenient. Since I was already dressed I could save my goose-pimpled flesh from the clammy morning ocean air. In my groggy state I became remotely aware that I was supposed to stand fog watch, as we had become enveloped in the stuff on our way up the coast of Maine. We had all been looking forward to sailing past all the familiar Maine islands, and especially at seeing the Owls Head and

Rockland Breakwater lighthouses. All we could do was hear them through the gray wispy walls. However, it was somewhat heartening to see the familiar land formations on the radar and to have our home port on the chart.

It was not until the fog had lifted a bit and we were actually inside the breakwater on our mooring that we could make out Rockland's shore line. After that misty veil lifted we truly realized that we had made it. The four of us had sailed our 60 ft. gaff-rigged schooner from our home port of Rockland, Maine to the Caribbean and back with our limbs and vessel intact.

We had made it with a few days to spare before my dad had to leave to catch his ship. But for another date we'd been too slow. My boyfriend and I had only overlapped by a few short hours after I came ashore, and we didn't get to see each other before he had to leave for the airport. It made our triumphant return bittersweet.

Eventually we both returned from our respective adventures and shared our experiences. We went sailing on Koukla in the summer, and skiing with his family in the winter, although he was more at home on the ocean than I was in the mountains. We were a safe haven for each other in the stormy seas of high school. Life went back to normal, for a time.

Ten+ Years Later

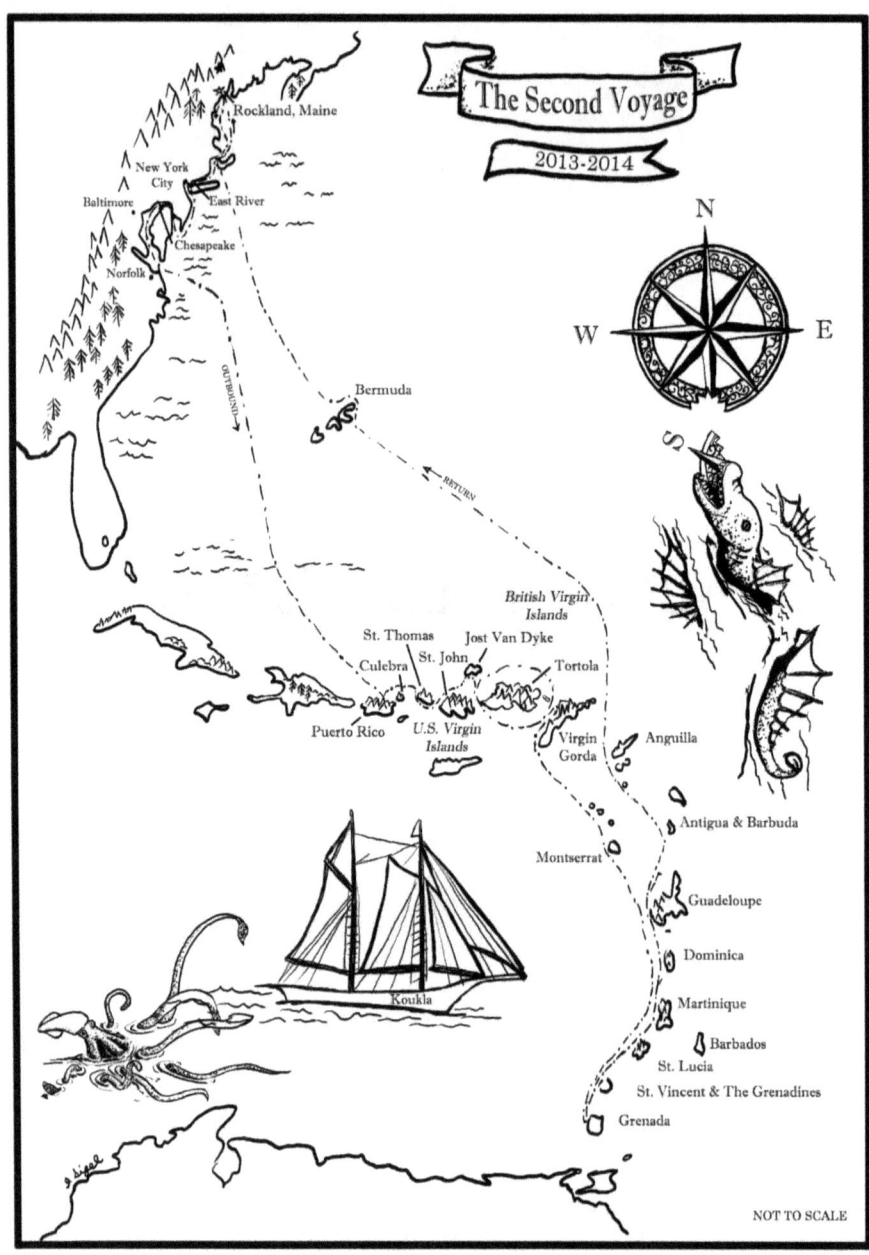

Second Voyage

17 Sea Fever

July 10, 2010
Brooklyn, Maine

For years, that Caribbean voyage became the barometer for all of life's joys and sufferings. The stress of high school, standardized tests and teenage drama, applying for college and leaving behind my boyfriend yet again, and the eventual amicable but still painful end of our relationship—all of it was made a bit easier after receiving that gift of blue water sailing.

Why did that relationship end? Lots of good reasons. First of all, almost nobody ends up with their high school sweetheart, and if you're considering this you should proceed with extreme caution. But ultimately we wanted different things out of life. The best advice my mother ever gave me—probably the best advice anyone has ever given me—is that love is not enough, you have to want the same things out of life. We didn't.

I knew I wanted more adventures. I'd been living far from the ocean for years. I had lost some of my sailor identity, and needed to reclaim it. I knew what an immense gift that trip had been, and I wanted to give it to someone else.

It's crazy to think how events that don't feel important or momentous at the time actually are. When I first met the man and the boat that would forever change my life for the better, I was unaware and unimpressed by both initially. I first met Isaac standing in line at freshman orientation. I wish I could say there was some spark or connection, but there simply wasn't. He was just some random guy. Much like with Koukla, a significant amount of time passed between our first unassuming meeting and eventual connection. We had a few friends in common and crossed paths occasionally, but it wasn't until senior year that he asked me out.

On our first date I talked about sailing. I drew pictures of the different types of sailboats on a napkin—schooner, ketch, yawl, brigantine, and sloop. I described the types of adventures I'd been on, and that I planned to have in the future. I was very up front. I essentially said this is the life I want—if you're interested, great, if not get out now. He was interested.

The summer after we graduated he came to Maine to meet Koukla, and fell in love with both of us. Two years later, we got married in Maine, not far from where I grew up, so my wooden sibling could be there too. After a few years of normal adult life, Isaac followed me to sea. I'd warned him.

18 Hauling Out

August 20, 2014
Rockland, Maine

While I was away at college, my family continued working on Koukla. While I was working on my master's degree (in biochemical and molecular nutrition), the three of them all earned their captain's licenses. Ever since the first trip we'd all talked about the possibility of a second. My family tells me that I was the driving force of making this happen. Perhaps it was because I'd spent several years far from salt air, and needed to breathe it again. But it had been just over a decade since our last trip, and I think we were all ready for a new adventure. We all agreed that the first trip was the best thing we'd ever done, so why wouldn't we do it again?

While we'd planned to recreate that first trip, much had changed. We were different and so was Koukla. Nearly all of Koukla's features and systems were functional. We had electricity, running water, flushing toilets, HAM radio email, shower, and even a small washer/dryer! And this time, thanks to the advances in technology over the past decade, we hoped to be more connected to friends, family, and the world at large.

My brother and I were very different too. We were no longer squabbling children. Teenage Danica did not want to talk about that very much, but oh it happened. She didn't really want to write about her annoying little brother very much either, beyond acknowledging his existence. Our mother, like most good mothers, had always said if you don't have anything nice to say, don't say anything at all. However, twenty-something Danica is happy to talk about her grown-up brother.

My brother, Horatio, is no longer the slightly pudgy 12-year-old you all met last time. He's now a 6-foot-tall beardy dude with practical engineering and craftsmanship skills to rival my dad's. He just finished his BS in mechanical engineering, along with his girlfriend Molly.

Horatio and Molly had been dating for about a year when she decided to come on the sailing trip, and we were all a bit surprised she'd agreed to do so. But after getting to know her a bit better it made more sense. We weren't sure if she was brave or crazy or a little bit of both, but eventually it dawned on me. She and her whole family are big Doctor Who fans, and as any good Whovian knows, if someone offers you the chance to go off and see the world/universe and have exciting adventures, you take it!

People often ask us how we managed to find the time and resources to go on this trip. Honestly, we just made it happen. There is no perfect time or infinite resources. You just do it. I imagine it's kind of like having kids—although I don't have any. (I didn't at the time of the trip, back in 2013). They say there's no right time to have kids, if you want to do it, you just do it. I imagine having kids is a much scarier and more expensive endeavor than taking an extended sailing voyage. Ask me again in a few years, which is scarier and more difficult and I think my answer will still be kids. (Can confirm, 30-something Danica does have a kid. Kids are scarier and more difficult.)

Before we set sail there was a lot of preparation to do. Isaac and I boxed up our lives in Boston, took the essentials and left the rest in my parents' empty house. We gave our pets to family members to watch while we were gone— our cat went to my grandparents, and our hedgehog went to my cousins. Yes, we had a pet hedgehog. No, I would not recommend getting one.

Thanks to my freshly minted nutrition degree, I was assigned the role of chief steward and put in charge of provisioning. I purchased, stored, and took an inventory of canned and dry goods, and frozen foods. I made jam, granola, and tested recipes to adapt to cooking at sea, such as yogurt, chicken curry, and beef stew. A fellow cruiser had recommended a kitchen gadget called a thermal cooker. It's basically a giant thermos you can use as a slow cooker. You heat up a special pot on the stove, then put it in the thermal sleeve, and it keeps cooking. Quite handy for preserving your propane stores, and limiting your stove use at sea.

We also had to haul out Koukla, and scrape and paint the bottom. All boats must be periodically hauled out to remove the excess marine growth–barnacles, seaweed, mussels, etc, and put on a fresh coat of antifouling paint to discourage future sea creatures from making a home of the bottom of your boat. It's a nasty business, and all crew members were required to help, even the newbies.

The first time we'd hauled out Koukla after we bought her, she'd sat dormant for years, and an entire ecosystem had developed below her. She'd grown a beard of muscles, seaweed, and barnacles. When we hauled her out of the water, several eels dropped from her forested bottom. We'd had to hack away at it with rakes, shovels, and other gardening implements. This time wasn't quite so bad, but still gross. We all suited up in our foul weather gear and took turns with the industrial pressure washer. But the marine grime found its way past our protective gear.

Shortly after Koukla was back in the water with a clean bottom, we all moved on board. Our first evening settling in, it was just us kids. My parents were busy with the work of readying the house for a Maine winter sitting empty. We made ourselves at home—Molly made her special cardamom rice pudding with the leftovers from dinner. The main saloon was warm and humid from cooking, and smelled like an Indian restaurant. We turned on the 90s alt rock station, while Molly cooked, Isaac and Horatio played a board game, and I wrote. It felt like home.

Landmine Chicken Curry

1 lb chicken

1-3 Tbs coconut oil

1 can coconut milk

1 can tomato sauce

1/2 to 1 bag frozen peas or veggies

2 cups rice

Tbs curry powder (or to taste)

5-10 cardamom pods (can also use ground, but there won't be any landmines)

Chop chicken into bite sized pieces, sauté in coconut oil until cooked. Add 1 can coconut milk, 1 can plain tomato sauce. Add curry powder until mixture turns yellowish. Add a small handful of whole cardamom seeds. Heat to gently boiling, then let cook in thermal cooker for about 3 hrs. Just before dinner time, reheat to simmer, and add whatever frozen veggies you have—peas, broccoli, cauliflower, or all of the above. Cook until veggies are heated through. Make rice. Serve curry over rice. Whoever accidentally bites on a cardamom seed has to do the dishes. Everyone will know who this is.

Cardamom rice pudding

The extra rice from dinner (about 1/3 of a cup)
3/4 cup milk
1 egg
7 green cardamom pods
1/4 teaspoon cinnamon
pinch of nutmeg
2 Tbsp raisins (optional)
1 tsp vanilla extract
2-3 Tbsp sugar

Make too much rice. Add milk to the pot the extra rice is in until it forms a thin slurry when stirred, about 3/4 cup of milk per 1/3 cup rice. Add egg, cardamom pods, cinnamon, nutmeg, and raisins. Beat thoroughly. Slowly heat, stirring until the mixture starts to boil. Reduce to a simmer. Stir constantly until it reaches desired thickness, about 5-10 min (it will continue to thicken). Add vanilla and sugar in last few minutes of cooking. Top with additional cinnamon or nutmeg if desired. Serve hot or cold.

19 Adventure Science

September 12, 2013
Blue Hill, Maine

The first trip had been so much more than a family vacation, and I wanted the second voyage to be as well. But I was no longer 16. The world was not quite so new and exotic anymore. I needed to figure out how to wring more from this experience. I'd just spent the last several years being trained as a research scientist, and I felt like I ought to put those skills to good use somehow. Thanks to Google and a bit of luck I found the non-profit organization Adventurers and Scientists for Conservation (or ASC for short, later renamed Adventure Scientists), which had been founded by a National Geographic fellow. The organization connects environmental researchers to adventure travelers who frequent remote corners of the globe. ASC had partnered with the Marine Environmental Research Institute (MERI, now renamed The Shaw Institute) for their global microplastics initiative, and was in need of sailors to collect data.

Both in college and after, I'd worked in cancer research labs, and I'd learned about problematic compounds in plastics like BPA and phthalates. Microplastics was a new topic to me at the time, but I was very interested. Having tiny bits of plastic out there in the environment seemed like a problem very much worth studying, and I was excited to contribute.

During our preparations for leaving, Isaac and I left behind the rest of our crew and drove up to Blue Hill to meet Abby Barrows, who was heading the project. It was pure luck and coincidence that the main base of operations of the microplastics project was located just a few hours away. Abby had invited us to her lab, and we got to see how she analyzed the water samples—with a microscope, painstakingly, by hand. I was no stranger to this sort of academic gruntwork. A shocking amount of scientific research is simply staring through a microscope and counting things.

Abby gave us a personal demonstration of how to properly collect samples. Our required equipment included a bucket on a rope, a 1 L screw cap bottle, and a log sheet. The bucket and collection bottle were both to be filled and rinsed three times to remove any detritus that might invalidate the sample. We then had to collect the latitude and longitude, water temperature, and label the bottle with the sample number.

Abby explained the potential threat of microplastics. As the name implies, microplastics are miniscule bits of plastic garbage that have broken down and invaded our ecosystems. They're lipophilic, and attract fat-based toxins in the environment. When filter feeders like mussels or baleen whales consume them, they could cause both malnutrition and toxicity, and concentrate up the food chain to humans. The more we knew about them the better. We'd be collecting water samples for Abby and her colleagues throughout our travels. They didn't yet have many samples from offshore, and none from the Caribbean, so they were just as excited to work together as we were.

20 Leaving Maine

September 18, 2013
Rockland, Maine

Off the bat, things didn't go as planned. When we first started telling people that we were going on this crazy trip, we said we'd be leaving the first week of September. As the months went by, that turned into the first or second week of September, then "early" September. At some point we decided on September 10th. Nice round number. But as the 10th loomed closer it became more apparent we wouldn't be leaving by then either. There was simply too much to do—things to hook up, houses, cars, bills, and obligations to take care of. Shore stuff.

A week later we were ready. Or so we thought. We took off the awning, sail covers, and sail stops, ready to take in the dock lines, turned on the engine and…nothing. The engine cooling water pump wasn't working. It'd be a few hours delay, if we were lucky. We weren't. Two welds and two breaks later, we realized we'd need a new part. Finally, on September 18th we were ready to go. The new part was installed, the engine was working properly, and we were leaving. For real this time.

We raised the sails as a crew of six for the first time. My mom was at the helm, my dad was tending the sheets, and the rest of us were on the bow. Once the sails were up, Isaac and I went and sat on the bowsprit, our bare feet dangling above the water, bouncing with the waves, as we began our journey south.

There's nothing quite like raising the sails on a blustery gray morning to make you feel alive. We'd hopped down the craggy Maine coast for several days, and were now headed toward a narrow passageway called The Gut. There's something about slightly dangerous and unpleasant tasks that can be exciting and enjoyable. It felt good, familiar, to stand on the bow, feet firmly planted to stay upright in the rolling seas, and raise the sails on an empty belly.

We spent the rest of the day in rolling seas. Not terrible, especially considering the weather we'd had on the first trip, but enough so that cooking lunch would have been rather difficult. We all had saltines and candied ginger, which I'd stocked up on. We motored almost all day to get us into Portland harbor at a reasonable hour, before the predicted evening storm arrived.

Shortly after we picked up our mooring in Portland Harbor a man in a red hoodie and jeans came alongside Koukla, much like the red hoodie and jeans my dad frequently wears, only without the motor oil stains. He came up alongside, remarking on Koukla, as people often do. We invited him aboard, along with his wife and daughter, who were there with him. As he introduced himself and his family I saw a glimmer of recognition on my dad's face when he said his name was Boyd.

Perhaps the red hoodie and jeans is the off-duty uniform for marine engineers, because it turned out Boyd was also a marine engineer. We started talking, and they were former cruisers with a 47 foot ketch, and Boyd had an extensive knowledge of ham radios. During our first trip we had chronic issues with ham radios. They never worked properly until someone who already knows what they're doing showed us what to do. While my mom, dad, and Boyd were engrossed in radios, Boyd's wife and daughter took the rest of us over to their boat for snacks and a tour. While we were all talking, it came up that apparently Boyd's grandfather used to be captain of the Victory Chimes, which is out of Rockland. My brother and I glanced at each other and my brother slyly asked, "What's his name?" and she said something something Guild and my brother and I said in unison, "No way!" My dad worked on the Victory Chimes under Captain Guild after college, and that was how our parents met. If not for The Victory Chimes my brother and I wouldn't exist.

In addition to the enlightening conversation, Boyd's wife Faith made us some tasty snacks. The best was her bruschetta, with pesto in place of fresh basil. I preferred it this way, and makes much more sense for the ocean-going crowd, as we're often without fresh produce let alone herbs.

Boat Bruschetta

Slice baguette, top with shelf stable pesto, mozzarella, and chopped tomato. That's it. Heat it up if you like or eat it cold.

When we came back to Koukla and mentioned our new friend's familial relationships to my parents, their minds were thoroughly blown. As we were saying goodbye to our new friends, my dad said to them, "I believe that our paths will cross again."

21 Drinking Moxie

September 27, 2013
Gloucester, Massachusetts

When we finally left Maine's waters, we shared a ceremonial bottle of Moxie. For the uninitiated, Moxie is a regionally popular soda that kind of tastes like a cola with a strong, medicinal aftertaste contributed by the bitter gentian root. It harkens back to when sodas actually had, or at least claimed to have, medicinal benefits. Gentian root does actually have some purported benefits, however I would not consider it a health drink, not by a long shot. It is an acquired taste to be sure, but a local point of pride.

After we downed our Moxie, we anchored in Gloucester harbor. (Pronounced glaw-ster, because nothing in New England, or old England for that matter, is pronounced the way it's spelled.) We've always felt at home in Gloucester. For one thing, Koukla is designed after the Gloucester fishing schooners. And like Rockland, it is largely a gentrified fishing village.

Our stay lined up with free museum day sponsored by the Smithsonian. The Cape Ann museum right there in Gloucester was one of the many participating around the country. The best part was the permanent installation on the history of fishing and sailing in the region, which included the story of local hero Howard Blackburn. Blackburn, a fisherman, had been caught in a gale. His ship had been lost and he was alone in a rowboat hundreds of miles offshore. He had the foresight to realize he wouldn't be able to hold the oars to row for very long and lashed his arms to the oars, which then froze tight. He rowed for days without food or sleep before being rescued off Nova Scotia. Unfortunately he lost all of his fingers, but he returned to Gloucester a hero. No longer able to continue fishing, the town helped him set up a shop which became very successful. He went on to get his own sailboat and sail solo across the Atlantic twice—the first (and only?) person without fingers to do so. When he died he had been planning yet another voyage.

Just as we were preparing to leave the next morning, we had a visit from the captain of the local charter schooner, Thomas E. Lannon. He was an engineer as well. The frequency of sailor-engineers is no coincidence. If you're going to venture off hundreds of miles from shore, with only your vessel separating you from the briny deep, you'd better have at least one person on board who knows how to fix the various systems that keep it afloat and moving.

The captain of the Lannon had also been cruising with his family, and had been successful chartering as well. He was very proud that since he'd begun, every kid who graduated from the Gloucester public high school had been out sailing with him. We had to cut our visit short, as we all had to be getting under way. As we left Gloucester, we passed the Lannon under sail, and he gave us a cannon salute.

The next day we were shipping off to Boston! Isaac and I had been living there for the past three years, and it had become our home. While we were anchored in Boston, Isaac and I had the chance to meet up with some of our friends. Three of my classmates from grad school came over to see the boat, and caught me up on their latest research. With a boat full of engineers, I realized I'd missed being able to talk about science, biology, and nutrition, so it was really nice to have my friends around. This was my first time away from academia since, well, ever. After college I worked in a cancer research lab at a university, then went to grad school. When we left I was in the process of switching from nutrition research to clinical nutrition.

I was partway through the prerequisite coursework to become a Registered Dietitian when I left for my sabbatical at sea. I remembered discussing this with my academic advisor. I'd already made up my mind to go when I met with her, and I was prepared for a bit of resistance to the idea. But I was met with unwavering support. She spoke of the importance of family, of spending time with one's parents while you can. There was a subtle air of sadness about the way she spoke. She was around the age when most people start losing their parents, and I wondered if she had recently.

Being back in Boston with my science geek friends reminded me that even though I had my family and my partner by my side, I still didn't have everything. Being one of the only non-engineers on board reminded me of this. As much as I loved Isaac and my family, there was still a piece of myself they didn't share.

A few more hops down the coast brought us to Nantucket Island, a new destination for all of Koukla's crew. Much like any other quaint, tourist-driven New England town, Nantucket was filled with galleries, restaurants, and boutiques. But Nantucket was different somehow—it felt like a living time capsule. The cobblestone streets were lined with weather-bleached wood shingle houses, many of which were topped with distinctive rooftop porches. You could easily picture a Victorian lady up there staring longingly out to sea. Or not.

While we were there we learned some of the history of Nantucket and its famous ties to the whaling industry as well as its less famous ties to the feminist movement. Due to all of the men off at sea, early Nantucket had been as close to a feminist utopia as you could get, at least in that century. With their husbands often gone for years at a time, sailor's wives enjoyed far more rights and privileges than your average 19th century woman. The verses from Nantucket Girl's Song captures this early feminist movement well.

> *I have made up my mind now to be a Sailor's wife,*
> *To have a purse full of money and a very easy life,*
> *For a clever sailor husband is so seldom at his home,*
> *That his wife can spend the dollars with a will that's all her own,*
> *Then I'll haste to wed a sailor, and send him off to sea,*
> *For a life of independence is the pleasant life for me,*
> *But every now and then I shall like to see his face,*
> *For it always seems to me to beam with manly grace,*
> *With his brow so nobly open, and his dark and kindly eye,*
> *Oh my heart beats fondly towards him whenever he is nigh,*
> *But when he says Goodbye my love, I'm off across the sea*
> *First I cry for his departure, then laugh because I'm free,*
> *Yet I'll welcome him most gladly, whenever he returns*
> *And share with him so cheerfully all the money that he earns*
> *For he's a loving Husband, though he leads a roving life*
> *And well I know how good it is to be a Sailor's Wife.*

I wondered how my mom felt about this. I knew my family tree was full of sailors, sea captains, and whalers. I'd often thought about the trials and adventures of my sea-going, male, ancestors, but I'd hardly ever given a thought to the independent women they'd left behind, even though I'd been raised by one of them. Perhaps I never thought about it this way because previously I had been the one to go to sea and leave someone behind.

While we enjoyed the beaches, bike trails, and historic sights of Nantucket, including the Nantucket Whaling Museum, my favorite of the historical sites was a place called Greater Light. It was basically just an old barn that had been converted into a home by two wealthy, eccentric sisters. The two sisters were world travelers and had amassed quite the collection during their lifetime of adventures. Their former home was a physical biography, telling the story of their lives in objects. I think we would have got on well.

22 Leaking Decks

October 9, 2013
Nantucket, Massachusetts

Isaac and Molly had both had it pretty easy so far. Other than some initial engine trouble, all of Koukla's mechanical systems were in good working order—perhaps because there were now not one but four engineers present. Refrigeration, electricity, plumbing—almost all the comforts of home. Horatio even had amassed a decent collection of downloaded movies and TV shows we could watch on laptops. I think my brother and I were almost resentful of our partners' easy time of it. Well, they were about to get the authentic cruising experience.

Within an hour of leaving Nantucket Harbor, we all donned our bright yellow foul weather gear. The ship rocked and rolled from the swells coming in off the open ocean, many of which were over 10 feet. They would rise up level with the deck, and crash against the hull like surf against a rocky cliff.

We were taking so much water over the bow that it had begun to rain in spots in my cabin. It leaked around the mast and right onto the middle of Isaac's bunk. It wouldn't have been so bad if he'd bothered to make his bed. Perhaps he would remember now. Molly's bunk was the worst. Water would crawl up under the railing when we rolled to one side, and pool right in the leaky spot over her bunk. She was a good sport about it. Or at least she hid any frustrations very well. The seas were the largest and roughest we'd encountered on this trip thus far, and Molly and Isaac were feeling it. We drugged them both (with antiemetics) and they were fine for the rest of the day.

Just when things seemed to have calmed down, a huge wave crashed over the sailing dinghy on deck and washed back over the boat, flooding the stern where I happened to be sitting. I jumped up to avoid being soaked, when Mom and my brother yelled "Danica, secure yourself!" I saw a second bigger wave coming on, so I grabbed the handrail over the wheelhouse, swung through midair, and flung myself feet first through the gap in the cover into the cockpit. And then Dad yelled at me for risking damaging the cover... sheesh.

Isaac used the words "exciting," "dramatic," and "like a movie," to describe the day's sail. The following seas would creep up behind us and swamp the deck. Waves curled up alongside Koukla and rained down ocean on top of the dinghy serving as a storage container on the forward section of the boat. Back aft, the inflatable in the davits would touch the water when the bow was up and the stern was down. All the while we were doing 6-9 knots with a 3 knot current against us. At this point in my sailing career I found the conditions unremarkable. I'd told him this wasn't a vacation, but I'm not sure he fully believed me. Maybe he was starting to.

Nowhere in Isaac's list of adjectives did the words "fun" or "enjoyable" come up. But I think this sort of minor ordeal can actually be good. It hadn't exactly been easy living with my parents and brother for the first time in my adult life. And I think all of them had struggled to remember that I was, in fact, an adult, and not the same person I was when we'd last cohabitated. Bad weather strangely helped this. When the weather declines and conditions are dangerous, shit gets real. You have to put aside all petty arguments and deal with the situation at hand. And once you get through it, it brings you all that much closer.

I thought back to all the "you don't even know"s I'd written to my high school boyfriend. Perhaps now Isaac knew. Or if he didn't, he would before long.

145

Another rough, wet, rolly sail brought us to Newport, RI—decked out in our foul weather gear yet again. Newport is allegedly the yachting capital of the US—and based upon their facilities for sailors I think I believe it. The facilities were clearly designed with sailors in mind, both the yacht club variety and unwashed liveaboards like us. With well maintained showers, laundry, free WiFi, weather channel on the TV, vending machines (with toothbrushes, razors, laundry detergent, etc) they really thought about what boaters need.

Another of Newport's claims to boating fame is the International Yacht Restoration School, or IYRS. The IYRS is a traditional trade school that instructs its students in classic yacht building, restoration, and repair. You can go right in and watch first year students at work restoring beetle cat boats up through graduates and instructors restoring the 130 ft "schooner yacht" Coronet—the last of the classic pleasure schooners in existence. Back in 2001, my dad and brother had seen the boat before restoration had begun, and it was in extremely rough shape. Since then they'd entirely dismantled the thing and a new frame filled the warehouse. A collection of odds and ends pulled from the boat, from blocks and tackle to a full-sized piano, were scattered in the corners. They seemed to have crossed the point where a restoration becomes just a rebuild. However, from the frames and scrap alone you could tell that once restoration was complete, it would be the impressive yacht it once was yet again. Or will it be an entirely new boat?

I knew I was the same person who had gone on that first voyage. I had the same name and social security number. It had been such a formative experience, but sometimes it felt like it had happened to a different person. Was I a rebuild or a restoration? Or was I building from scratch?

We heavily debated staying in Newport another day, but decided to keep going. I wished we'd stayed put. We had yet another rough, windy sail, but worse. We had our first sailing-related injury. We were jibing the main in 25-30 knots of wind, the main sheet popped out of the winch, and I instinctively held on. I usually wear sailing gloves when tending lines, especially the main sheet, but of course I wasn't that one time. It gave me a bad case of rope burn, and removed several layers of skin from patches of my palms and fingers. I was furious with myself for making such a rookie mistake. Right after it happened Mom and Dad acted extremely concerned, saying "it's going to be okay, Danica, you're going to be okay." I replied, "I'm fine, it's ok, it doesn't even hurt." But about 10 minutes later it hurt like hell. Since we were sailing in such rough conditions I had to wait a good 20-30 minutes to get bandaged up. My hands were marginally usable mittens for the following week. But I got out of dishes and line handling duties, so it wasn't all bad.

Thanks to my recent injury I gained an increased respect for Blackburn, the fingerless sailor from Gloucester Mass. I have no idea how he sailed across the Atlantic without the use of his fingers. Twice! If it had to be anyone, it was probably best it was me. Dad and Horatio are too important to sailing the boat, mom knows where the medical supplies are and how to use them, and well, we wouldn't want to traumatize the newbies too much. But I think they now knew how dangerous sailing could be, and have a healthier respect of the sea and ship.

In spite of recent frustrations—living with family in tight quarters, injury, lack of privacy, etc. I'd been reminded of how much I love being out on the water. I'd missed the smell of the salt air, the wind on my face, the sparkle of the sun on the wrinkled sea, and the music of the ocean.

The sounds of the wind and water combine with wood, rope, and canvas to create a symphony. The lapping of gentle waves against the hull, meow-like creak of the blocks, slapping of halyards against the mast, and the luffing of sails make up the percussion section. The whistle buoys, foghorns, and roar of the wind funneling through islands are the brass and woodwinds. One must be well attuned to the sounds of the ship and constantly vigilant for aberrant pathological noises. Unusual creaks, hums, slaps, or crashes could mean something is about to break or has already broken. Or the continual din of the sea can mean all is well.

Approaching New York City from the water is a sight to behold. In the many intervening years between our voyages I had frequently visited this city, as two of my best friends now lived there. But traveling by water, viewing the city from a different perspective changed things. I had never seen the industrial fringes of the city before—factories, power plants, and barges lined the shores. On our previous voyage we could not stop at New York City due to the then still very recent events of 9/11, and we'd taken a slightly different path. This time we were going up the river and into the city.

We carefully timed our passage through the notorious tidal confluence known as Hell Gate, to avoid the dangerous currents that can form here. We passed through without issue, and were surrounded by that famous skyline.

Massive skyscrapers lined the shores for miles, grouped in clusters that each could have been a city in its own right. Barges barreled down the narrow channel, forming a chaos of ricocheting wakes. Highways full of cars zipped by within feet of the water's edge.

Although New Yorkers are notoriously unflappable, our presence caused a bit of a stir. It's not every day that a classic wooden schooner passes through the East River. All the while we waved to the people on shore, and many waved back. Construction workers, men in fancy suits, and a gaggle of uniformed school children behind a playground fence all waved at us as we proceeded down the river.

We rounded Manhattan for a long four mile chug up the Hudson to our anchorage at the 79th Street Boat Basin Marina. From there it was an easy walk up to Central Park. I was surprised at how isolated you could feel from the surrounding metro within its wooded paths and sheltered glades.

That evening, a few friends from college came to visit us and see the boat. They were only able to take a short time out of their busy lives, and the rapid pace of life here reminded me of one of the beautiful gifts of traveling by sail—time. Time to read, time to write, time to think, time to converse, time to dream. I'd spent the better part of the past decade in large cities. The busyness, the rush of life became my norm. Our friends reminded me how different the roving sea life is to "normal" life on land. I knew I wouldn't be doing this forever, but I'd enjoy the change of pace for as long as I could.

23 Reefing Sail

October 24, 2013
Delaware Bay

After a short but pleasant stay in New York City, we headed out toward the Delaware Bay for our first overnight sail. It had been blustery all day, with moderate seas, and we made about 7 knots. The winds and seas picked up that afternoon, and gradually pushed us farther from the coast. The motion of the boat became rougher and increasing amounts of spray hit the deck.

Just as the sun was setting, we decided to put a reef in the main. Reefing means reducing the size of the sail, typically in response to high wind. Historically, we have not done much reefing, even when we really should have. For instance, when we were in gale/near-hurricane-force winds out in the open ocean during the first voyage we didn't reef. However, my dad had recently finished redoing the reefing system to make it easier, and this was an opportunity to try it out. After the six of us reefed the main in heavily rolling seas, high winds, bombarded by spray on all sides, I understood why we generally don't do it.

All the while the sails, the main included, were flapping thunderously, as we had to spill the wind from the sails and point into the wind in order to do our work. We lowered the main and tied off the dozens of little ropes, called reef points, around the boom. The boom is quite aptly named, as it's constantly crashing back and forth as you're trying to hold onto it and do your work. The rear part of the boom extends beyond the stern of the boat, out over the water. My dad did that part.

But it was a good thing we went through all that trouble, because if we hadn't the force on the sails wouldn't have been balanced, and it would have been too much for the autopilot to handle. And that would have meant someone would have had to steer. All. Night. Long.

Before it got really rough, Isaac and I briefly attempted to take a nap in our cabin. Each time we hit a wave, we'd lift off our bunks as we crested the wave and come falling down onto our thin foam mattresses as we plunged into the trough. The motion didn't bother me as far as seasickness is concerned, but it was still very unpleasant, and sleeping down there was virtually impossible.

After dusk, when the ability to sight the horizon had disappeared, a few members of the crew started feeling ill. Horatio started to feel a bit nauseous, and wisely took some dramamine and was fine throughout the remainder of the passage. Isaac foolishly went back down to try to sleep in our cabin again, which was pitching even more violently, and was subsequently very seasick.

When Isaac was violently ill and in need of medication, water, and general assistance I had to do laps from the wheelhouse to the main saloon. While this distance is only maybe 20 feet, going back and forth on a pitching vessel is incredibly taxing. Every muscle of your body is engaged in keeping you upright and stable when the boat and seas are doing their best to knock you over. The motion down below in these conditions is typically too severe for any significant stay. Thanks to my sailor genetics I could accomplish several tasks with only the faintest twinge of nausea. After about five laps from wheelhouse to galley I wasn't nauseous, but I was exhausted.

The 10 foot seas were hardly the largest my family has ever encountered, but because they were spaced so closely together the bow was constantly plunging into the surf, and we were taking a lot of green water over the bow. Every so often we would be hit with a wave from the side, sending water in through the slits between the wheel house and its back cover, soaking the cushions to the point of uselessness.

Deck leaks are a constant battle for all boat owners, and for wooden boats especially. We'd been successful in addressing several, but as we try to fix one, another seems to crop up. The most disruptive ones are over our bunks, and there is at least one over every bunk. While our bunks were among the driest, Isaac and I were without a usable cabin due to the constant crashing of the bow.

Isaac and I were on separate watches, so that a "captain" was present for each watch. My mom, dad, and brother have all passed their captain's license tests. So I was paired with my mom, Isaac with my dad, and Horatio and Molly got to stick together.

We had made the wheel house into a big bed, thinking we'd be able to nap a bit in there, but the boat was at such a slant it wasn't possible to lay down comfortably, and it was quite moist on top of that. And Isaac was so horribly seasick that when he wasn't in the head he was taking up half the wheelhouse trying to sleep it off. He was also pretty much useless for keeping watch, so it was probably for the best he was paired with dad instead of me.

I felt guilty that Isaac was having such a rough go of it, that I'd done this to him. I worried that karma might come back to bite me when and if we ever had kids. (It didn't! Fun fact, there's a genetic link between susceptibility to motion sickness and morning sickness, and I was pretty resistant to both.) But if he'd just taken the freaking dramamine he likely would have been fine.

When I was off watch I was allowed to sleep with mom in her cabin on their double bunk. Due to the heeling and deck leaks I spent the whole time trying to avoid wet spots and from rolling into my mom. It was just as well I had to sleep in my clothes. It was too cold for proper pajamas anyway.

Three hours later, I was kicked out of bed to make space for dad, who'd just finished his watch. I was allowed to sleep in Horatio's cabin, who was just beginning his watch. Although Horatio's bunk was comparatively more comfortable and dryer—and lacked another person to avoid disturbing, sleep still eluded me. It was not until after my second watch, at around 6am that I finally slept. Mom had decided to stay up on watch with dad, so I had their bunk to myself.

Finally, dawn came. The seas calmed, and we sighted land. We made it to the Delaware Bay. We anchored behind the breakwater of the aptly named Harbor of Refuge. The sun was shining, and we all pulled our sheets off our bunks—which varied from slightly damp to soaking wet. We cooked a meal and scarfed it down. And we slept. We were all ready for bed before it was even dark out.

The next day, we continued up the Delaware Bay and anchored just outside the entrance of the C&D (Chesapeake and Delaware) Canal. It was Isaac's birthday. Growing up, Isaac's favorite birthday cake was a giant chocolate chip cookie. When we first started dating, his birthday had come just a few weeks later, and we were in that phase where it was too soon for a proper present, so I baked him a cookie cake. There's a photo somewhere of me holding that candle-topped giant cookie, and Isaac blowing out the candles wearing a moose antler hat. Why was he wearing a moose hat? Good question.

I made his traditional birthday cookie cake this year too, and Horatio made a special treat to go with it. When we were last at Trader Joe's I'd found a box of shelf-stable whipping cream for a special occasion such as this. I'd even purchased a whisk to whip it with. But, after about 5 minutes of whipping by hand, we realized this was not going to work. Horatio jokingly suggested we use the electric drill. After chuckling about the idea for a minute, we figured why not! So Horatio brought out the huge cordless drill and duct taped the whisk to it. And wouldn't you know, it worked like a charm. We could have made the cream into butter with that thing.

Birthday Cookie Cake

Follow the recipe on the Tollhouse chocolate chips bag. Smush ball of dough into a circle on a baking sheet. Bake until no longer raw in the middle.

Bright and early the next morning we set off for the C&D canal. We were up before sunrise yet again. It seemed that every morning for about the past week we were up and under way before sunrise. I think I'd seen more sunrises in the past few weeks than in the past few years. I was starting to get sick of them.

When we entered the narrow passageway, the sun hadn't even thought about coming up yet. Lines of airplane runway-style lights dotted the shores on both sides of the canal, guiding our passage. We had gotten up at such an ungodly hour to time our passage through the canal to align with the tide. The water was like a sheet of satin, just a few wrinkles here and there. The ripples from our wake reflected the red, orange, and gold streaks of the now-rising sun to dramatic effect. There was a sense of peace and stillness about us. Few other boats passed. There were few buildings and little activity ashore, and almost no motion about the water. The very air about us was still asleep. Herons took flight along the shore, their long legs dangling awkwardly as they gained altitude. A few hours later, while the sun was high in the sky, we finally made it to the Chesapeake Bay.

24 Visionary Art

October 29, 2012
Baltimore, Maryland

The exit of the C&D canal is hard to notice, as it slowly widens into the upper branches of the Chesapeake Bay. The gentle sailing in the bay was an enjoyable change from the rough passage we had just weathered. This would be our home for the next few weeks as we continued to move south and wait for a good weather window to cross to the Caribbean. Shielded from the open ocean, we didn't need to seek out good harbors anymore, we could just pull off to the side nearly anywhere and drop anchor. We did this for the first night in Still Bay.

The next day we took a shortcut away from the main channels, saw few other boats, and by the afternoon passed through the industrial expanse around Baltimore. Many factories, processing plants, and cargo ships lined the wharves. Eventually we made our way downtown. Based on our lack of company, it seems to be a little-known fact that there is an officially sanctioned, though small, anchorage area right in the middle of Baltimore's attractive Inner Harbor. We had anchored in the same spot on our last trip. With confirmation from the harbor master, we settled down right in front of the National Aquarium, just alongside a WWII submarine (which constantly called out "Dive, Dive! Ooga! Ooga!"), and not far from the USS Constellation (which shot off an amazingly loud signal cannon).

Our stay in Baltimore this time around was just as pleasant as the last—more so, in fact. The showers and laundry facilities had been updated since our first voyage, and a free bus system was now available—the Charm City Circulator.

In addition to enjoying the city, we were able to complete some odd projects on Koukla. Isaac did some repair work on the mast hoops and other bits of rigging from the bosun's chair. I think he felt like a proper sailor now, as a tourist novelty pirate ship circled around and the captain shouted "looking good, matey" while he was at his work.

My favorite outing in Baltimore was a visit to the American Visionary Art Museum, conveniently located near the marina we frequented. It was unlike any other museum I'd ever visited. The place was filled with amazing pieces by self-taught artists with inspiring, often heartbreaking backstories. Many artists had been poor, homeless, mentally ill, or outright institutionalized. Some were just middle class Americans with talent and passion.

Isaac and I had made something of a hobby of seeking out this sort of artwork. We had visited Watts Towers during our time in LA, and took a road trip to visit Salvation Mountain—both of which are massive, multi-year artistic endeavors created by extraordinary ordinary people with a passion for creation.

The museum even had the hot air balloon created by Leonard Knight, the creator of Salvation Mountain, who we got to meet several years ago. The goal of both his creations was to spread the message of God's love in an accessible, nondenominational way. His work is inspiring, regardless of your beliefs. (Sadly, he's since passed away. There's a documentary and Wikipedia page about his work.)

We took a mini vacation from our sailing adventure, and Isaac and I took the train from Baltimore to Washington D.C. Horatio and Molly followed suit after we returned. We visited a wide variety of attractions during our 2-day whirlwind tour, but the best part of it was having a brief moment of privacy to enjoy just being a couple and not crew. And visiting as many of the amazing (free!) museums as we could. We did a whirlwind tour of The Museum of American History, Museum of the American Indian, Natural History Museum, and Air and Space Museum. We also visited various historic monuments, including Washington, Lincoln, and the Declaration of Independence Memorial before we had to return to Koukla. On the train back, surrounded by commuters returning from their jobs, we strongly felt the oddness of our wandering waterbound lifestyle. In a few more days we picked up anchor to continue our course down the Chesapeake Bay.

After three days gunkholing down the Bay, we made it to Norfolk, our last stop before the Caribbean. We were all enjoying a leisurely afternoon ashore, using WiFi at a local marina when all of a sudden Dad announced we needed to be ready to head offshore either that night or the next morning, first thing. The weather window we'd been waiting for had arrived. We quickly jumped into action and divided tasks. Isaac and Molly were assigned laundry duty; my brother, Mom, and I caught a cab to the grocery store for final provisioning. Dad was glued to his computer monitoring the weather. Mom, my brother, and I bought two full shopping cart loads of foodstuffs, including a small turkey we'd measured to ensure it would fit in our tiny oven and all the fixin's for a Thanksgiving dinner. After the tasks ashore were completed we set about securing everything above and below deck, as we were told to expect a couple of rough days as we went through the gulf stream.

25 Knock Down

November 19, 2013
The Atlantic Ocean

For our newest crew members, the offshore passage had loomed like a dark cloud on the horizon. Having technically done three offshore passages already, I wasn't particularly looking forward to it, but I wasn't exactly dreading it either. I knew what I was in for, more or less. Or so I thought. To keep track of the days, which can almost imperceptibly blend from one to the next, I made sure to write at least a sentence or two every day out at sea.

Day one: On November 19th, we left Norfolk and headed out for blue water. We were quickly off to a rough start. Isaac, Horatio, and Molly all took anti-nausea meds not long after leaving. I wasn't nauseous, but I was exhausted. We'd been up shortly after sunrise and under way before breakfast.

I was determined to take a water sample at least once a day while we were out in open waters. But that first day out Isaac was too seasick to help. I ended up collecting the sample by myself. Everyone else was either too queasy or too busy. Actually, I think my mom could have helped, but she said it was too entertaining watching me. I had to time it just right for the starboard side to be closer to the ocean. To pour the water into the collection bottle I had to sit on the swaying deck and hold it with my bare feet. I pulled up my pant legs so I didn't get my clothing wet, as I inevitably spilled a lot.

The drugs didn't seem to be helping Isaac much, as he spent a lot of time in the head. I wondered if I was going to be served divorce papers when we hit land.

Day two: Isaac had mostly acclimated to the motion, and during our 8-12 AM watch we crossed the gulf stream. The seas are rolly and uncomfortable, but we're making good time, and we don't seem to have too many leaks. At our current speed we'd be there in 10 days, but we're likely to be becalmed in the next day or so. I wouldn't mind an extra day of mild wind and seas if it meant catching up on sleep. Sleeping has been difficult, and our forward cabin is out of commission due to the motion. It warmed up a lot after we crossed the gulf stream. I'm going to have to take off my thermal underwear.

And, so much for hoping for mild seas…. The waves have been pretty incredible. It's like falling into a pit, but on a boat, with water for walls, then climbing up a hill of water. Repeatedly. We're out in the blue water now. It's that deep purple cobalt blue that I remember. In spite of the seas, I couldn't help but feel welcomed by the familiarity of the open ocean.

Life at sea continues to have its challenges. We lost a few dishes when a cabinet we'd thought had been secured came flying open suddenly. And the head broke, so that's fun.

Day three: The seas have calmed a bit. Still rolly, but we can sleep and eat more easily. Isaac and I took another water sample, much easier with two people and smaller seas. I'm still hoping to take daily samples as long as the weather cooperates. Horatio made hot dogs this morning, and while I'm generally not a processed meats kinda gal, they tasted really good.

Day four: Conditions not great, but tolerable. I poured a large bowl of cereal for me and Isaac to share, but he didn't hold up to his end of the bargain. I think he's not feeling well again.

The boat creaks considerably. It sounds like someone is pacing back and forth constantly down below. A dozen ghosts could be having a party down there and we wouldn't know the difference. I made spaghetti for dinner, and that was quite the ordeal. The gimballed stove is at about a 45 degree angle from the rest of the boat, and flames and boiling water moved continuously with the waves. I think everyone was grateful to have a full meal for a change. As basically the only person aboard with both resistance to seasickness and decent cooking skills, it was kind of up to me.

That evening on watch, Isaac and I talked about the passage so far. I don't think Isaac has enjoyed offshore sailing very much, other than the stars. He pulled out his astronomy field guide and was able to identify a few different constellations. If it hadn't been for the rest of my family in close quarters, it would have been quite the romantic evening.

Day five: We're becalmed. The generator broke so that it's harder to recharge the batteries. We have to conserve power, primarily by not using the autopilot during the day. Still no functional head. It's rather disheartening that we're not even half way there yet. We've been doing pretty well with our daily water sample collection.

Today is the 50th anniversary of Doctor Who, and tomorrow is my birthday. Despite the lack of wind we've still had an awful lot of seas.

Last night we had great stars and we got to see bioluminescent sparkles trailing behind the boat.

Day six: Worst. Birthday. Ever. It started out as just another day at sea. It was tiring simply moving around doing everyday tasks on a pitching vessel, but I'd gotten used to this brand of unpleasantness.

My dad had told us to expect a couple of gusty fronts to pass through–no fun but nothing to worry too much about. The first passed through as predicted. There was a 10-15 kn increase in wind speed, and about 15 minutes of heavy rain, but that was it. The second was trouble.

The skies darkened and we all realized this one would be different. My dad shouted, "everyone get ready, we're dropping sails before we break something." My brother and dad harnessed up and went out on deck to lower the sails. My mom was at the helm, and Molly, Isaac and I were in the wheelhouse handling lines. We did not have harnesses, as we only had three and those were reserved for the deck crew. As the most experienced of the three of us, I had the main sheet.

In the middle of lowering the sails–the fore was down, but not the main–a huge downburst struck us like a freight train. In seconds Koukla was nearly on her side–masts at a 45 degree angle. My dad and brother were instantly waist deep in ocean. My dad recalls having an out of body experience as we were pummeled, viewing the boat from above. My brother was frantically pulling in lines that were washing overboard. If one of the lines made its way into the propeller and we lost the engine, the situation would get much worse. Without the engine we wouldn't be able to round up into the wind to get the sails down. Meanwhile, I'm in the wheelhouse swearing like the sailor that I am. When that gust hit, I felt my sympathetic nervous system kick into high gear like never before. My system flooding with more adrenalin than it's ever produced. This was what the fight or flight system was designed for–real physical danger. My heart raced, my senses heightened, I could practically feel my immune system preparing to deal with incoming injuries. Time slowed down.

It felt like ages, but it couldn't have been more than a minute or two in real time before the wind decreased and Koukla righted herself. The relief was short-lived. Another downburst forced us onto the other side.

As water filled Koukla's decks, my mom shouted for me to release the main sheet. And I hesitated. This hesitation, brought on by the significant injury I'd suffered handling the same sheet in much less severe conditions, likely saved significant damage to Koukla at best, us from severe, possibly life threatening, injury at worst. Seconds later my dad and brother frantically shouted not to release the sheet.

All the while, gear was crashing from below. I heard glass shatter. Isaac and Molly were likely questioning their life and partner decisions. Isaac later said he was envisioning boarding a lifeboat. Molly said she was grateful we were not a catamaran–a very astute observation, as if we were we would have almost certainly capsized.

The downburst ended before Koukla was pushed into the sea. She righted herself, we got the sails down, and counted our blessings.

That glass shattering? That was my birthday cake. My brother had made me a cake for my birthday, and left it in the oven for safe keeping, with the gimbal on the stove to keep it safe. At some point my dad had seen the oven swinging around and turned off the gimbal, forgetting that there was a cake inside. The knockdown forced open the oven door, sending the cake in its glass pan onto the floor. Happy birthday to me…

Day seven: We all slept poorly, our systems still flooded with adrenaline from the knockdown. Isaac and I were on extra daytime watch, as my dad had taken over most of our watch the night before. He'd done more work on less sleep than anyone, with the least negative symptoms. I definitely didn't get those genes.

Day eight: It's been rolly and blustery. Horatio and dad put up the rest of the sails this morning, with a reef in the main. Isaac is out steering, with dad's assistance. I am exhausted, as usual. I am so tired of feeling tired all the time. Thankfully there's coffee. We've been taking on a lot of spray from all sides. It's kind of like going through a salty car wash. Buckets of water are constantly thrown at us from all directions.

I think we're all pretty exhausted and worn-down, but starting to get hopeful about arriving in a few days. Dad, Isaac, and I started to talk about the cleanup and errands we'll need to do when we get there, and I'm actually looking forward to the work. If it means the boat will stop moving and I can sleep at night, I'm all for doing a bunch of chores.

While we're still several days away, it's starting to feel like the end is in sight. The air is starting to feel warmer and more tropical. Several of us have traded in pants for shorts. I've swapped my soggy jeans for my synthetic hiking pants. I think it's helping to prevent a chronic case of swamp butt, as basically everywhere is wet. The whole boat ranges from damp to sopping wet, and that is unlikely to change for a while.

Day nine: Well, that was too much excitement before breakfast. I hadn't even finished eating my bowl of cereal this morning when Dad decided to take the reefs out of the sails. There's a fair amount of wind (15-20 kn) but it's not from a great direction, so we're not going that fast. Just as Mom was going to the wheel to steer, we hit a wave and she went tumbling down and fell on her butt and cut her finger pretty good on something. Then, after some bandaging and a brief rest, Mom went back out to steer, and Dad and Horatio went to let out the reefs and I did most of the line handling. Mom is probably going to be resting the remainder of the day. I think she's pretty bruised. Isaac and I are basically taking over Mom and Dad's watch as Dad is down on the computer trying to get some weather reports.

This passage has reminded me how hard of a life the sailors of times past have had it. This blustery, bouncy, unpleasant passage would have been a walk in the park for those old sailors.

The passage hasn't been without a few pleasant parts. Steering is kind of a mixed bag. It is rather exhausting, but also exhilarating. Frustrating, yet empowering. There is nothing quite like being at the helm of a schooner out in the open ocean. The vastness of it is beautiful and terrifying. The all encompassing nothingness.

Day ten: Thanksgiving. Along with my birthday, Thanksgiving had been postponed till we arrive. We have a turkey in the freezer, stuffing, cranberry sauce, and pumpkin pie ready to be made. But that won't be for several days still.

It's starting to feel like the home stretch, although I'm not entirely sure where our destination is anymore. We charted a course for Puerto Rico rather than St. John. The winds weren't really doing what we wanted them to do. But I was fine with stopping pretty much anywhere.

I've been sleeping better lately, the seas seem to have died down a bit so the motion is better. And I washed my hair in the sink this morning. Mom and Molly did yesterday. I didn't get the chance to because I was on watch.

We're officially in the tropics. We passed the Tropic of Cancer sometime early this morning. It's a pleasant day today, nice temperature, comparatively moderate seas. I've rather been enjoying steering today.

When you're in the open ocean, there is no reasoning with the waves, arguing with the winds, and no amount of money will persuade an oncoming storm to change its course.

Day eleven: We're practically in the home stretch. We should be getting in sometime tomorrow, as long as nothing bad happens. I'm probably jinxing myself with that sentence. Yesterday was pleasant but last night on Isaac and my watch the winds started picking up and we were doing 7-8 kn, and by Mom and Dad's watch we were doing up to 10 kn fairly steadily with sizable seas. So at 6:30 this morning Dad got everyone up to take down the main. This was one of the smoother procedures we've had. We first sheeted in the fore, staysail, and jib, then went partially into the wind and let out the main, at which point dad and Horatio lowered it. Then we sheeted it in and put stops on. Molly, who was all suited up, put on the climbing harness and went out to handle the jib.

Day twelve: Almost there. With only 15 nautical miles to go, we should be there around noon. Yesterday was fairly uneventful. We put the main back up with a reef.

It feels like Christmas. The excitement and anticipation. The end of a long and tiring voyage is in sight. I should even get presents today, since I never got them on my birthday. And maybe we'll have Thanksgiving tomorrow.

26 Cheesy Chocolate

November 30, 2013
San Juan, Puerto Rico

After twelve unrelenting days at sea we had finally made it to the Caribbean. While our original goal had been St. John (USVI), we did make it there in a sense, as San Juan is Spanish for St. John. And after no showers, little sleep, and barely sufficient food we were willing to stop just about anywhere.

We had looked forward to vividly green islands, white sandy beaches and swaying palms welcoming us to the Caribbean. Instead we were greeted by a gray, mist-shrouded expanse of coastline, and couldn't make out anything until we were practically inside the harbor. But it didn't matter, we had made it. The mist parted as we entered the fort-lined harbor of Puerto Rico. All six of us were happy and cheering at our final arrival. My mom hollered, "Hola, Puerto Rico!" in a bad Spanish accent.

Shortly after anchoring, we all jumped ship in search of our first shower in nearly two weeks. Unfortunately, all we found was a cold-water shower in a bare cement stall in a ramshackle marina. At least it was free and we were clean. As soon as we finished with showers, there were even more showers. We were trapped in the locker rooms in a torrential downpour with no sign of letting up. By then it was nearly dinnertime, so we made a run for it and ducked into the closest eatery—a Sizzler—to wait out the rain. We were all soaked and very thankful that the place wasn't overly air conditioned. We were pleasantly surprised with the quality of the food. The buffet had surprisingly decent Puerto Rican-style food and was popular with the locals. I'm not sure if it was actually good, or if we were just happy to have something that wasn't the same canned beans, premade spaghetti sauce, or curry we'd batch cooked and frozen.

The next day the real work began. We had taken a beating during the offshore passage and everything above and below deck varied from damp to sopping wet. My cabin was in bad shape after being damp for nearly two weeks with no air circulation. This provided excellent conditions for a healthy crop of mold to grow in our closet and under Isaac's bunk. So things were removed, closets scrubbed, laundry done at the marina, and before long we were starting to get back to some semblance of normalcy.

After Koukla had aired out a bit, Horatio, Molly, Isaac and I had our first Caribbean outing—to the San Juan SuperWalmart. Lizards scurried into the shrubbery as we passed. Sidewalks were sometimes absent, sometimes occupied by parked cars. With crosswalks rare or non-functional, we had to nervously run across streets between narrow gaps in the traffic. We passed men at work painting walls or washing or repairing the cars on the sidewalk. All signs and storefronts were in Spanish. Near the end the streets became small and residential, lined with boxy pastel cement houses in various states of repair, from brand new to decrepit and crumbling. Though a part of US territory, it felt like a foreign country.

The San Juan Super Walmart was quite impressive, and we all had a great time examining the unusual tropical products. We even had a great lunch of local fare in the cafeteria-style restaurant. While we had brought at least a month's supply of food onboard for the offshore passage, we were all craving fresh fruits and vegetables. We would soon discover that lettuce doesn't do well in the Caribbean (it turned to slimy mush in about a day, even in the fridge) but found cabbage, a sorely underappreciated and underutilized vegetable, makes a serviceable replacement for many applications. We also enjoyed fresh local papaya, pineapple, and mango, and taught ourselves how to prepare fried yellow and green plantains. Our trick was to look at how the restaurants we frequented prepared them and tried to copy them.

Sweet Yellow Plantains

Yellow Plantains

Coconut oil

Slice into ½ inch chunks, or whatever size you like. Leave them whole if you want, it'll just take longer to cook. Melt 1-2 T coconut oil in frying pan. Add plantains, cook on medium heat until golden brown and caramelized.

Smashed Green Plantains

Green plantains

Oil

Slice plantains into large chunks, smash gently with a fork. Fry in oil like tiny pancakes. Cook until golden brown and slightly crunchy.

Old San Juan is the touristy area of the city, although this is not necessarily a bad thing. There are large stone forts, a few museums, and lots of restaurants, cafes, and shops. The narrow streets and comely squares speak of the city's Old World Spanish heritage. We explored the many levels of El Morro, a fort strategically located near the mouth of San Juan Harbor. We had lunch at a Puerto Rican restaurant our guidebook recommended, but found we'd preferred the meal at the Walmart cafeteria.

One highlight of the visit to Old San Juan was the Museo de las Americas, with exhibits and art focusing on the native peoples of the Americas. We particularly enjoyed the exhibit on the many tribes that are native to

North, South, and Central America. Each tribe had its own diorama with details on customs and livelihood of that tribe, complete with a life-size bronze statue of a real tribe member. Swedish artist Felipe Lettersten has traveled around the Americas, making plaster casts of Native Peoples (with permission, of course), which he turns into exquisitely detailed statues. He always returned to give a statue to each tribe.

After lunch it rained. And rained. We ate much more than we'd intended as we kept needing to duck into cafes to avoid the downpours. The most interesting place we unintentionally visited was a restaurant called the Chocolate Bar. We ordered a Puerto Rican hot chocolate and a churro, and we were confused when the hot chocolate came out with a slice of cheddar cheese and a square of chocolate. We ate half the cheese and chocolate before the waitress told us it was supposed to go in the beverage. So we plopped it in, but half thought that the waitress was just pulling a prank on the stupid American tourists. However, the internet later confirmed it is in fact a Puerto Rican tradition to put cheese in hot chocolate. But I'm not sure I'd recommend it. The cheese just created a mucus-like film on top of an otherwise excellent cup of hot chocolate.

By the time we finished our chocolate and churro it was starting to get late, but still pouring. We tried to hop in and out of shops to make our way back toward the boat, but by the time we were almost out of town, and almost out of shelter we realized this was not going to work. We tried to hail a taxi, but we weren't able to pop out of our shelter fast enough. Thankfully, the friendly security guard at the random government building we were taking shelter under hailed a taxi for us.

While Isaac and I decided to catch a cab just as it had really started to pour, Horatio and Molly had left a bit earlier and were already about half way back to the boat at that point. This meant they still had about a mile to go, and little to no available shelter from the rain. Veritable rivers popped up alongside or instead of roads, often dotted with large pools, some of which went past Horatio's knees or nearly up to Molly's waist. By the time Isaac and I arrived back at the marina we were quite wet, but Molly and Horatio were utterly soaked.

The four of us had exhausted all the easily reachable attractions and decided to rent a car, so we hit the road to the rainforest. El Yunque National Forest is the only tropical rainforest in the US National Forest system. The attractions of El Yunque string out along a switch-backing mountain road that ascends into the forest. We decided to drive to the top first and then work our way down. But first, we needed lunch. A cluster of food shacks lined the road just at the entrance to the forest. We stopped at one and found that it served a variety of odd-tasting fried things, including two forms of ground beef stuffed into banana and fried.

After lunch we headed down a stone path meandering through the rainforest, up toward El Yunque peak. Dense canopy, massive leaves, hanging vines and epiphytes, rain constantly dripping down on us—it was exactly what a rainforest is supposed to be. A few miles into the hike, we took a short side trek to Mount Britton Tower at the top of a ridge, just in time to shelter there underneath a violent downpour. Without any obstructions to slow it down, strong winds flung rain horizontally, while dense white mists rushed over the mountaintops. It looked as if we were in an airplane. Occasionally the clouds would shift and we'd get a glimpse of the forest.

We enjoyed this dramatic experience for a while, and continued our hike once the rain let up, despite a passerby warning us the trail was a river of mud. That turned out to be an exaggeration, but the climb was long, wet, and overall not pleasant. A stone platform waited for us at the peak, but it wasn't really as exciting as the previous tower. Cell phone and radio antennas loomed abruptly out of the mist, surprisingly large and disturbingly close. This clutter on the peak ruined the feeling of isolation.

After the hike, we went swimming at the base of a waterfall. It was a cold, rocky, and somewhat painful, but completely incredible experience to have a rain-swollen waterfall pounding down around you.

For our last day with our rental car, we decided to go to Rio Camuy Cave Park. Puerto Rico was the largest, most populous place we expected to be for six months, and on this drive we really felt it. The residential area of San Juan was soon left behind as we passed many miles of industrial sprawl lining the southside of San Juan Bay. This was soon replaced by billboards, fast food joints, and outlet malls lining the highway. Eventually, the development lessened and we turned inland to the sharp green hills of central Puerto Rico.

After we reached the park, a guide led us through the toothy cave entrance through a series of massive underground caverns. I don't know if we knew exactly what to expect, but it was actually really cool. We saw many interesting rock formations, explored huge chambers, woke up some bats, saw creepy insects like a "scorpion spider" (google image search at your own risk—I did not care to take a photo of it), and heard an underground river. You could see the stalactite/stalagmite formation process in action, as many continuous drips fell from overhead in concentrated spots. On the way back, we picked up a papaya and grilling peppers from a roadside food stand before returning to Koukla.

One final attraction that Isaac and I managed to visit before leaving Puerto Rico was the Museo de Arte de Puerto Rico. The sculpture garden contained a pond full of enormous carp that schooled towards us at our approach. They had learned to associate human proximity with the arrival of food. The museum included many peculiar installations, from a musical typewriter you were allowed to play with, to an entire room set up like a surrealist barbershop. It reminded me a bit of the American Visionary Art museum in Baltimore, Maryland, although these exhibits were a bit more polished. As we were leaving the museum, we were approached by a local art enthusiast working on putting together a comprehensive art tour of San Juan. Apparently the Puerto Rican art museum is more popular with the locals than tourists, and we didn't exactly blend in with the locals.

I wanted to share with Isaac the side of the Caribbean I'd seen over a decade before. So far I hadn't. When we made it to Culebra it felt like we had finally arrived. The well protected harbor was full of anchored cruiser boats, surrounded by a sleepy town of pastel houses and scattered one-room shops, and even a dockside restaurant.

Puerto Rico is not just a single island, but also includes two other populated islands, Vieques and Culebra, east of the main island. Although technically a part of Puerto Rico, Culebra felt worlds away from San Juan's urban sprawl. Here were the white sandy beaches, turquoise waters, and swaying palms we had been looking forward to for months. Culebra was the Caribbean as I remembered it from our first trip 12 years ago, despite the fact that I'd never been here before.

We were told a trip to Culebra would not be complete without a trip to Playa Flamenco, allegedly one of the most beautiful beaches in the world, so off we went. The only bad thing about it was the location—a solid 2 mile hike along shoulderless roads from where we were anchored, with little to no shade. There were taxis available, but did we take them? Of course not!

So Horatio, Molly, Isaac, and I set off with swimsuits, towels, and water bottles in our backpacks. We apprehensively went onto the unmowed shoulder whenever we approached a blind turn. At least one taxi slowed down and offered us a ride at a discount, but we were determined to walk. We were joined by small flocks of chickens scurrying into the undergrowth. We even saw several crossing the road! Although we're not sure why. We passed several crabapple-like trees that we inspected, and were unable to identify. Later we learned they were the poisonous Manchineel tree, or death apple. After making a bit of a wrong turn, we reached Playa Flamenco.

With its big U of white sand, with turquoise on one side and vibrant green hills on the other, we could definitely see how this beach had earned international notoriety. Isaac enjoyed body surfing on the large rollers, while I somehow always ended up with water up my nose. Borderline-tame fish would curiously swim right around your legs if you stood still long enough. Horatio and Molly built a sandcastle, with a moat to protect it from the oncoming tide. Because of the beach's popularity, small restaurant shacks had popped up a short ways inland. Isaac and I sipped piña coladas while chickens and feral cats scurried about. We particularly enjoyed watching one rooster apprehensively peck at a Hostess cupcake someone had dropped. He would peck at it and run away, peck, run, peck, run. Eventually some other chickens that were not afraid of cupcakes showed up and ate it, wiping their cream covered beaks on the ground.

Farther along the beach were campgrounds. Beyond that were art-covered tanks, leftovers from Culebra's use as a marine base, one on the beach and one a bit further inland with flowers stuffed into the gun barrel. Both were completely covered with colorful graffiti.

That evening we ate at the local cruiser hangout, the Dinghy Dock restaurant, which is literally a dinghy dock. The restaurant's dock was overrun with inflatables and dinghies of all sizes from the cruising boats in the harbor. A school of enormous fish lived right off the dock, waiting for someone to throw a piece of their dinner. I think they may have been grouper, as that is the biggest fish I can think of that lives in this region. I had grilled mahi-mahi with a cilantro-lime aioli and tostones—fried flattened green plantains. It was like the Caribbean on a plate. We watched bats dive after insects as we ate.

At the Dinghy Dock, we met a delightful British couple and made a date to exchange info with them, as they were making our route in reverse. They came up through the southern Caribbean, and were headed to Maine this summer. They came over for drinks the following afternoon and we exchanged information and sea stories. It was quite the tête-à-tête, as charts and guidebooks of Maine and the Caribbean were hauled out and copious notes were taken.

Meanwhile, we had yet another visitor from a neighboring boat—a dismasted high-tech racing yacht, apparently with the mast intentionally left off. He was a yacht designer/refurbisher and his unconventional ideas were fascinating. He had gotten a great deal on his boat due to the dismasting, but left the mast off, covered the exposed area with solar panels, and had plans to rig up a large kite to further increase the boat's already excellent fuel efficiency. He made enough electricity from his solar panels to run his refrigeration, and planned to have air conditioning. Unheard of!

"Now the only thing this place is missing are some showers," my mom remarked to a local. Ask and ye shall receive. Apparently the owner of a hostel lent out his bathroom to cruisers. So off we went with our soap and towels to the plant-covered building in search of the proprietor. Since there were six of us and only one bathroom, we spent quite a bit of time chatting with the Tennessee native. While he'd been a resident of Culebra for over a decade, his southern twang was still intact.

27 Retracing Steps

December 20, 2013
St. Thomas, USVI

Our next destination was Charlotte Amalie, St. Thomas. This had been our first landfall last time around, and it wasn't exactly my favorite before. Following a short, rough sail (as usual), we dropped anchor in the middle of the large harbor. Charlotte Amalie was quite a change from quaint Culebra. The huge harbor filled with dozens of boats of all varieties: charter catamarans, cruising boats (some of them disused and rotting away on their mooring), tourist "pirate" ships, enormous mega-yachts, and towering cruise ships. On the first trip, on the east end of the harbor there had been a run down hotel with disgusting showers. Since then, it had been cleaned up and had been replaced with a high-end megayacht marina. We were no longer welcome there.

Charlotte Amalie is the largest city in the Virgin Islands, but has more the feel of a cruise ship amusement park than a real city. It was block after block of jewelry stores, watch shops, high end clothes and accessories, a Belgian chocolatier, and other luxury items, all cashing in on Charlotte Amalie's status as a "free port," meaning no sales tax. It was more or less the same as I'd remembered, if perhaps slightly more polished.

One evening we decided to go out for dinner, and found the downtown area shuttered up and deserted. Sometime around 4 or 5 in the afternoon the cruise passengers return to their ships, and the city shuts down. Despite the many restaurants lining the streets, by 6 pm we had a hard time finding any place open to eat.

Far from the cruise ship docks and megayachts, we went to get our propane tanks refilled before moving on. A long semi-industrial expanse of scrap metal dealers, welding shops, construction material depots, and used tire vendors eventually dumped us at the place to get propane, right at the doorstep of a large power plant. The engineer crew members marveled to see that the tanks were filled based on weight, using purely mechanical old cast iron beam balance scales. The proprietor haphazardly vented large amounts of propane in the process of filling our tanks.

We'd found the best spots in the Caribbean are often those only accessible by (small) boat. That was the case for Solomons Bay, St. John, and technically the whole island. St. John does not have an airport or cruise ship dock. Solomons Bay is even more inaccessible, as you cannot drive there by car. Instead, most people get there from a one mile hiking trail from St. John's main town of Cruz Bay. Or, as in our case, arrive by boat. We had a great time swimming, talking with some other cruisers, exploring tide pools in the rocks, and snorkeling.

We unpacked our wooden sailing dinghy that up until now had been a storage container. Horatio had spent a lot of time and effort varnishing and painting the lapstrake tender, and it got a lot of attention. Hauling the immaculately restored dinghy up on the beach felt like arriving at a party in a Rolls-Royce. Many people stared, some sneakily or not so sneakily took photos. I wonder how many people's vacation photos featured that tender.

Other than just trying to get to St. John for the fun of it, we had to get here for logistical purposes. First Isaac's mother, and then Molly's parents, were coming to visit. I'm not sure if Isaac and Molly's parents visited just as an excuse to go to the Caribbean, or to give them a way out if needed. Probably a combination of the two.

Since you can only get to St. John by boat, Isaac had to take the ferry back to St. Thomas to meet his mother at the airport. The Charlotte Amalie-to-St. John trip that we had done over the course of two days took just 40 minutes by high speed ferry.

One thing Isaac's mom wanted to do while visiting the U.S. Virgin Islands was visit the British Virgin Islands. So one day the three of us took a ferry over to Tortola for the day. In the U.S. we are used to expecting most places other than the post office or banks to be open during all regular daylight hours. In Tortola, they still close pretty much the whole island down on Sundays. Oops! We wandered around town fruitlessly for a bit, unable to get into the botanical gardens, or pretty much any shops or restaurants.

So we took a taxi to the top of Sage Mountain, the highest point in the Virgin Islands (US or British), and had some excellent banana smoothies prepared by an eccentric British man who runs a restaurant up there (thank goodness he was open, because his shop was also the only source of trail maps to the peak). The taxi ride down was an adventure in itself. The serpentine roads wound around the coast mere feet from the ocean, all while the driver blasted a video of a concert he'd

just attended. Did we ask for said entertainment? Nope. Overall, the Tortola visit wasn't what we'd expected, but in spite of this (or because of?), it was quite memorable.

One day we decided to make a circuit of St. John, visiting the Annaberg sugar plantation ruins, then Coral Bay (St. John's other town, on the southeast end), and then back to Cruz Bay. Taking a taxi on St. John is not the same as in the U.S. Taxis are all large safari-style trucks, and the drivers like to wait until they have a group all going to the same place (since fares are per person). A crowd of taxi drivers was waiting around the ferry dock in Cruz Bay, but when we asked for someone to take us to Annaberg, no one wanted to do it, and it nearly started some arguments about who would get stuck with us. Finally, someone did start driving us out of town, only to pull over just a few minutes later and pass us off to a different passing taxi coming from the opposite direction. However, when we finally got to the ruins, it was worth it, because the Annaberg sugar mill was great. We saw the ruins of a windmill, a horse mill, and the sugar processing buildings. A park interpreter showed us how coral had been used as a building material by the Danish, and not only explained the

history of the sugar economy on St. John, but also what it is like to live there in the present day. We ate some traditional bread prepared on site, and got to smell or eat examples of local plantation food from the gardener (sugar cane, lychee, bay rum leaves, and coconut).

Our taxi adventures were not over yet. Coral Bay is a bit beyond Annaberg, but the drivers don't like to go that way, and one driver advised us that we would wait a month before finding someone to do it. One did pick us up, but then it turned out that he was conducting an island tour, and the group (and now us as well) was getting taken to the Cinnamon Bay beach and campgrounds to have lunch. We skipped out at this point and were taken to Coral Bay, where we had our lunch. Getting back to Cruz Bay, we flagged a passing safari bus, but it turned out it wasn't a taxi at all, it was a family from Maine of all places. The rental place had run out of cars and given them this brightly colored open air jeep, identical to the tourist taxis throughout the island. People had been hailing them down all week. But, they kindly decided to give us a ride back to Cruz Bay anyway.

Shortly after Isaac's mom left, Molly's parents arrived. We did a lot of the same sorts of things we did with Isaac's mom—beaches, hiking, visiting some historic spots. Unlike Isaac's mom, who stayed in a hotel on shore, Molly's parents—Bruce and Cathy—stayed with us onboard Koukla. The whole 8-people-to-one-bathroom thing was a challenge, but otherwise it was fun having them stay with us. Bruce and Cathy are both teachers, and didn't stop teaching during their visit. Bruce is an electrical engineering professor and taught the engineers how an AM radio works. He lost me when he started talking about sine waves. Cathy plays the Irish flute, and brought it with her. Isaac and Molly had both brought their instruments—banjo and French horn—but neither had played them much up until this point. But they brought them out to play with Cathy.

One day on St. John, Isaac and I had been ashore in Caneel Bay using WIFI, and were in the dinghy headed back to Koukla, when we saw a little sailing dinghy dead in the water. It was the type the resort rents out, and there was no one nearby we could see. So we motored over and it turned out there was an older gentleman in the water trying to get back onboard. So we maneuvered next to the boat, and I held on to the side of the boat to keep it steady while he climbed back onboard. Meanwhile, a motor boat from the nearby resort headed out to see if everything was ok, but we had already done their job.

Shortly after Molly's parents left, we set off for the British Virgin Islands, not far from the U.S.'s Virgin Islands. Other than being British, the biggest difference is that they are generally smaller and less populated. However, there are a lot of them.

Our first stop was Jost Van Dyke, home of the legendary Foxy's Bar and Restaurant, which is practically the only thing of note on the entire island. On our first trip twelve years ago, I had particularly enjoyed meeting Foxy himself and listening to his singing and jokes. We weren't as fortunate this time, and didn't get to see him perform.

Shortly after we arrived on the tiny beach-lined harbor of Jost Van Dyke (pronounced yost), Horatio, Molly, Isaac, and I set off up the steep, almost ladder-like hill overlooking the harbor. Twelve years ago, we did this same hike, and I had remembered it as being hot, sweaty, and difficult—yet rewarding. And it was pretty much the same this time around, only perhaps a little more difficult. The dirt road often gave way under foot, which often added up to two steps forward, one step back. But the view of the harbor and neighboring islands was quite spectacular. During the hike, we were constantly running into groups of goats grazing on the grassy hillside.

After we left Jost we hopped over to Great Camano Island for the night. In our anchorage it seemed as if we'd left the Caribbean and were transported back to Maine, with its steep rocky shores and gravely beaches, and peaceful evening silence with just a handful of houses visible up on the hill. The biggest difference was the wildlife. Flocks of pelicans flew in formation, hovering over the water. Every so often, one would plummet into the water after a fish, splashing water far into the air.

The next morning, as we pulled up the anchor, I heard an eerie scream of someone in distress. I looked around, saw no one in imminent danger, and realized it was the goats on shore, with their near-human-like screams. On our way out of Great Camano Island we had to go through a very narrow passage. We lacked detailed charts for this area, so Horatio was sent aloft to look for water color changes indicative of sudden depth changes, while Isaac, Molly, and I were on the bow doing the same.

There were several shoals in the vicinity, but we made it through intact. That evening, we anchored in Spanish Harbor, the main town on Virgin Gorda, and treated ourselves to WiFi and nachos ashore. It had been a while since we'd had internet access, and we all pulled out laptops, iPads, smartphones, etc. and munched silently and checked emails, completely ignoring the scenery. Another bar patron, clearly on vacation and not suffering from internet withdrawal thought we were a comical sight and took our picture.

The next morning we were off to the Baths! We had been ill-prepared the last time we were here, and hadn't brought swim suits or cameras. We did not make that mistake this time. The ancient rock formations were the same as they'd been a decade ago, but I wasn't. I enjoyed myself much more this time. I wasn't fighting with my brother or missing my boyfriend. I had my partner by my side to share the experience, and my relationship with my brother had improved over the years as well.

Climbing and swimming around the boulders was like crawling through an excellent natural jungle gym. Inside the dimly lit sea caves, tiny white fish would play about our waists and jump if we moved too quickly.

We crawled and swam amongst the giant boulders, and scrambled up them chasing scuttling crabs. They were everywhere—the boulders, not the crabs, although there were a lot of those too. There were boulders along the sandy path, on the shoreline, partially submerged, creating labyrinthine pools in the water.

You are not allowed to anchor at the Baths overnight, so after we were done exploring, we set off for Peter Island. We anchored in a pleasant bay, surrounded by nothing but a few other sailboats. But it wasn't quite as peaceful as you'd expect, since the everpresent goats were soon bleating ashore.

Shortly after we'd dropped anchor, a floating grocery store came alongside us. The overgrown dingy was sitting low in the water due to its hefty load of fresh produce and other goods. It looked like it hadn't been hauled out in a while, and needed to be scraped and repainted with a bit more anti-fouling paint, as marine growth went halfway up the hull. The whole thing was topped with a crown of flags from around the world. We had provisioned recently, so we didn't need anything, but we couldn't say no to ice cream bars, a rare treat for us due to our inability to keep frozen desserts onboard.

That evening we were treated to some fantastic bioluminescence. We could see comet-like streaks of light left by fish darting through the water and we splashed about with an oar, filling the ocean with stars.

Next up was Salt Island. As the name implies, the island was once used to manufacture salt, with the two salt ponds on the island. The island seems to no longer be used for this purpose, as it reeks of dead fish in the high salinity ponds. The island is now all but deserted. The few small, ramshackle houses on shore were slowly breaking down, with doors missing and rooms empty of all but scattered debris. The highlight of Salt Island was the snorkeling. We were surrounded by creepy schools of squid or cuttlefish (we weren't sure which), and Horatio and Molly found an octopus atop his garbage heap of empty conch shells. Horatio dove down and snatched one off the pile. Since there was little else to see on Salt

Island, but more than we cared to smell, we quickly moved on.

Norman Island is almost synonymous with pirates and buried treasure. On our first trip, we had set out in our dinghy to snorkel the famous sea caves on Norman Island, but rough weather and outboard motor troubles prevented us. But the twelve year wait was worth it. It was easily the best snorkeling of the trip thus far. We saw blue tang, small-mouthed grunt, sergeant major, rainbow parrotfish, squirrel fish, and fairy basset. (I looked them up on our fish ID card as soon as we got back.) The aptly named rainbow parrot fish was my favorite, with its bright plumage and beak-like mouth.

The sea caves themselves were a unique experience. We'd read that it gets quite dark, so we'd come prepared with a waterproof flashlight, but even with that it was creepy. The narrow cave was quite deep—deeper than we cared to venture. It is the sort of place you might see at the start of a horror film, where vacationers are slowly picked off by a human-fish hybrid monster. Something very primal pricks up in dark, enclosed, natural spaces and tells you to get the heck out of there. So we did.

28 Midnight Mooring

February 4, 2014
Saba, Netherlands Antillies

After our swing through the BVIs, it was back to St. John to wait out bad weather. There is a sizable gap between the dense clump of Virgin Islands and the rest of the Caribbean island chain. Since it was also to the east, into the prevailing tradewinds, it was going to be an overnight beat into the wind. When traveling by sail, you generally want the wind to come from behind you, not blow directly at you.

After a bit of a wait, some good wind did show up and we were off. For once, the weather predictions actually held in our favor, and we made the whole run in one tack. In a way, it was too good. We arrived at Saba just before midnight. So there we were, in front of the huge dark mass, sparsely dotted with lights in the pitch black, with spotlights on the bow looking for a mooring ball—a veritable needle in a pitch-black haystack.

Due to its status as a protected marine park, anchoring is prohibited, so we would need to pick up a mooring. A mooring is a chain attached securely to the ocean floor for tying up a boat. A buoy—usually round and about two feet across—holds the other end at the surface of the water. To pick up a mooring, a boat passes slowly alongside the buoy while someone at the bow snatches it up with a boat hook and ties up to it. Usually there is an additional length of rope attached to the buoy to make tying up easier. When it's light out, it's easier than anchoring. At night, not so much.

Isaac and Molly took turns with the spotlight, scanning the water, while Horatio was ready with the boathook, and I was prepared with the cowhitch—a braided loop at the end of a rope—in hand to tie us up quickly, while my parents were steering back aft. The wind that had got us here so quickly whipped around the sheer cliff face of the island and made both communication and steering difficult.

Meanwhile, fish were jumping everywhere. In the act of scanning the ocean surface for a mooring buoy, we'd caused a frenzy of activity for the marine park's aquatic inhabitants. Our spotlight illuminated schools of small fish—better enabling large predatory fish to see and eat them. Fish of all sizes jumped out of the water, I couldn't believe how many there were, and how far they could launch into the air. We were mesmerized. It was like watching a live nature documentary. The only thing missing was narration by David Attenburough.

My dad shouted back from the stern, "We're looking for moorings, not fish!" So we kept sweeping the area with our spotlight, and we finally found one. We were all intently staring forward trying to keep an eye on the mooring when, Bam! something struck me right in the thigh. I yelped in surprise more than pain. I looked around to see what it was, and there was a silvery winged fish flopping on the deck by my feet. I was too startled to process, and Isaac nabbed the wriggling thing and tossed it overboard.

We came around again and approached the mooring. Horatio leaned over and reached out with the boathook and I stood ready with the cowhitch as we shouted directional signals over the rushing winds. After three attempts we finally managed to hook it, but there was no rope to tie up to! So we had to abandon it and start all over again, heading to the next mooring over. Thankfully, we were able to pick it up on the first try. By then it was 1am. We cooked up a can of beans for a very late supper, and went to bed.

The next morning, we awoke to the startling view of Saba. Little more than a sheer cliff thrust up from the sea, the coas twas flat and absent of any sort of harbor or habitation. If we didn't know better, we would have believed this was just another unpopulated rock. Having been here before did not diminish my awe of the place.

My favorite islands (from both trips so far) had been those off the beaten path, places friends and family had never heard of. Saba was one of those elusive places, and I was excited to share it with Isaac. I was pleased to find it was almost exactly as I'd remembered.

Molly and Isaac marveled at the Road that Could Not Be Built. We hiked up Mt. Scenery as before, so Isaac could check off another tallest point on his list. He'd made it his goal to reach the highest point on every island we visited, and he'd reached a high percentage of them. This location had the unique distinction of being the highest point in all The Netherlands. The white houses with red roofs amongst the green hills looked like a clutch of toadstools on a mossy forest floor from our aerial vantage point.

Next up was Stacia, the nickname for St. Eustatius, another small Dutch island about a day's sail east of Saba. As soon as we dropped the mooring and raised the sails we were hit by a huge gust of wind before we had a chance to check the portholes. We heeled to port, and a huge amount of water came into the galley. Several inches of water accumulated on the floor. The stove was wet and not working properly. The pantry of cans was wet and would need to be washed off and dried so they didn't rust. The compartment where we kept the pots and pans got wet too. The wind was so strong and flaky that Dad had to steer the whole four hours there. Isaac briefly took the helm, but he had a hard time keeping course.

We pulled into Stacia before sunset. Despite being a small island with little development, there were tons of huge fuel tankers anchored all around. Apparently it is used as a major fuel depot for the Caribbean region. Perhaps that was a development in the past decade, as I did not remember this being the case previously.

Ashore, a single road runs through a thin strip of flat land along the coast, lined by near-vertical cliffs. This flat bit is known as Lower Town. To reach the top, where the main town of Oranjestad spreads out, we walked a steep cobblestone path called the Old Slave Road, as it was once used to lead enslaved people up from ships that had just survived the middle passage. I was haunted by this place the first time around, and I felt its dark energy still. I was perhaps even more affected this time, as I had a better understanding of history in general. Violent images flashed through my brain, imagining the horrors that this beautiful location had once seen.

Oranjestad spread out on the plateau above. At the top of the Old Slave Road, we overlooked terraces lined with potted plants being grazed by goats. What was the story on this? We don't know. There was no explanation available, as overall Statia seemed to be not at all designed for tourist visits. We wandered around the streets, passing occasional small restaurants and bars, some corner markets (but no tourist shops), and many residential houses. Every house seemed to have at least one dog. One of these canines joined our wanderings for the day and barked in our defense at any other dogs we passed.

The main attraction on Stacia is The Quill, which we'd just learned (or remembered?) is a mispronunciation of a Dutch word that means pit. My brother and I had remembered it fondly, and were excited to share the experience with our partners. My parents and their knees decided to sit this one out. At the top of the peak, just before climbing down into the crater by rope, was a sign, "Hike at your own risk or use a guide," with a rooster standing in front of the sign. The rooster didn't seem interested in escorting us, and my brother and I had been here before, so we continued on. I marveled at the delight and excitement on Isaac's face as we explored the ancient rainforest as much as the forest itself. We found ourselves in a thick jungle, sealed off from the outside world and ringed on all sides by the crater, like the sort of place you might find a small band of surviving dinosaurs. Many gargantuan trees filled the crater. After visiting many of them, we scrambled back up with the help of the ropes and went back to the boat.

29 Spectacular Devastation

February 10, 2014
St. Kitts, St. Kitts and Nevis

It had become tradition that my dad and I always go to clear customs together. In a boat, it is only mandatory for the captain to go and declare the other passengers, that is why not everyone needs to go in. But my dad had encouraged me to accompany him once or twice, and he quickly noticed how much smoother things went when I was with him. Did I actually do anything to make things go more smoothly? Not really. But somehow the customs agents—usually young and male—were more polite to me than when it was just my grizzled sailor of a dad. And I relished this one-on-one time with him.

It is interesting, and often telling of the island culture, how their customs procedures are set up. In St. Kitts, we got to listen to the customs lady singing along to "Make Time for Jesus" and see immigration officials aggressively playing candy crush on their smartphones.

As we exited customs, we were met by a friendly yet aggressive tour guide named Veronica wanting to sell us a tour of the island. It was late in the day, so we said we'd think about it, but really we'd just intended to pass. When we arrived on shore with the whole crew, she was waiting for us at the dock, and began dropping her price, eventually telling us to just get in her van and pay at the end only if we liked the tour. She was fiercely proud of her island home and wanted to show it off to anyone willing to come along. How could we refuse?

So we all piled into her lovely air-conditioned van and off we went. Our first stop was Romney Manor, originally owned and built by Thomas Jefferson's great-grandfather, Samuel Jefferson. It is now the site of a well known batik factory, where we got to watch the waxing and dyeing process of making batik fabric art, which involves using wax and sequential dying to create intricate designs. We had come to this same place twelve years ago, and I had purchased some lovely pillow covers that had since turned to ribbons from overuse, and I was anxious to replace them. Outside the batik shop, we walked around their lovely manicured gardens and saw monkeys playing about in the branches above us. St. Kitts is one of only a handful of Caribbean islands with monkeys, as they are not native to the region.

Soon we were off to our next destination—Brimstone Hill Fort. We had also visited this location on our first trip, but this time around, it was a much more pleasant experience. The first time, we had not taken a taxi, but a local bus and hiked up the considerable hill to the fort in the searing midday sun. I remembered the distinctive suffocating sulfurous stench for which the fort is named.

Thankfully, this time it was a pleasant temperature for late afternoon, and the smell of brimstone was noticeably absent. Since it was near closing time we practically had the place to ourselves as we wandered about the huge complex and enjoyed the spectacular views of the sea and villages below.

Then we were off to the opposite end of the island—a favorite spot of Veronica's—where you could see the Caribbean sea and Atlantic ocean separated by a thin strip of land. The contrast was striking. We passed through shanty towns with brightly colored yet crumbling clapboard or concrete structures. What they lacked in financial resources, they made up in natural ones. Just about every house had papaya, mango, and breadfruit trees in their yard. The far side of the island was a whole other world with McMansions and all-inclusive resorts. It was beautiful but soulless. As we returned to the dinghy dock, we thanked Veronica, #1 tour guide in the Caribbean, for her knowledge and hospitality, and before long it was time to be moving on.

In fact, we were incredibly anxious to move on from St. Kitts because of the terrible anchorage. It never stopped rolling the entire time we were there. The constant side-to-side motion made everyday actions incredibly difficult, especially eating dinner off of our gimbaled table. However, it was somewhat pleasant for sleeping. I'd come to enjoy the rocking motion of the boat as I drifted off to sleep.

Montserrat was one of the few islands we didn't visit back in 2002, as it was actively erupting at the time. We had watched steaming boulders rolling down the mountains as we sailed past. Now, things had calmed down enough that we had decided to stop here.

Our visit was immediately off to an exciting start. As soon as Dad and I were heading back to Koukla after clearing customs, a man at the dock pointed to a small sloop and asked if it was our boat, as it was drifting out to sea! We raced back to Koukla as fast as we could to get our dinghies and more people to help. (It's the code of the sailor: if you see a fellow sailor in need, then you go help.) We have two outboard motors for dinghies, a 25 and a 2.5 hp as backup that could be used to rescue the sloop.

Since the little outboard motor hadn't been used in a while, we had put it on for a change to let it run for a bit to keep it in good working condition. When we were almost back, our little outboard motor died. It seemed we had picked the wrong day to run the little motor. Dad started to paddle while I kept pulling the motor's start cord over and over. Eventually it restarted, we got back and switched to the 25 horsepower motor in record time (this involves hoisting the heavy thing over the side and onto the dinghy using our anchor burton), and Horatio, Dad, and I went off after the boat in distress.

Another neighboring boat had also gone over to help, so the three of us plus the two of them worked on a plan. Horatio and I, along with Samaritan #1, hauled up the anchor by hand, while Dad and Samaritan #2 tried to get the motor started. It was no use, their engine appeared to be dead. Either that or we simply didn't have the key. Thankfully, we had our 25 hp outboard motor now in place, so we pushed the boat back in. Horatio was at the helm, dad was driving the inflatable, while I held it in place next to the sloop.

We weren't sure how to re-anchor the thing, so we tied it off Koukla's stern, and said our goodbyes and thank yous to the two Samaritans, while we rushed back ashore to notify the authorities in hopes of finding the owner.

We gave the name of the boat to the customs official, just before they were about to leave for the day, and miraculously they managed to get ahold of the owner. He came over soon after, and expressed his deep gratitude.

Our second day on Montserrat was almost as dramatic as our first. We took a taxi tour of the island, specifically to see the volcano and its destruction. First we went to the volcano observatory, and watched a short film on the history of the volcano and its recent eruptions. On a clear day you could see the peak of the volcano from the observatory. It was not a clear day.

Before we went into the exclusion zone, the area of the island that has been surrendered to the volcano and deemed uninhabitable, we had to check in with the police station and sign our names and nationalities into a big leatherbound book—should anything happen.

It was a bit unnerving being in the shadow of an active volcano. Over the past several decades, 90 people had died due to volcanic activity. Although nearly all had been due to their own ignorance and negligence, not heeding scientists' warnings.

The devastation was spectacular. The gray ash-covered hills stood out in deep contrast to the lush green vegetation. We walked through a formerly posh resort, now piled thick with ash. The swimming pool, half filled in, was now home to aquatic plants and numerous tadpoles. We were allowed to roam freely in the post-apocalyptic setting, into hotel rooms, lobbies, backrooms, and so forth, now wrecked and filled with ash and mud. Melted shower curtains still hung from their rings. In other areas, houses were filled with ash up to their roofs. We were able to peer into second story windows.

On our way back, we stopped at Runaway Ghaut, a fresh mountain stream with mystical properties. Next to the stream it says, "If you drink from this burn, to Montserrat you will return." So apparently we will all be back someday.

30 Boat Kids

February 14, 2014
Guadeloupe, France

Our next sail took us across the channel between the United Kingdom and France, but we didn't need to go to Europe. We were crossing from Montserrat (a British Overseas Territory) to Guadeloupe, which, along with Martinique, are fully incorporated parts of France, with all the same rights and status as the mainland, similar to how Hawaii is for the U.S..

We arrived in the village of Deshaies in the northwest of Guadeloupe, and it was soon clear that it was very different from most of the islands we had been to recently. There were large fast roadways full of cars, lots of boutique shops and restaurants, and just development in general. There were numerous French bakery and pastry shops, a large modern library, and even recycling, which sadly, most islands lacked. We ate many baguettes and croissants and lots of government subsidized brie. (High quality, affordable cheese is a high priority for France, so they purposely reduce the cost in their territories. I had trouble fact checking this, but many other sailors believed this to be the case.) Unlike the other islands we'd visited that are administered by a distant nation but still had a Caribbean character, Guadeloupe really did feel more European.

Also, everyone spoke French. It turned out they usually knew English as well, though they weren't always willing to admit it. In the French islands, they have farmed out customs check-in for boats to private businesses, which basically just provide a computer terminal for you to fill out electronically. In Deshais, this was in a tourist knick-knack shop. My dad asked the shopkeeper if she spoke English to help clarify some things on the form. The shopkeeper replied, "Oh, no no no no no." while waving hands. Minutes later, while hovering over, she interjects in English, "You filled this part out all wrong."

When we returned from clearing customs, my mom had prepared a breadfruit we'd purchased in St. Kitts. Molly aptly described it as a cross between a potato and a squash. I thought it was quite tasty. Dad added the factoid that apparently breadfruit was a cause of the mutiny on the Bounty, as Captain Bligh was watering breadfruit trees with water intended for the crew. They were transporting the breadfruit from the South Pacific to the Caribbean, where they hoped to cultivate it as a cheap food for enslaved people. The breadfruit trees on the Bounty were tossed overboard by the mutineers, but breadfruit made it to the Caribbean eventually. This was a lot of heavy history for what was essentially a fruity potato. I enjoyed it boiled and mashed with a bit of butter.

We didn't stay long in Deshaies, and moved on to Basse-Terre, the capital of Guadeloupe. There we met the crew of Elida, a fellow cruising family. Elida was made up of a well-known boat-builder, Ross, a former commercial fisher, Kristen, and their 13-yr old twins, Greta and Olin. Despite more than a decade's age difference, Horatio and I felt an immediate kinship with Greta and Olin. They were boat kids, just as we had been. We both keenly remembered how lonely it could be, rarely encountering anyone close to our own age on our first voyage. Even though Horatio, Molly, Isaac, and I were in our mid to late 20s, to a couple of 13 yr olds we were as close to peers as they were likely to get. They were outgoing, precocious, friendly, and excitable.

And honestly, they were more fun to hang out with than many of the adult cruisers we encountered, as we were closer in age and life stage to a couple of teenagers than the retirees we often encountered. They were both quite talented. Greta showed off her impressive collection of handmade stuffed animals, with even, intricate stitching. Olin frequently brought his specialty—homemade gingerbread—to our game nights.

Our next destination was a clump of small islands known as The Saintes just south of the Guadeloupe "mainland." It was much as I'd remembered. Quaint red-roofed houses dot the green hills. The main part of town borders one continuous beach. Many sidewalk cafes offered delicious yet inexpensive baguette sandwiches and free WiFi. And all the grocery stores!

I enjoyed seeing and buying all the high quality French products—breads, cheeses, yogurt, cookies, jams, fancy canned beans, frozen vegetables! After bringing our loot to the dock, the rest of the crew headed back to Koukla, while Isaac and I continued exploring.

A short walk out of town the scenery became positively rural. These tiny islands had a balance of civilization and nature that is quite rare in the Caribbean. For one, there is a house shaped like a ship bursting out of the cliffside, built by the island's single resident doctor many decades ago. Why? Who knows, but it looked cool. It is still a clinic to this day. A short walk took us over to the large beach on the east side of the island. Exposed to the open ocean, massive rollers crashed violently against the rocks and sand, so it wasn't really a swimming beach. We had the dramatic expanse of rugged shoreline all to ourselves. The pounding waves threw many things up on shore, which makes for great beachcombing with many sea fans and shells, but unfortunately also including a lot of trash—bottles, motor oil canisters, flip flops, and other detritus spoiled this tropical paradise. I'd be willing to bet almost none of this came from the island itself. We made sure to get extra water samples for the microplastics researchers here.

Before heading back to the boat we picked up a few baguettes from the hole-in-the wall bakery. My high school French still wasn't that good, but I'd gotten pretty proficient at ordering baguettes and croissants.

Those baguettes went to good use when we had Elida's crew over for dinner. They had followed us to The Saintes. My mom made pizza (using Cathy's pizza dough recipe). Isaac and I made Italian dunkers (you know, those cheesy breadsticks with meat sauce that your school cafeteria used to serve). Horatio made a cake, and they brought a salad. I was excited about their salad with fresh crisp lettuce and homemade dressing.

31 Bananaquit Smoothie

February 20, 2014
Portsmouth, Dominica

Dominica is quite simply one of my favorite places in the world. It is one of the Caribbean's hidden gems. I've been both baffled and somewhat thankful for its lack of popularity and notoriety. In my opinion, this island pretty much has it all—beaches, pristine rainforests, waterfalls, a bounty of fresh fruits and vegetables, unique geothermal attractions. This is

probably why it was chosen as a filming location for several of the Pirates of the Caribbean movies. Everyone on Dominica seems to be quite proud of that fact, as all of the tourist maps point out the various filming locations.

We anchored in front of the white sandy beaches of Prince Rupert Bay, in northern Dominica. As soon as a cruising boat came close, while often still a couple miles out, it would be met by one of the local wooden work boats, rushing out to offer tours, produce, laundry service, garbage disposal, Dominica flags, etc. This hadn't changed in the decade-plus since we'd last been here.

The first boat out to greet us was manned by Alexis, who is a member of PAYS (Portsmouth Association for Yacht Security), an organization that works to keep Prince Rupert Bay safe for cruisers. They patrol the harbor at night and keep watch for potential boat robbers. We decided to book a tour with Alexis up the Indian River, one of the main local attractions.

The following morning, Alexis came right out to our boat to pick us up for the tour. It was just four of us—Horatio, Molly, Isaac, and me. At the mouth of the river, Alexis turned off his outboard and switched to oars. It's quite impressive that these river guides can row these heavy boats full of people for long distances, multiple times a day.

As he rowed, Alexis told us all about the various flora and fauna around the river and the island at large. He mentioned that there is nothing poisonous on Dominica, and joked that if there was, he'd be dead by now. He especially liked to talk about all the different birds, fish, lizards, and amphibians he grew up eating but are now protected. He always followed with, "And you know what it tastes like… chicken." Even with many species protected, there are still plenty of wild fruits, vegetables, and animals to feed just about anyone on Dominica willing to go and get it: mangoes, breadfruit, papaya, bananas, plantains, and grapefruits grow wild throughout the island.

Our first stop on the tour was a small shack with a dock along the river, which looked almost exactly like the voodoo lady's from the second Pirates of the Caribbean movie. It was a re-creation of the same shack, in the same spot, for a different pirate movie, since the first was taken down. This time, the Dominicans made them leave it up. Apparently many of the river guides had been involved in filming. Alexis puffed up a bit when he said he knew Johnny Depp and Keira Knightley.

As we proceeded on down the muddy brown river, the trees crowded overhead to form a bright green canopy. Crabs scuttled about in the roots of mangrove trees along the shore. The river gradually narrowed as Alexis rowed along. Where it became quite narrow, we rowed over to a small dock, which led to a bar covered in thatched roofing with rough-hewn wooden seats. We all ordered banana smoothies, made from bananas picked right around the corner. While we waited for our drinks, we watched as several fearless little birds munched on fruit specifically left out for them. When Horatio had finished his smoothie and left it briefly unattended, a yellow-bellied bananaquit hopped up on his glass rim and stuck its beak in his straw.

As we relaxed and drank our smoothies, Alexis made tiny birds out of palm fronds, which he artfully stuck into flowers and presented to us as souvenirs.

After our river tour, all six of us spent the afternoon ashore, exploring Portsmouth. The town is stretched along an expansive white sandy beach and made up of concrete buildings with flaking paint or gray weather-worn wood. To get from the dinghy dock inland, we had to walk down narrow alleyways and over wooden planks across drainage ditches.

It was getting late by the time we finished exploring, and we decided to get a pizza for dinner. They had some unusual topping options—including corn on the veggie pizza. By the time we finished, it was almost sunset. We watched through a chain link fence next to a hardware store as the sun set, and we all saw the famous green flash. The four of us had seen it several times on our first trip, but it was a first for Isaac and Molly. It can be a bit of a let-down for some, as the small green dot at sunset would be a better name.

The next morning we sailed down the coast to Roseau, the capital of Dominica, on the southern coast of the island. We had now officially gone farther than we had on our first trip. Last time we didn't make it past Prince Rupert Bay. We visited the nearby botanical gardens. It was unlike most botanical gardens, as it was more of a public park with a scattering of strange looking trees that may or may not be labeled. The highlight was a school bus that had been smashed under a tree in a hurricane. A large tree had fallen on the (thankfully) empty school bus and went right on growing.

We decided to postpone exploring the waterfalls and hiking trails of Dominica's interior until we were heading back north, so after a short stay in Roseau we sailed off to Martinique.

32 French Preservatives

February 27, 2014
St. Pierre, Martinique

After leaving Dominica, our next stop was Martinique, home to the deadliest volcanic eruption since Krakatoa. In 1902 Mt. Peele erupted and wiped out the entire population of St. Pierre—30,000 people—except for one man. (Actually there were two other survivors, but their stories are less interesting and history has largely ignored them.) The night before the eruption, Luger Sylbaris got into a bar fight and was thrown into prison. This was the best thing that could have happened to him, as he survived thanks to the prison's poorly ventilated, dungeon-like cell. He later joined Barnum and Bailey's circus, billed as The Man Who Survived Doomsday.

When we visited, very little suggested its tragic past. We found it to be a nice place to stay due to the many attractions in walking distance. The beaches were full of seaglass of all varieties and colors, extending into unusual things such as a fair amount of sea-smoothed ceramic tiles (remnants of the former city?), and even some sea glass marbles. We enjoyed visiting the quaint French town, but we were all aware of the active volcano looming in the distance.

In St. Pierre, you can still go see many ruins of the disaster, including a

ruined theater, several crumbling walls along the waterfront, and the wreck of nearly a dozen ships that were in harbor when the disaster struck (we didn't actually get to see those because you need to scuba dive). We visited the bomb-shelter-like cell and imagined what it must have felt like to survive the apocalypse inside it.

Finally, one day we made the longer trek to the nearby Depaz Rum Distillery. On the way up the road, the town development drops away to be replaced by rolling fields of sugar cane—all part of the Depaz estate. On arrival, we were met with a strange, smelly mixture of alcohol and burnt sugar. The distillery provided an excellent free self-guided walking tour of their facilities, where with very little restriction you get to see the whole factory operation. I'm always surprised by the lack of guardrails and caution signs when traveling abroad, but I appreciate the lack of litigiousness. The engineers among Koukla's crew enjoyed seeing the hundred-year-old steam-powered sugar cane crusher.

From St. Pierre we motored down the coast to the big city of Fort-de-France. After the months of small island towns, it was quite a change to be in a congested, gridded metro again. We spent a day just wandering around and seeing the sights: a big park with many food vendors, a beautiful library, and a church designed by Gustave Eiffel.

We decided the next day to take the bus to the nearby Jardin de Balata. It had many amazing landscapes of manicured plants, including some interesting cactus-like things, and tons of hummingbirds. The gardens were beautiful, but the series of rope bridges really set the place apart. The bridges rocked and swayed under our feet, as we took in the gardens below.

Our main reason for traveling to Fort-de-France was Carnival, the festival that occurs just prior to the start of Lent. It is perhaps best known in Brazil, but it is celebrated throughout the world. It is a part of the culture of the Caribbean and is celebrated on many islands. In the U.S. we are more familiar with Mardi Gras, but that is just one day of the Carnival season.

Going to the parade on the first day, we didn't know quite what to expect. In some ways it was similar to a normal American parade, but in others it was very different. There were marching bands, although the type of music they played was very different. Some businesses had floats or cars. No candy was tossed out, but one car did hand out preservatives, which looked a bit like candy in the packaging. Molly shared a funny story from her high school French teacher. She was in France (her teacher, not Molly) and was buying bread and wanted to know if there were preservatives in the bread, but didn't know the right word, so she just said the English word with a French accent, and the baker just laughed. Apparently preservative is French for condom.

Despite there being tons of children and families the parade was rather risque, even a bit raunchy at times. There was a surprising amount of cross-dressing. Even the parade-goers were often scantily clad in neon colors.

I'm sure there were a lot of cultural references that went over our heads, but still a fun time was had by all. I didn't understand a word anyone said (shouted?) despite knowing some French.

There were people in red robes, white head wraps, followed by people covered from head to toe in what I assume was molasses, many holding sugarcane. One of them (intentionally?) rubbed up against me and got some of the sticky dark stuff on my arm. I was pretty sure it was molasses. The theme of the parade was red devils, and there were groups of them here and there. There were also people in the classic Carnivale style bikinis and headdresses.

I was impressed by how many people in the parade were middle aged, some even quite old, as well as small children. There was one stooped old woman who looked as if she was about 100 dancing and marching in the parade and having a grand old time. The happiness and vitality was infectious.

One image that will be burned into my memory was of a man in an electric blue thong, holding a neon green lace umbrella, and standing bouncing on the hood of an old car revving its engine. That was one distinct thing about the parade—old, beat up cars, painted, with dented hoods that people would bounce on while they revved their engines. One of the highlights was a giant wicker puppet of a woman with electric eyes marching down the street.

33 Unicorn Potluck

March 5, 2014
Rodney Bay, St. Lucia

There is a saying that whenever two boats are going to the same place, they are racing. Elida, the family with the 13-year-old twins, was also headed from Martinique to St. Lucia. Since their vessel was much smaller and sleeker, we figured we didn't have a chance in our heavy gaff-rigged vessel, but we passed each other several times. At one point, they came right up alongside Koukla, such that the teenage kids could have swung over and boarded us pirate style. We had a great time waving and shouting to each other each time we passed, but eventually they pulled ahead and beat us into Rodney Bay, St. Lucia.

We almost skipped out on St. Lucia due to a recent event on the island. A cruising couple had been boarded and robbed in the middle of the night, leaving the man dead and the woman severely injured. But it would be a long way to skip the island, and supposedly the perpetrators had been apprehended, and we'd be going nowhere near that area.

Despite that recent unfortunate event, we were surprised to find one of the most active and rewarding cruising communities in the Caribbean in Rodney Bay, and we had a full social calendar for our entire stay.

On our way to shore the next day, we swung by our racing buddies to see if they would like a lift. Their son came along with us to refill their propane tank. Meanwhile, Mom and Dad went to get a small puncture in our inflatable repaired. They found out that it could be repaired that day, but this meant that we were all stuck on shore for the day, including our young friend, who had no way to get word back to his family. Basically that meant Horatio, Molly, Isaac, and I were charged with accompanying a rambunctious 13-year-old boy for the whole day who liked to roll around on the ground, touch everything in the stores we went to, catch rides on passing custodian golf carts, and asked everyone we met where to get kittens.

He and his sister were obsessed with finding a boat cat. Everywhere we went that day, he asked, "where are the kittens, do you have any kittens?" He was obsessed. At lunch, when he was ordering, he said, "I'll have a burger with no onions, a milkshake, and where are your kittens?" The waitress didn't know how to respond.

Eventually the rest of his family made it to shore, and that evening all ten of us went out to dinner at what was basically a Caribbean Chuck E. Cheese. There was good pizza and an excellent playground where all the kids got to run around and play, including a free-spinning metal platform of a type likely banned in the U.S. by this point. My mom called it a kiddie killer. It was great fun for the kids, including some local kids who made fun of us and said their grandmas could spin them faster. There were also slides, swing sets, a jungle gym, a trampoline, and even a bouncy castle. As the other families left, we 20-something kids could play on the equipment without getting dirty looks.

The whole time the kids had been going on about catching a cat we really didn't take them seriously. Then their family showed up to dinner with cat food and a litter box. They asked a local where the best place was to catch kittens, and sure enough, it was right next to a rather upscale restaurant.

So after our pizza, while people dined a few feet away, the father opened up a can of cat food and not five minutes later a kitten came out from under the porch and started eating. Then another, and another, and another. He snatched up the first one out, because clearly that was the smartest and boldest and would therefore make the best boat cat. The father had it cuddled up in his shirt while they dinghied back to their boat.

Sure enough, within just a few days, the kitten was adjusted to its new home, climbing all over the boat and running along the boom.

The next evening we went to a cruisers' potluck aboard the Unicorn. The Unicorn was a well-known boat (to people, like my dad, who know about boats), built in 1948 and had appeared in the Pirates of the Caribbean movies. It had recently sold, and was being refitted as a floating bar/restaurant for tourists. It was a bit sad to see it being retired as a true sailing vessel, but at least it was being well kept and maintained.

The potluck itself was great fun. There was tons of good food and fellow cruisers from around the world. Isaac and I found another couple close to our age. They were from Sweden, and we talked with them for quite a while. They both worked online, in web and graphic design, thus enabling them to sail around the world while still earning a living.

The most interesting people we met were a family from Seattle. I got talking to the mother and a friend of hers from France while waiting in the (very long) line at the buffet. Most live-aboard cruisers have some sort of tie to sailing. In my family, there have been lots of seafaring Cowans going back many generations. Not so with this family. It all started when the husband was at home watching TV, recovering from minor surgery. He saw a report about a 16-year-old girl who'd sailed around the world, and thought, well, if a 16-year-old can do it, then I can do it. He had never been on a boat before. A few months later, he and his wife sold their house and most of their belongings and flew to France to buy a boat, taking along their two children. They spent a year cruising the Mediterranean, learning how to sail in the relatively safer waters of an enclosed sea though that gives no protection against freak accidents—like having their mast struck by lightning. Some of their electronics got fried, but everyone was fine. They figured it out, and now with their sea legs, crossed the Atlantic without major mishap. From St. Lucia they were headed to Panama, through the Canal, and then on to the South Pacific.

Whenever people would find out about my seafaring childhood, I would often get the response of "I want to do that!" And people would often ask me for tips about how to get started. My advice is typically don't rush off unprepared. Those people are invariably the ones who—best case scenario—get rescued by the coast guard. You need at least one person who knows how to sail, how to fix all the systems that keep your boat afloat and moving, and someone with some medical/advanced first aid training. I was really impressed with how much this family had done and learned basically starting at zero. So it can be done, but these stories are rare.

34 Spice Island

March 11, 2014
St. George, Grenada

The next island-nation south of St. Lucia is St. Vincent & the Grenadines. However, St. Vincent itself (not the Grenadines) has a bad reputation among the cruising community, for both being unsafe and uninteresting, so we made the jump all the way down to Grenada. This required yet another overnight sail.

This passage to our southern-most destination was unusually pleasant. When one sailor wishes another well, they often use the salutation, "fair winds and following seas." It basically means best wishes, as these are the

best possible conditions one can have. Maybe it was all the fellow cruisers wishing us well in St. Lucia, because this was one of the most pleasant passages we had. We did in fact, have fair winds and following seas. The rare goldilocks zone where you have enough wind to move at a decent rate, but not so much to make things uncomfortable. Koukla moved with a gentle, rhythmic motion. Water sloshed gently at the hull as we made way. Our propeller cage gave off a pleasant, reassuring hum, telling us we were going fast, but not too fast. Isaac and I watched the stars move through the night sky, and kept an eye on the radar to watch for other vessels. When our watch was over we slept soundly in our bunks, rocked by the cradle of the deep.

Isaac and I woke for our 8 am watch to the calm and islet-studded waters of the Grenadines archipelago, and continued south on to Grenada.

Grenada is famous for its nutmeg. Much like the Native Americans are known for using every part of the buffalo, Grenadans use every part of the nutmeg plant. It is their number one commodity. Beyond just nutmeg and mace (a second spice from the same plant, made from fibers around the nutmeg), on the island they've come up with several other uses. The

nutmeg's fruit is turned into nutmeg syrup, nutmeg jelly and jam, and even used to sweeten barbeque sauce. Nutmeg husks are used like wood chips to cover walkways. Many billboards advertised medicinal products made from nutmeg, called Nut-Med (supposed to ease joint pain). Grenada is so proud of this little spice they put it on their flag.

After clearing customs, we set off on a day-long taxi tour of the island. Our first destination was a spice estate. The estate we visited did not let you see the actual fields, but they had a showroom where they gave demonstrations of the spices they grow. In addition to nutmeg and mace, they grow bay rum, cocoa, cinnamon, cloves, and anise. The demonstration showed us the spices in their raw form, including a very strongly scented branch of cinnamon wood.

Next up was the Belmont Estate, the only chocolate-producing facility in Grenada. The previous spice estate produced cocoa, but only in the raw form. An extremely energetic tour guide took us out to the orchard, where he told us the nearby mango and citrus trees help give flavor to the cocoa. Did it really? I have no idea. He climbed a tree and broke open a cocoa pod for us to try the raw seeds, still covered in white pulp. The taste was very strong, but of fruit and citrus, not chocolaty at all.

The tour continued through the various stages of chocolate production, which includes a long fermentation in wooden bins covered with burlap and palm leaves, then drying in the sun or greenhouses, and finally roasting. The cocoa beans can then be sold, or turned into chocolate right there (by grinding and mixing with other ingredients). At the end we were served strongly spiced Grenadian hot chocolate. It was delicious. I also bought several of their chocolate bars, produced on site. (Belmont Estates has a website where you can order their chocolate bars. I may have done this a few times.)

Next we went to a unique attraction: an airplane graveyard. First, some background. In 1979, Maurice Bishop came to power in Grenada through a coup. In 1983, other members of his party, favoring more radical policies, seized power and executed him. The U.S. then invaded, claiming they were protecting U.S. students at the medical school and concerned about Cuban participation in construction of a new airstrip. Ultimately the country returned to the pre-1979 system of democratic government. How do Grenadians feel about this? I suspect he would avoid saying anything disagreeable to customers, but according to our taxi driver Grenadians had "loved Maurice Bishop," so after his execution they were in favor of anything that would get rid of the people responsible, and so supposedly most people viewed the invasion positively.

A strange result of all this was that due to the U.S. invasion, a couple of Cuban airplanes were stranded in Grenada. Afterwards they were not allowed to leave and left to molder away in a field outside of the old airstrip. There they still sit, surrounded by goats and other animals that local farmers graze on the land. They are not fenced off in any way, so we were able to go right up and examine the exposed engines and broken dashboards.

Finally, we drove back towards the boat, but only after first passing through the forested center of the island. This offered us some good views, but unfortunately no sight of monkeys, which are usually around earlier in the morning. There was also a neat waterfall just a short walk off the roadside, which also included a small garden, and a group of guys that wanted us to pay them to jump off the waterfall. To cap off the excellent tour, our driver agreed to swing by a grocery store so we could use his van to load up on provisions to bring back to the boat.

After the tour, we visited the capital city of St. George's, which had an enormous Saturday market with a large variety of produce and spices for sale. Also in town, a stone tunnel ran under a hill to connect the waterfront to the rest of the city. It is just big enough for one lane of traffic and one lane of pedestrians. When we had to pass through we found ourselves nervously squeezing against the wall to stay out of the way of the cars.

We had enjoyed our visit to Grenada, especially the island tour, but it was soon time to leave. As we rounded the "toe" of the vaguely boot-shaped island, after many months of cruising, we turned north. We still had a few more places to visit, but we had officially reached our southernmost point and were now headed homeward.

35 Turtle Tales

March 20, 2014
Union Island, St. Vincent and The Grenadines

In the Caribbean, the ocean is constantly changing from one vivid shade of turquoise to aquamarine, to purply shades of dark blue in deep open waters. I thought I had seen every shade possible until our final approach to Union Island, the southernmost island in the Grenadines chain. As we entered the harbor, the ocean turned an unbelievable shade of vivid, electric blue. It was like the ocean was glowing.

We anchored in between two coral reefs, one of which had a tiny man-made island on it, home to a bar called Happy Island. That evening we sipped drinks there and watched the harbor fill up with acrobatic kite surfers, doing tricks right in front of us.

The next day we were off to another tiny island, Mayreau. It was such a short sail from Union Island to Mayreau that even though Horatio grabbed a banana right after we got the sails up, he hadn't finished eating it before dad gave the order to start flaking down halyards.

Once the anchor was down, it was off to the beach. Isaac and I headed to explore the island, prepared with our bathing suits on under our clothes.

Off we went up a steep cement road, lined with ramshackle houses and hole-in-the-wall eating establishments. One of these was completely and artfully covered with nautical bric-a-brac and other assorted flotsam and jetsam. We continued up the hill to enjoy the scenic overlook. The view was spectacular. Nothing but white sand,  green palms, and ocean in various shades of turquoise as far as the eye could see.

On we pressed, in search of Salt Whistle Bay. When we arrived more than a little hot and sweaty, the bay did not disappoint. This place was picture perfect. The water was swimming pool calm, clear as glass, and refreshingly cool yet still pleasantly warm. We spent a glorious afternoon in relative solitude floating around and lazing on the beach. This was peak Caribbean.

After we were good and pruney we headed back to Saline Bay, where everyone else was swimming and then back to Koukla. That evening, we invited aboard one of our neighbors, captain of Snoozle, who we had seen off and on throughout the trip. (Yes Snoozle is a very silly name. We were told it means a short nap, I don't think that makes it better.) The Swiss gentleman was single-handing a specially designed yacht so he could comfortably sail himself around the world. But we thought he might like some company, so we invited him over.

To look at him and his boat, it would seem like he had it all. But he had a rather sad tale. He had realized his dream—to sail his own boat around the world, but it cost him in other ways. He had fallen in love with a woman

 who was very much not a sailor. She had even given it a go, and joined him for a spell, but she was miserable due to persistent motion sickness. Now he had to choose between the love of his life and the life he loves. Hearing his story, I think we all felt incredibly fortunate that we did not have to make such difficult decisions.

We also had rather a lot to thank this man for. The next island in the

Grenadines, or rather collection of islands, was the Tobago Cays. We were all itching to go there and visit the sea turtle sanctuary, except for the captain, who thought it would be too tight a spot for Koukla and not worthwhile. Thankfully, after talking to this man who'd just been there, he was convinced otherwise. So next stop, Tobago Cays!

As they were described to us, the Tobago Cays are what people picture when they think of the Caribbean–perfect sandy beaches, half a dozen different shades of turquoise, and palm trees. With no settlements, they are the classic image of island paradise. The Tobago Cays are so close to Mayreau we didn't even bother putting up the sails, and just motored over. As soon as Koukla was settled on her anchor and the standard afternoon rain shower had passed, we hopped in the dinghy to head to the turtle sanctuary, snorkels in hand. Snorkeling with wild sea turtles in the sanctuary is not only legal, but incredibly popular. The tiny coves were jam packed with boats. It was amazing how many people were in such a remote location.

Snorkeling with sea turtles in the Tobago Cays is pretty high on the list of amazing things we did on the trip. It was incredibly peaceful, almost surreal, watching these graceful creatures munching sea grass and swimming around. It looked like they were flying. It was almost a bit eerie how close you can get to them.

Along with the turtles we saw a couple huge manta rays. Isaac and I were swimming back to shore at a decent clip, and all of a sudden there was a huge ray right in front of us, and we had to suddenly put on the brakes and try to swim backwards, which was a bit tricky. Ever since the whole Steve Irwin incident, I think people have had a much healthier respect/fear of manta rays, myself very much included.

That evening we enjoyed the significant lack of light pollution thanks to the uninhabited islands we were anchored next to. Isaac had been studying our field guide and had learned to identify several constellations, and we could see a good portion of the Milky Way. We spent quite a while laying down on top of the wheelhouse enjoying the sights and sounds of that balmy night.

We had heard good things about Bequia from many cruisers and we were all looking forward to getting there, but we didn't really know much about it. Ultimately, what made Bequia special wasn't any particularly amazing attractions, but just the pleasantness of everything: a nice-sized town, good restaurants, not too crowded or built up, and most important, a popular cruising destination where we reunited with friends we'd made elsewhere. It felt like the perfect island community.

There was a unique grocery store with odds and ends shoved into every nook and cranny. They made their own chocolate croissants there, which were ultimately the best of the trip (even better than the French islands). After trying them, my dad put in a special order for a dozen to pick up the next day, and informed us that four were for him, and we could figure out how to divide up the rest.

In addition to the green sea turtles we swam with in Tobago Cays, we had a chance to see another species. The Old Hegg Turtle sanctuary on Bequia was founded by Oreton King, as a personal mission to save the hawksbill sea turtle. His idea was to gather turtle eggs from the beaches and raise the turtles in captivity until they are 3 years old, and then release them to the ocean. This avoids the high-mortality period when the turtles are small and have many predators. He has raised and released over 2000 three-year-old turtles. Before releasing them, he marks his turtles' shells with a small hole in the back end of their shell. Divers have reported seeing his marked turtles throughout the Grenadines.

In the middle of one misty night while we were all asleep in our bunks ... CRASH. Everyone scrambled up on deck in pajamas, and found a boat smashed t-bone style across our bow, with our bowsprit broken through their railing.

"IS THERE ANYONE ON THIS BOAT!" Horatio shouted. It took time for them to appear, dazed, unhelpful, one just curled up and clutching his head. It was going to be up to us to get out of this mess. Their boat's weight in the wind and current pushed us tight on our anchor, the chain was straining and we couldn't back up. With barely a word we jumped into action.

My brother and I jumped in the dinghy and maneuvered into position against their port side. Bracing myself in the bow of the dinghy I held onto the other vessel. I kept us as close to the center of gravity of the other boat as possible. My brother let loose with the 25 horsepower motor. Normally when an outboard motor is running at full throttle, you are also moving through the water quite quickly. The fact that we were held back by a large boat broadside to the wind meant we were not. The propeller churned the water behind the dinghy and it soon began to splash over the back side. My brother held the throttle fully open with one hand and bailed out the dinghy with the other. Slowly but surely we pushed the other boat sideways, getting them off without getting our bowsprit any more tangled up in their railing or rigging.

Their boat then began to drift slowly out into open waters. My dad decided that we better go find out their name for insurance purposes. And so he and Isaac, who were both in their underwear, got in the inflatable and chased them out of the harbor. Their vessel's name was hidden behind a swim platform, so they wrote down their hull number and left.

Ultimately everything turned out okay. They hadn't really been running away. We later learned they were all severely hungover, which is why they were no use during the crisis. I still don't really understand why they had seemed to be leaving, but they eventually came back and re-anchored. I'd probably chalk up that decision to the presumably large amounts of alcohol the crew had imbibed that evening. Though part of their rail was destroyed, Koukla sustained no real damage. But one thing we did come away with was one of the most memorable experiences of the trip.

36 Boiling Lake

March 30, 2014
Rodney Bay, St. Lucia

As much as we enjoyed Bequia, getting rammed into in the middle of the night felt like our cue to leave. We left first thing the next morning. We were on a broad reach doing 7-8 knots, which is pretty unheard of for us. A broad reach is the point of sail schooners really like, yet it seems like we're never on that point. We made excellent time, the seas were calm, and we were barely heeling. My dad said, "this is the type of sail you pray for, so savor it."

We were now on the return leg of our trip, and mostly going to places we'd already been before. After a brief, uneventful stay in St. Lucia, we moved on to Dominica. On our first voyage, Dominica had been my favorite island. While we had been to Dominica previously on this trip, it was a relatively short visit, and I was looking forward to seeing more of the island, in particular the boiling lake. Due to volcanic activity, Dominica is home to one of a very small number of geothermal lakes around the world. It is the second largest boiling lake in the world.

On the first trip, our guided tour around Dominica was such a major highlight that we attempted to repeat, unsuccessfully. I wasn't sure if it was Dominica that was different, or if it was me. Was I too old and jaded to experience that magic and wonder anymore? I hoped not.

We found ourselves in a difficult situation hiring guides–more than once. We mentioned a few of the attractions we'd been to before and wanted to revisit, but somehow this didn't pan out. We said we wanted to see some waterfalls, but we ended up at a spot where you really needed to be a goat to get up and see it. Only Horatio made it to the falls. We went all the way to the Carib village, only to find out after the fact that it's only open on cruise ship days. We spent more time in a vehicle than out in nature. Our previous tour of Dominica had been one of my favorite memories of the whole trip, and I was pretty disappointed. We'd planned to use the same guide to go to the boiling lake, but we decided at the last minute to hire someone else. That also didn't work out so well.

It wasn't really an option to traipse off on our own. The trail there is not well marked and a bit dangerous due to the geothermal features. We did not get a chance to meet our guide before the beginning of the hike, and I wish we had. He barely spoke a word to us the whole time.

The hike started out in the rainforest, with the lush, vibrantly green jungle I've come to expect from Dominica. Perhaps I wasn't so old and jaded. The trail quickly became increasingly steep with wooden stairs set into the mountain. Before long, my knees told me that I was, in fact, getting old. At one point there were several "fake outs" where I would think we were about to reach the top, only to be met with more stairs. Once we did finally reach the peak, we were met with an impressive panoramic view of the island and ocean beyond. Then down the mountain through more rainforest, and into the Valley of Desolation.

We passed through a geothermal river, which had several small pools, which our guidebook said you could go in, but our guide said you couldn't. I think our book was correct and our guide didn't want to stop, and I was a bit bitter about this. I wanted to soak for a bit, and my knees would have thanked me for it. Our guide seemed annoyed at us, like he had somewhere else to be and just wanted to get there and back as quickly as possible. (On the way out, we saw other hikers in said river, confirming my suspicions.)

The Valley of Desolation was a bit like it sounds. Few plants grow there, and steam billows out from various holes in the ground. This was just about the only part it helped having a guide for, as it was a bit confusing to follow the trail. Then the Valley of Desolation led us to the boiling lake itself. Horatio accurately described it as like a videogame rendering of water. It really did look almost fake the way it bubbled like a cauldron in the middle and the way the ripples spread across the surface of the cloudy grey water.

At times you could barely see the lake through the thick clouds of steam. There was a small waterfall feeding the lake, and when the steam cleared you could see where the water flowed out. It was cool, but reaching the boiling lake felt anticlimactic. I'd wanted to come here for ages, and this was it? Would I have been more

excited a decade ago? Was it just our wet blanket of a tour guide? While the four of us were watching the bubbling lake and eating lunch, our guide was off on his own toking up. I think I'll blame our guide.

After we hiked out of the jungle, we ended at Titou Gorge. We rented life jackets—they came highly recommended, as we'd been told there was a very strong current channeling through the narrow gorge. It varied from about ten to three feet wide, and the top overflowed with a canopy of green. Beams of light streamed down and were outlined in floating particles of dust. The walls were coated with algae, and seemed to glow green and pulse with life. I felt that electricity of the rainforest yet again. We floated on our backs and looked up at the steep rock walls rising on either side of us. When we approached the opening where the waterfall came into the gorge we were thankful for our lifejackets. After swimming we ate homemade coconut candy. It tasted just like I remembered.

37 Classic Regatta

April 15, 2014
Antigua and Barbuda

Why is nothing ever easy? We had arrived at Antigua for the classic yacht regatta, and were all excited to actually be at a dock as part of the event. Horatio had come up with a plan for how we'd maneuver into the dock, drawing out a play-by-play diagram like a football coach. We were all in position, ready to back into our slip and...no reverse. I should probably mention that on our way into the dock we all heard a loud clunk come from the engine. We didn't think too much of it at the time, but that was almost certainly the source of the trouble.

This was a huge let-down, as docking was really a special treat. It might sound like nothing, but living aboard at anchor with only one dinghy for six adults with differing interests and priorities had been a bigger challenge than we'd anticipated. On the first trip, Horatio and I were 12 and 16 respectively, and weren't about to be going off on our own. But now, with four 20-something adults instead of two children, it had been a significant logistical challenge to balance and coordinate multiple shore-related activities.

Unwilling to give up on the luxury of docking, we pulled off into the harbor to regroup. We realized we couldn't do this on our own, so we called for backup. Regatta volunteers—almost exclusively fellow cruisers—in dinghies ferried our dock lines to additional volunteers waiting on the dock, and we winched Koukla into her slip. Unfortunately we had to repeat this process every time we came back into the dock, but we all thoroughly enjoyed our hard-earned freedom.

We'd been assigned a slip next to a very expensive, very fancy Italian yacht with a professional crew. I don't think the owner appreciated being next to a bunch of ragamuffins like us, and gave us the stinkeye as we pulled ourselves into place with a spiderweb of lines.

The first night of the regatta we met several colorful sailors, but perhaps the most remarkable was Mark. Mark was a talented boatbuilder who had just finished building a beautiful sailboat for himself. In his plans to set sail he'd neglected a critical detail— learning how to sail. The captain of Elida, Ross , as a fellow boatbuilder, had taken him under his wing. However, what Mark lacked in sailing skills he made up for in appearances. He had an actual parrot on his shoulder! However, we learned why this practice has fallen out of fashion. Mark's crew member described the mess—and horrible smell—this bird made all over the boat.

The first official event of the regatta was the concours d'elegance— basically a beauty pageant for boats. To prepare, we frantically cleaned and hid junk in various places—mainly the foc'sle and lazarette, the equivalent of shoving everything in the closet before company comes over.

There were multiple categories in the boat beauty pageant. We weren't up against the modern multimillion dollar yachts, but against the other crusty liveaboards. The judges seemed to like our wooden bathtub and folding rocking chair on deck, but ultimately we didn't win anything. Dad thought we were robbed, and I have to agree I think we at least deserved 3rd place.

One afternoon when Isaac and I were heading back to Koukla we walked past Elida—home to those mischievous, cat-catching twins. We saw someone bent over, looking in the water next to their boat. We asked if they needed help, and said there was a cat in the water, and sure enough there was the kitten swimming towards the dock. It was the same kitten that had been first out to the tuna can back on St. Lucia, and had quickly adapted to her new life as a boat cat. But it was low tide and she couldn't climb the steep walls to get ashore. I jumped down into a nearby inflatable, and scooped up the kitten. Isaac swung aboard Elida, and I passed the wet little furball to Isaac. The twins' mom, Kristin, came by shortly, and had him swaddled in a dry towel, just his little face poking out.

Boat people are an eclectic bunch. There was the aforementioned Mark, the parrot-clad wannabe pirate, and there was Nichole, who in addition to her talents as sailing crew, was also trained in the circus arts. One evening she performed an aerial acrobatic routine hanging from the cross trees of one of the boats docked at the regatta, and on another evening she did a fire dancing routine. Isaac was given the task of holding a wet towel just in case she accidentally caught fire. I think he felt important. Elida was docked right next to the boat of the acrobatic performance, and they invited us over. We had a front row seat and we got to play with the kitten and eat gingerbread while we waited for it to start.

Sailing and living aboard was a way of life for us, we'd forgotten to the majority of sailors it was a sport. Cruisers treat their boats like winnebagos, yachties treat them like Ferraris. We figured with all these fancy multi-million dollar classic yachts, they'd be more concerned with scuffing their paint job than winning. Not so. But we cared much more about avoiding a collision and chipping our varnish work we'd done ourselves, than winning. So we hung back. Even without any sort of competitive spirit, just going through the course was physically taxing. We realized after the fact and seeing how many crew members were on similarly sized vessels that we were significantly under-crewed.

Typically there's at least one person per sheet at all times in a race, and maybe an extra hand or two. I was on the jib sheet the whole day and we were constantly tacking back and forth through the course. I was constantly winching away. By the end of the day my arms felt like rubber snakes.

Even though we weren't in amongst the fray, it was still exhilarating. It was blowing about 20 knots, we were heeling about 45 degrees, and Koukla had a bone in her teeth—there was a perpetual churn of white ocean waves beneath the bow.

The sea was full of magnificent vessels of the past, present, and future. Several boats would have looked familiar, even antiquated, to Horatio Nelson himself. A few looked oddly advanced to my modern eye.

As we were finally about to cross the finish line (second to last), we had to take one last embarrassingly large tack back in to round the final buoy. We'd made it in, were about to drop the sails and start the engine and…no water was coming out the stern as it's supposed to. We had to quickly drop anchor with no sails. Dad felt like Koukla was talking to us, and didn't appreciate what we'd just put her through. Thankfully it was just an air bubble in the water pump, but we got the message.

Never a dull moment at the Antigua classics! Isaac and I were walking around the docks one balmy evening well after sunset when a harried looking man came up to us and asked if we were from the Adventuress. Smoke was coming out of one of the hatches. Many sailors nearby quickly noticed the rising smoke and jumped into action. Those that felt competent enough climbed aboard, braving the toxic smoke to go down below. The captain of the Greyhound rushed into the fray with fire extinguisher in hand—and no pants. Crises always seem to happen when you're not wearing any pants. We were asked for torches (I was momentarily confused, but realized the British man meant flashlights), so Isaac and I ran back and also retrieved flashlights and my dad who would likely be more useful to them. My dad went aboard to help. He came above a few

minutes later and told us it was an electrical fire. While it wasn't out yet, it was contained and the captain was on board. He was not having a good day.

This was a good example of the sailing community at large—good in a crisis and always ready to help. As you may have noticed by this point, crises, mishaps, storms, accidents, malfunctions, etc. are quite frequent at sea. When they happen, you almost automatically go into emergency mode—you scan your environment, clear out unnecessary thoughts and emotions to the best of your ability, and either give or follow orders depending on your rank.

We made the decision to attempt one last race. It was a simple back and forth course. We didn't push Koukla too hard and nothing broke. We were still last, but by a smaller margin. And that was the end of Koukla's racing career.

 The next day we moved from Falmouth to English Harbor for our final events: cream tea and gig racing. We docked in historic Nelson's dockyard. We were one slip over from Greyhound which was modeled after the 18th century luggers, so it wouldn't have been too out of place in Nelson's time.

The cream tea was wonderful, if a bit hoity-toity. Scones with clotted cream and finger sandwiches were served with proper English tea served on white china. The fact that most of our compatriots had British accents added to the effect.

And we finally won something! We won the concours d'elegance for dinghies—the prettiest dinghy contest. Horatio got a bottle of rum shaped like a skull, as he'd done all the brightwork in our sailing dinghy. Collectively, we even won a few of the dinghy racing events. Horatio and dad got second for men's doubles rowing and Horatio got second again for sculling.

38 Airplane Sandstorm

April 28, 2014
St. Barts, France

St. Barts is a well-known holiday destination for the rich and famous. The quaint little buildings were all the traditional white with red roofs. The downtown area was neat as a pin and full of designer shops I didn't dare enter. The grocery stores we encountered were super deluxe gourmet shops to provision the mega yachts in the harbor. A box of cereal, which we typically used as a benchmark of affordability, was a ridiculous $20. I eyed a beautiful bottle of olive oil in a rainbow striped bottle. It was $50. There was even a molecular gastronomy section, full of unusual colorants, flavorings, and additives for making foams, gels, spheres, or otherwise changing food from one form of matter into another. We didn't buy anything there. We splurged on some homemade nougat and candied nuts from a street vendor. The island itself was lovely, but not significantly more beautiful than your average tropical island. We did particularly enjoy the immaculately clean and modern showers, free at the local marina. We speculated these were provided so a bunch of grubby sailors didn't go stinking up their exclusive island. This place was not meant for the likes of us, so on we went.

At this point we had been living aboard for about 8 months, and were approaching our final leg home. I found myself daydreaming of Boston— about bay-windowed apartments, large beds (I'd been sleeping on a less-than-twin-sized bunk the whole time), of rainy fall weekends with hot cups of tea. I dreamed of farmer's markets, and getting to cook whatever I wanted.

This daydreaming was likely fueled by my general disappointment with St. Martin. St. Martin had been among our favorite spots the first time around. I remembered the French side being full of brightly painted, quirky boats, interesting shops, restaurants, and bakeries. Now it was full of identical looking fiberglass boats, and many shops had gone out of business. Thankfully there were still a number of restaurants. But the whole place seemed more weather-worn, not as vibrant as I'd remembered. I had remarked that back then, St. Martin and Antigua were in competition as the boater's hub of the Caribbean. Back then St. Martin was winning, but I think now Antigua, or possibly even St. Lucia, was taking the lead.

One day, Isaac and I were out on our own exploring the French side of the island. We'd just finished brunch at a cafe when a man approached us with an iPad and asked if we wanted to enter a contest. There didn't seem to be any harm in playing along, so we spun the little animated wheel-of-fortune app. Suddenly he started exclaiming excitedly that we had won the grand prize, it was so amazing, he'd never seen it before, we just needed to go to this condo resort on the Dutch side. At this point it felt like a scam, but we had nothing else to do for the day so figured, why not?

When we got to the condo complex and presented our "winning ticket", the prize was... a timeshare presentation. Oh well, at least we weren't kidnapped. But as we were being given a tour of the grounds, a gigantic rat ran right in front of us. Our guide was red-faced with embarrassment and quickly said, "I've never seen that happen before!" Needless to say, we didn't buy a timeshare.

Since we got to St. Martin we'd been trying to connect with our local friends Lynn and Andrew, who had volunteered us in the Heineken Regatta in the first trip. Due to limited forms of communication it took a while. They picked us up and took us back to their place, which had been under construction 12 years ago, but now was a beautiful showcase of their travel mementos and Lynn's beautiful pottery work. Their daughter, I'd remembered as a spunky little kid obsessed with honey, was now a vivacious young chef obsessed with food in general. I felt old. She'd also invited some of her friends over to help make sushi. They artfully displayed their handiwork on Lynn's beautiful platters.

My parents and Lynn and Andrew reminisced about their decades-long intermittent friendship, which started with their visit to Rockland not long after we'd first bought Koukla, our last Caribbean voyage, the Heineken Regatta, and our return over a decade later.

While the older generation reminisced, the younger got into a bit of hijinks. Horatio and one of Gwen's male friends got into a friendly but heated wasabi-eating contest, for which there are no winners.

At our friend's suggestion we headed over to Maho beach the next day. Maho beach is a famous destination for aircraft enthusiasts, as it is right under the airport runway. It's on the Dutch side of St. Martin, and right in front of the Princess Julia International Airport. There were multiple warning signs not to get too close, but they were largely ignored. Watching the planes landing was incredible—the low-flying aircraft would majestically glide overhead. It felt like you could reach up and touch them.

Takeoffs were another story. As the planes revved their engines for takeoff, right in front of the beach, the jet wash created a massive sandstorm. It felt like every inch of my skin was being buffed by a belt sander. We ran to the safety of the water, and ducked below the waves until the sandstorm had passed. You might have noticed that we took photos of planes landing, but not taking off. If we had attempted any, we would have lost our camera. Any items in the path of the jet wash would get blown out to sea.

Some crazy idiots would stand at the fence directly in front of the runway, receiving the full force of the jet engine's blast. They would hold on to the fence and get lifted off the ground, and a few with poor grip strength would get blown backwards. This is particularly dangerous because there is a public road dividing this fence and the beach. (Sadly someone actually died doing this in 2017, and St. Martin officials have since added more fences.) I didn't think about this at the time, but I've since spent a lot of time worrying about just how much jet fuel exhaust we all inhaled that day. But our trip to St. Martin wouldn't have been complete without a traumatizing beach visit.

39 Living Meditation

May 21, 2014
The Caribbean Sea

After a long wait for weather in St. Martin, it was finally time to head out to sea for our last big offshore passage. Offshore sailing is at its best when it's dull and monotonous. One day drifts almost imperceptibly into the next, following the four-hour watch cycle. For the low-risk passage Isaac and I got to go on watch together—the only couple that didn't come with a captain's license. But we got the easy 8-12 watch. Horatio and Molly had 12-4, and my parents had 4-8.

My schedule for the whole passage was as follows. Wake up and go on watch from 8am-12pm. Have coffee and breakfast, maybe read and write a bit while on watch. The daytime watch shifts are a bit more relaxed as typically everyone is up and about. At noon, go off watch, eat lunch, afternoon nap from around 1-2, get up, take a water sample, read, help cook dinner. Dinner 6-6:30, clean up 6:30-7, after dinner nap 7-8. On watch from 8pm-12am. Go to sleep and start all over again.

There were very few deviations from this schedule the entire passage. Depending on the wind, weather, and waves I might sleep better or worse some nights. For ocean crossings, and really life at sea in general, your entire living environment is constantly moving—and not just forward, but on multiple axes. Mine and Isaac's cabin was the furthest forward, and therefore the most sensitive to the bouncing and rocking of the waves.

Being out to sea is like a living meditation. There's nothing but ocean surrounding you—just a vast expanse of wet nothingness. At night there is the most to see. We could see the night sky as it was seen by the ancients who named the constellations. Most of them still don't make much sense to me. But the name Milky Way does. It's like a splash of cream across the black canopy of the sky, each cloudy pinprick a potential sun with potential solar systems surrounding it. The nothingness during the day and the vastness of the universe at night does odd, introspective things to the brain.

Over the course of our four-hour watch we could see the stars rotate in the sky. The change in orientation of the big dipper from horizontal to vertical was the most obvious.

While the vastness of the universe was hidden during the day but revealed at night, the alien mystery of the deep is never revealed. I knew just enough about marine biology to imagine the monsters and marvels that could be beneath us at any moment, Sperm whales, giant squid, the Burton-esque nightmare fish of the midnight zone where sunlight never penetrated. My love of science fiction filled in the gaps left by science fact.

I did something incredibly stupid while out to sea. I decided this would be a great time to read a true story about being shipwrecked. Not smart to read In The Heart of the Sea, while actually in the heart of the sea. It's about the true story of the whaling ship Essex that inspired Moby Dick. It gets into some pretty grisly details. It describes the physiology of dehydration–what it's like to basically dehydrate to death. And it discusses cannibalism, a dark and often ignored part of the history of sailing. It's a great book, but I only recommend reading it from the comfort of dry land.

On the 6th day out, around 6:30 am I heard shouting up on deck, and ran up to see a clutter of glistening backs keeping pace with us. It was a large pod of dolphins—a good omen.

I spent many hours staring off into the empty horizon. While we may have been frustrated by the lack of wind and lack of progress towards Bermuda, the sight of a calm ocean has a calming effect on the soul.

I had a thought as to why I'm so drawn to the sea—perhaps why so many adventurous souls are drawn to it. It is constantly different than it was before. It changes colors and textures from minute to minute, hour to hour, and day to day. I love a certain degree of change. Too much can be disorienting, but without change you have stagnation. Within a certain area in a certain time, land doesn't change much. Land changes too slowly for an average human life to witness.

While I love the sea, I found myself longing for the unchanging land, for something concrete, for a home base.

The sea has an odd sense of humor. After being becalmed for several days, after we were finally in range of Bermuda, the wind picked up to the point that we had to reef in order to get in after sunrise and not in the middle of the night. Of course, not long after we'd finished reefing the wind died down again so we had to undo all our work.

We made it into Bermuda, but we didn't get in dry. I was literally tossed out of bed when we hit a rain squall and a gust of wind pushed Koukla on her side. We all donned our bright yellow foul weather gear as we took the sails down before entering the harbor.

The change in climate signaled that our tropical voyage was at an end. It was time to put away our swimsuits, shorts, and sandals and get out the jeans and sweaters. I could finally wear the sweater I'd knitted months ago.

Mentally, many people think of Bermuda as part of the Caribbean, but geographically it isn't. With its mixture of pines and palms, sandy beaches and rocky shores it very much feels halfway between Maine and the Caribbean.

We all felt the nearness of the end of our voyage and wanted to get as much as possible out of our remaining time. Our first trip ashore we gathered up an assortment of tourist brochures to plan our sightseeing.

We were most interested in seeing the network of caves that make up the innards of Bermuda. We went on both the crystal caves and fantasy caves tour. We'd visited one cave during our first trip, but we couldn't remember which we'd been to before, so we visited both.

Our tour guide told us that back in the early 1900s, two 12-year-old boys were playing cricket, and lost their ball down a hole. They got some rope, climbed down the 100-something feet into the cave, went swimming for 3 hours, then climbed back out again before telling anyone.

The fantasy caves tour had a campy, over-the-top tour guide who was hamming it up for the cruise ship passengers. The four of us felt having an amateur standup comedian for a guide detracted from the ancient splendor of the caves. We enjoyed the crystal caves tour more, both from the lack of campy tour guides and the addition of pontoon bridges over the water filled caves. I imagined those little boys swimming in these caves without the addition of modern lighting and how eerily wonderful that must have been.

Off in the corner of the island brochure map, we noticed a couple of miles out of town a dot labeled as the Bermuda Institute of Ocean Science (BIOS). It turned out, they gave public tours once a month, which by luck coincided with our visit. We had a pleasant walk over the flat, country lanes outside of town over to the institute, and it was fun to be exposed to labs and research again.

While on our tour, I had the chance to talk with some of the people from 5 Gyres project—a nonprofit organization working on ocean pollution. A gyre is a system of wind and ocean currents where plastic may accumulate. I was happy to be contributing to the cause in some small degree through our water sample collections for the MERI/Adventure Science microplastics project.

The Institute also had labs on coral growth, ocean acidification, marine bacteria, and sea urchin longevity. Sea urchins are a well-known model organism for biology research. I learned to hate them in college as I once had to write a 100-page lab report on the embryonic development of S. purpurata, or the purple sea urchin. To this day I find sea urchins slightly anxiety-inducing.

Dad had been closely watching the weather for our entire stay in Bermuda to find a good weather window for our final offshore passage. Isaac and I bought all day bus passes to explore the entire island before the final leg of our trip back. It was a rather cold, rainy day and many of the buses were unnecessarily air conditioned. We took one of those chilly buses to a lighthouse with an outdoor observation deck all around it. The views were spectacular, but feeling like I might be blown over the edge at any moment detracted from the experience. From above it was even more apparent we were no longer in the Caribbean—the multicolored foliage reminded us of that.

After waiting for the bus with neither smartphone nor bus schedule, we managed to catch one from the lighthouse to the royal navy dockyard, which had become a tourist plaza of shops and cafes. At some point we went over the world's smallest drawbridge, which is a blink and you'll miss it attraction. Unfortunately I blinked. I did see a lot of men in bermuda shorts and knee socks, which is harder to miss.

∽∽∽

We left Bermuda in a hurry. Horatio and Molly had decided to copy our bus tour idea and arrived back at 4:30, and we were weighing anchor by 5. We quickly fell into our offshore watch schedules, with Isaac and me on our usual 8-12 shift. As soon as we left the protection of Bermuda's harbors, the seas picked up quickly.

Before long we passed through the cold front we'd been dreading. Rain, thunder, lightning, but not too much wind. Despite the cold front, we all sweltered down below as we had to keep all the hatches and portholes shut. Once the front passed the seas calmed a bit, and Isaac and I could sleep in our own bunks.

We motored as much as we could given our limited fuel capacity. We didn't have enough fuel to motor all the way to shore. While we were stuck in the doldrums, it wasn't all bad. It was warm, sunny, and calm. It was calm enough that my brother was able to take on a serious baking project—homemade sticky buns.

Our fifth day out we exited the doldrums and entered the gulf stream. If the wind held out we'd hit land in just two or three days. My dad told us to all write lists of our purchases in preparation for clearing customs. It felt like a physical summary of our voyage. T-shirt from Antigua Classics, blue handmade pottery bowl from Antigua, handmade pottery silverware strainer from Bequia, map from St. Lucia, spices and chocolate from Grenada, baskets and calabash bowls from Dominica, dress from The Saintes, painted rainbow fish ornament made of scrap metal from Saba, batik pillow cases from St. Kitts, and sea glass bracelet from Martinique.

As we were mentally preparing ourselves for a return to shore life, we had a last hurrah at sea. We were a day from shore when a pod of dolphins joined us. I went up on the bowsprit, and four of them were right underneath keeping pace. I could feel the spray from them surfacing, and hear the little snorty puff from their blowholes. I'd been waiting the whole trip for a sighting like this. Now we could really go home.

40 Last Hurrah

June 16, 2014
Newport, RI

Land ho! We anchored in Newport, Rhode Island, piled into the dingy, and were ready to go ashore and get the American meal we had most missed: pizza. But first we needed to clear customs.

We'd cleared customs by boat countless times on our voyage, and Newport is an official port of call in the US, so we thought nothing of it. But when we arrived at the office ready to check in, no one was there. It turned out it's a rare enough occurrence in Newport that you're supposed to call ahead. My dad managed to get someone on the phone, but it was going to take an hour for them to get to the office. He asked if it was okay for us to go out for pizza while we waited. Their answer: no. Clearly, the Caribbean-style laid back approach to bureaucracy was behind us.

So we awkwardly sat on a bench outside of the custom's office, officially barred from doing anything until we could check in. Not quite the homecoming we had been expecting. But eventually we got the all clear, and got our pizza.

After a short stay in Newport, the wind shifted to the perfect direction, and we were off to Maine. Going south we'd spent weeks getting from Rockland to Boston, but we were impatient to be home and decided to make a straight-shot from Newport to Rockland with one last multi-day sail. As much as I'm tired of overnights, it'll be nice to get back. Rhubarb is in season, and I'd like to make a batch of jam before the patch in our yard goes to seed.

The first two days we had little wind and made slow progress, but we made good time the third day and by midday we approached the rugged Maine coast.

As we pulled into Rockland harbor, a fellow sailor from the wharf was just heading out. "Is that Koukla?" he called out, "Wait just a minute!" He proceeded to pull out a conch shell from storage that apparently he kept at the ready for just such an occasion. He let out a blow, and with the sound echoing out over the Harbor. We were home.

After

Koukla's Continuing Adventures

My brother and I had grown up and moved away, and so not long after our second voyage, it was time for Koukla to move on too. Shortly after our return, Horatio & Molly and Isaac and I departed towards different cities to pursue further education and our careers. My parents chartered Koukla for a few years, but it's a lot of boat for two people to handle regardless of age and fitness level. They knew it was time to let go, and they put Koukla up for sale.

Koukla was featured in the Maine Boats and Harbors expo, and caught someone's eye. Like my dad, Scott had been on the lookout for a schooner for quite some time.

Something about Koukla attracts wild, adventurous souls. With a quick wit and a million stories of his own shenanigans, Scott was just the right mix of competent and crazy to take on Koukla. Even his name felt serendipitous. In fact, my brother Horatio only started using his legal name in college, and he went by Scott his whole childhood. My parents and I are the only ones who still call him Scott now.

Scott (not my brother) took an afternoon charter with the agreement to credit the cost of the charter towards the sale, should he decide to buy her. More sails followed, and both my parents and Scott became good friends.

The sale was eventually completed the following spring. When my dad sold Koukla to her next owner, a former Navy SEAL, he said it was like selling it to himself.

Scott came up to Maine to retrieve Koukla. He had arranged for a couple friends to help sail her back to his home in Virginia. They flaked out on him, and he was prepared to single hand her down, when his partner Brittany (who had no sailing experience!) stepped up. I wish I could say they sailed off into the sunset and everything was peachy. But you read this book, that's not how things go on Koukla.

Koukla put her new owners through their paces. On that sail from Maine to Virginia they were in gale-force conditions. They had 60 mph winds and 27 ft seas. Koukla was testing them, as she had tested us. But ultimately Koukla deemed them worthy.

Under new ownership Koukla has been through three major storms during six round trips between Maine and Virginia. Scott never once felt concerned for his safety—he knew Koukla could take it.

Koukla continues to sail the waters of the Atlantic and Caribbean. On a recent visit to Martha's Vineyard, local children swam up to Koukla and spent the day jumping off the boat with Scott and his family. I'm happy my wooden sibling is still out there living her best life.

Danica's Reflections (The Journaler)

Several years after our trip ended, Isaac and I embarked on another adventure—parenthood. There are actually quite a lot of similarities to offshore sailing and the early stages of parenthood. Lack of sleep, losing track of what day it is, going on and off watch, constantly damp, having another human being rely on you for their safety. I've been through two ocean gales and one pregnancy, and given the choice, I'd sooner take another ocean gale. We're biding our time while our son, Everett, grows and plotting our next adventure.

This was the main reason I decided to write this book. As one does when one becomes a parent, you look back on how you were parented to figure out what you should and shouldn't replicate.

As a parent now myself, I realize how insane my parents were—in the best possible way. I knew I had to figure out how to replicate in some way the essence of that first sailing trip for my son. After the second trip, I knew there probably wouldn't be a third. Isaac has put his foot down and refuses to do another ocean crossing. While I'm a very capable crew member, as I've mentioned before I am not a captain, and I'm not interested in becoming one. I don't care to take on that sort of responsibility.

If you're now itching to head off on your own adventures, here are a few tips I've discovered from thinking far too long and hard about this topic. First off, you do not need to sail around the world to have great adventures. If your family struggles with motion sickness I would strongly advise against this. However, if your adventures take you far off the beaten path—without easy access to medical attention or repair shops—someone in your adventuring party needs to have basic knowledge of how to fix machines and how to fix humans. You don't need to have a doctor and engineer in the family (although it helps!) but someone needs to be able to do basic and ideally advanced or wilderness first aid, and someone (probably not the same person) needs to know how to fix whatever sort of vehicle you're traveling in. You'll find most cruising families are a combination of engineering and healthcare professionals—which was the case for our family.

But do not discount smaller adventures! Adventuring Together by Greta Eskridge is a great resource for figuring out what sort and what scale of adventures makes sense for your family. It should go without saying, but chosen family counts too! Whatever it is, or wherever you go, there is immense value in doing hard (and hopefully fun!) things with those you care about.

I still haven't figured out what my family's version of living on a boat and sailing to the Caribbean and back will be. But I plan on making it weird and memorable, on building relationships with each other and our community, and with nature. There will almost certainly be misadventures, discomfort, probably some frank suffering, possibly some fear and danger, although I hope to keep that bit to a minimum. I hope in the end it will make a good story.

Ted's Reflections (Dad)

I am grateful that Danica felt moved to put our story down in writing. It demonstrates to me that we were successful in creating an event that would help develop and shape her and her brother's characters, and leave them with a foundation of memories to draw on over their lives.

The decision to take the family sailing offshore was not made lightly or on a whim. I had a love of the sea, and a love for sailing, but that was not the only motivation driving me.

From the moment we decided to have children, I toiled over the task of how to prevent them from being absorbed into the inanity of modern society. How do I ground them in reality, responsibility, maturity, independence, and a work ethic?

Those desires eventually coalesced into a comprehensive plan to take the family sailing, offshore sailing to exotic locations. The original dream was to go around the world. This was at a time when such an endeavor was still relatively rare. Unlike today when it has become a common fad.

The plan included the choice of a profession, the search for a vessel, and devoting the time and resources to see it through.

The results can clearly be seen in Danica's writing.

There have been regrets. My decision to pursue marine engineering, put me at sea 6 months a year in the engine room of ships. And when home the remaining 6 months, I was in perpetual pursuit of finding, repairing, and maintaining a wooden vessel—an endless pursuit.

We found a great boat, a traditional wooden schooner, but it was in horrible shape. Its owner's health had failed, and the boat was neglected for years.

There was never enough time or money. As the years went by and the boat still needed more work, the clock kept ticking. We needed to go before the kids were out of high school, or it wouldn't happen. So we drew a line and said we go now or not at all. We'll finish things along the way.

By the end of the first trip, Bev and I felt immense satisfaction that we had succeeded in achieving the desired result.

With regards to the second trip, I am eternally grateful that it presented the opportunity for Bev and I to get to really know the mates our children had chosen. They both became integral parts of the family, in a very special way. Especially given the fact that they voluntarily submitted to our 2 stipulations. First that if you sign on for the trip, there is no backing out. You can't get to the Caribbean and decide you have had enough and want out; you start the trip you finish it. And second that this is not a democracy. As the captain responsible for everyone's lives, mine is the final say.

The regrets of missing 6 months of the kids' childhood each year, while I was at sea working, and then devoting so much of my at home time to the boat, will sting forever. But I would do it all over again to see how Danica and Horatio have turned out.

Bev's Reflections (Mom)

Having returned from our first trip to the Caribbean, I remember saying, "Ok, now what?" We'd spent all our time and efforts for so long in order to reach this goal. Many sailors dream of setting sail for the Caribbean and we'd done it. Eventually, I stopped checking for the anchor from our bedroom window believing we were still living on the boat. Yes, it took some time before I returned to normal.

As the saying goes, the two most important days of a sailor's life are the day you buy your boat and the day you sell it. Looking back, I agree. Getting a boat like Koukla didn't seem possible unless it was in bad shape, and indeed it was.

Our objective in buying a boat and sailing it to the Caribbean was centered on our kids' development. It was several years before we could set off for our trip with all the renovations that needed to be done. Time was running out as they were growing up fast. We wanted to give them the experience of a lifetime. Character building. You find within yourself qualities that life on shore doesn't challenge. Hard work followed by the gratification that you can accomplish more than you thought you could.

Danica and Horatio took the first watch while underway. They were instantly relied upon with a great responsibility for our safety. I had the last watch from 4 to 8am. The beauty and calm as the ocean sunrise appeared is a memory I'll cherish always. While the family slept below deck the new day of our adventure began on my watch and all was right in our little world.

We went back to life ashore and jobs after the first trip. We'd done it and didn't expect Danica and Horatio to want to go again, but they did. Apparently, they forgot the bad parts and wanted another adventure. We couldn't say no despite the months of preparation and expense. Everyone pitched in, this time with Isaac and Molly as new crew members.

I was often at the wheel while the crew raised the sails or the anchor. It was nice to have so many hands available for us to get underway. I loved it.

When you have a child, you see everything differently. Danica was precocious, sassy, and smart when she was little. When Horatio was born, we thought he'd have a hard act to follow, but he managed and he's still cute. They are great people, we're proud and love them.

Horatio's Reflections (Brother)

In Danica's account of the events of the first boat trip she used the phrase "you just don't even know" when trying to talk to her friends about the experience. I felt similarly about the trip. I had difficulty relating to my old friends and describing the events that transpired. When I tried to do so, I found my high school classmates to be largely disinterested. Over time I stopped talking about it because I found that it would hurt people's impressions of me more than it would help. Maybe it was because they thought I was bragging, or that I sounded like a spoiled rich kid. I mean it is true, not many people can afford to do something like this, and we are so extremely fortunate to have been able to do so.

It was only after I had been in college for several years that I would start to talk about it again. This was also around when I stopped going by Scott, and people started calling me Horatio. There was another Scott in my group of friends, so when we were discussing how to differentiate the two of us I said "well that's not my real name, my real name is Horatio." They gave me a puzzled look then said "Horatio?! Yeah we're calling you that." I had friends I knew in college for many years that when I would make some comment about when I lived on the boat, they would stop me and say "Excuse me you did what now?" To this day it remains a unique experience that piques many people's interest when I bring it up. Maybe the moral of the story is that kids in high school are mean. Who knew?

When we were younger, Danica and I did not get along. I don't know whether to say we mixed more like oil and water, or baking soda and vinegar. Writing this perspective now as a 34-year-old adult, my sister and I get along pretty well. Perhaps it helps that we live on opposite sides of the country. The fact that we had such a strong sibling rivalry shaped how I was represented (or not represented) in the account of those events.

For Danica and I, the first boat trip was a formative experience. We both lived through the same events, but we experienced them fairly differently. I willingly went out to work on the boat during the summers that Dad was at home. Dad was always out working on the boat, so how else was I going to spend time with him? I look back on those memories fondly. I enjoy building and fixing things. I can't say if that is a conditioned response, or if I have always been that way.

We set out on that first adventure just a few days before my 12th birthday. Unlike Danica, I was not leaving a girlfriend (or boyfriend) behind. I had friends, but they would be there when I got back. I admit I was a bit sad and lonely on my 12th birthday, but we managed to go ashore and get pizza that day, and I got used to my new status quo.

When we set out on this adventure, I was 12 and Danica was 16. At those ages that's a pretty significant age difference. From my perspective, despite the fact that Danica was quite a bit older, I was generally asked to do more. At the time I thought of Danica as a passenger and myself as crew. Reading Danica's record of the events, you get the opposite impression. I suspect the truth lies somewhere in-between.

The story about the starter motor breaking on our way to Jost Van Dyke was an example where Danica and I experienced the events very differently. Dad put the starter motor and its supporting cast iron bracketry into a canvas bag. Dad held one handle of the bag, and I held the other. To a twelve-year-old this was extremely heavy. We then proceeded to trek our way across two islands to get it fixed. I distinctly remember how much my arms ached after carrying that thing all day long. In my opinion Danica missed out on some of these adventures, even if it didn't seem that way at the time.

There are a couple of big events on the first trip that are forever burned into my mind. One of the biggest happened during the storm on our first offshore passage. I remember being in the doghouse during the storm, and Dad was exhausted. It was particularly rough right now and Dad had asked me to go on deck to tend some lines. I was too afraid to go. I probably shouldn't be too hard on my 12-year-old self, but I have always been ashamed that I couldn't bring myself to go out there at that moment. This was something I strived to improve on for the second trip, and for my life in general. I wanted to be someone you could depend on when things got tough. On our second voyage I made sure that Dad knew he could depend on me in a crisis.

The extreme nature of some of those events have forever shaped my perception of the world. However stressed out I may be about an exam, or a project at work, it never quite measures up to the feeling of being hundreds of miles from shore in a storm on a boat which at any given moment is $\frac{1}{3}$ boat, $\frac{1}{3}$ submarine, and $\frac{1}{3}$ airplane.

The second trip was probably the ultimate test of my relationship with Molly. She had no previous sailing experience, and was crammed onto a boat with the whole of her boyfriend's crazy family (and believe me they are crazy). She never jumped ship despite her bunk being constantly wet, her legs being constantly bruised, and her personal space constantly invaded.

Thanks for putting this book together Danica. I'll always love and be proud of my big sister, but don't think that means I won't still give you a hard time.

Molly's Reflections (Sister-in-Law)

I wouldn't say I loved sailing. Honestly, I found it fairly boring a lot of the time. I spent so much time on our offshore passages looking at clouds. Clouds over the ocean aren't different from clouds over land. They just seem more interesting because they're the only thing around.

There were amazing parts too though. I remember looking at the stars with Horatio on the offshore passage with nothing around us but water and sky. Venus was so bright it cast faint shadows on the deck. I loved the flying fish too, silver darts flitting over the clear blue water. There were rainbows and white sand beaches and the best bananas I've ever eaten. It was unlike anything I'd ever experienced, and overall, I'm glad I went.

It was also my first time living with Horatio, and I certainly jumped right into the deep end. It was frustrating, being such a beginner at sailing while he'd been around it his whole life. He taught me a lot, but I'm not sure he really understood how hard it was to be completely new to it. Horatio, on the other hand, was anxious about being one of the most experienced people on the boat. He felt responsible for everyone's safety, and responsible for stepping up when things went wrong.

Things went wrong a lot, too. As far as I can tell, nature hates boats, and does whatever it can to break them: waves slowly shake things apart, rain seeps into crevices and causes rot, the salt corrodes almost everything, even stainless steel. Boat ownership is a constant battle against these forces. It occurred to me that someday Horatio would probably want to get a boat of his own, and if we stayed together, I would have to take up that fight against the elements someday, too.

I married him anyway.

I feel like I should say that after that big test of our relationship, everything else has been comparatively easy. That wouldn't be true, though. Life can be difficult on land too, and we've had challenges thrown our way. But we've been able to face them head on, with both of us united against the problem instead of against each other. I think that's something we learned on the trip.

And I don't know if it's nostalgia, or just an appreciation for a slower pace of life now that I've reached my thirties, but I even recently told him that I'm starting to warm up to the idea of buying a boat someday—a small one though, fiberglass or maybe ferrocement. Horatio accepted these terms and added another requirement: not too much brightwork.

Isaac's Reflections (Husband)

It would be convenient if I could start with a story about how I had always wanted to go to sea, but the truth is, I had never once thought about it. Before knowing Danica, the world of cruisers with their nautical vagabonding is something I didn't even realize existed. So why did I want to embark on this voyage? After looking through all my old notes, or struggling to rethink the thoughts of my younger self, all I can say is... of course I did! Who wouldn't want to go on an adventure?

The funny thing about an adventure is, while there are many incredible experiences, they're separated by large stretches of in-between time: waiting for weather, slowly sailing along with low wind, or just being on the boat between outings. I remember realizing that even in classic adventure stories like Lord of the Rings, most of the time would have been people just walking all day with nothing in particular happening. That part doesn't get covered.

But the trip was not about just hitting a bunch of vacation highlights interspersed with the occasional sea story, it was a year of living differently. And those "between times" of daily living on a boat are in retrospect what most separated the experience from everyday life.

On hearing about the trip, many people's first reaction would be on the challenge of living in what was effectively a tiny floating apartment with my in-laws. That was actually fine, there's more ability to go off into your own space than one would expect. The real challenge was the dingy.

Because we would always anchor out, every trip ashore had to be coordinated. Think of it like living out in the suburbs with a single shared minivan for six adults that often wanted to do different things (and no uber). The ability to freely come and go at will was ultimately what I was most looking forward to on our return. I could say that learning to live with others and sometimes forgo my own wishes to the needs of the group was a valuable growth experience, or helped prepare me for parenthood. But if I ever go on a similar trip again, I'm making sure there's two (usable) dinghies! (or pay for docking).

Living on the water and being powered by sail makes one uniquely subject to the influences of the natural world. There were many times coming down the Eastern Seaboard where we had to time our passage to the tidal currents. If that was 6 am, we'd be up well before dawn, bundled in our winter gear to raise, clean, and stow the anchor and get the sails up while the world was still dark and cold. As we drifted along, the air would slowly brighten around us as the day began.

On the long offshore passages, I came to the unfortunate realization that nearly any wind speed was unpleasant for me: too little and we'd never get there, too much and the waves became rough and uncomfortable. The psychological experience of a storm is different when you can't just "go inside" to wait it out. What on land would be a minor nuisance defines your whole existence. To quote an old saying, it was long periods of boredom punctuated by moments of terror. Needless to say, I'm not planning to make another offshore passage (though I'm not opposed to a future shore-based or island-hopping sailing cruise).

But I don't want this to come off as overly negative. Enduring shared hardship was part of the point. Though I wouldn't want to go offshore again, I'm very happy and proud to have done it. And when the weather was just right, it was incredible. I'll always remember the experience of being at the wheel on a perfect day as the boat climbed up over the broad rolling hills of blue water. Sargasso weed stretched out in long ribbons, flying fish occasionally burst forth to dart across the swells, with no other object in view but sea and sky.

One thing I miss from being on the boat is the night. We had a portable hammock that we would string up between the stays. Lying there, the boat swaying at anchor, with the stars slowly moving overhead and the gentle sounds of the harbor, that is the essence of living at sea. I noticed how the moon rose about an hour later each night than the day before. And not just the moon, you can watch the stars rise from the horizon and travel across the sky as well, slowly wheeling around the fixed axis of the North Star. But wait a minute… the moon rising an hour later each night? That happens everywhere. But there's a difference between something that I may have known on an academic level, and the experience of noticing and (re)discovering it for myself. Something as obvious as when the moon rises isn't obvious at all when you're enclosed in the world of cities and jobs. And really, this is what the trip meant for me: breaking out of my normal existence and experiencing the world in a different way, a way that had to be lived and felt.

Distances expand on a sailboat. The one-hour drive from Rhode Island to Boston is a full day's voyage. Traversing the East Coast takes weeks if you never stop, or months if you do. The boat is full of relatively modern technology and conveniences, but this is the one area where the traditional nature of sailing comes through most strongly. I felt like I truly understood the wideness of the world in the era before steam. Shortly after the trip ended, Danica and I took a flight from Boston to Seattle, and the idea that you could travel thousands of miles in a matter of hours felt like strange magic.

The value of the trip was the experience of living life in a different way, containing both discomfort and joy, boredom and excitement, frustration and accomplishment, but more than anything, just a year that was totally unlike all the rest. At least until the next adventure.

Acknowledgements

Above all I must thank my parents for deciding to head off on our seagoing adventure in the first place, and spending decades making that dream into a reality.

I should thank (or apologize to?) my brother not just for helping to review and contribute to this book, and for being a better crew member than me, but for putting up with my angsty teenage self on the first trip, and becoming a friend and cool guy I actually enjoy hanging out with on the second.

I don't know if I would have been able to see this project to the finish line without the support of my husband. Thanks for being game to head to sea despite not exactly knowing how to sail in the beginning. Thanks for braving storms, seasickness, and for your calmness in the face of my crazy family. And for all your help reading multiple drafts of this book. (Also, Isaac wanted me to clarify that we don't drink alcohol, so any time I made mention to drinks we had on our travels they were all non-alcoholic.)

Thanks to my sister-in-law, Molly, for all your editing suggestions and sharing your memories and perspectives, and for playing peacekeeper along with Isaac when needed.

I must also give thanks to my high school boyfriend, Tim, for being cool about me writing about our awkward teenage selves decades later.

Thanks to Scott, Koukla's current owner, for the updates on Koukla's continuing adventures, and for taking care of my wooden sibling. We will definitely be taking you up on your offer to come sailing again!

Thank you to my beta readers—Lauren and Ariana. Thanks to my former student Mariah for all your help. Thanks to my editor Steph Ritz for your support and encouragement through this longer than anticipated project.

Thanks to my friend and illustrator Deb Siegel for contributing your amazing artwork, and telling me when I was using obscure nautical terminology.

Finally, thanks and apologies to anyone else I neglected to mention who had a hand in the creation of this book, an (unintentionally) uncredited photo, story, reference, etc. This book was decades in the making, and that is a very long time to remember and keep track of things.

References

Before

- Glossary https://en.wikipedia.org/wiki/Glossary_of_nautical_terms
- Halcyon youth: https://www.weather.gov/gyx/water_temperature_normals.html

First voyage

- Ch 2: Both the boat and the nonprofit are still around! https://soundwaters.org
- Ch 2: https://oceanservice.noaa.gov/facts/ocean-oxygen.html
- Ch 4: https://www.military.com/base-guide/naval-station-norfolk#:~:text=Naval%20Station%20Norfolk%20is%20the,or%20one%20every%20six%20minutes
- Ch 6: https://www.popsci.com/eat-pigeons-squab
- Ch 6: https://www.nps.gov/articles/petroglyphs-of-reef-bay.htm
- Ch 11: https://smn-news.com/index.php/st-maarten-st-martin-news/21192-sewage-pumpout-service-for-boats-now-available.html#:~:text=According%20to%20international%20law%2C%20boaters,hygienic%2C%20and%20environmentally%20responsible%20option
- Ch 13: https://en.wikipedia.org/wiki/Manchineel

Second voyage

- Ch 18: If you're an adventurer, check out their list of current projects! https://www.adventurescientists.org
- Ch 20: https://www.cntraveler.com/story/nantucket-is-for-feminists
- Ch 20: https://nha.org/research/nantucket-history/history-topics/what-is-the-nantucket-girls-song
- Ch 35: https://turtles.bequia.net
- Ch 39: https://www.5gyres.org
- Ch 39: https://bios.asu.edu

Afterward

- https://oceanservice.noaa.gov/facts/ocean-oxygen.html
- https://www.military.com/base-guide/naval-station-norfolk#:~:text=Naval%20Station%20Norfolk%20is%20the,or%20one%20every%20six%20minutes
- https://www.nps.gov/articles/petroglyphs-of-reef-bay.htm
- https://www.5gyres.org
- https://www.weather.gov/gyx/water_temperature_normals.html
- https://www.allatsea.net/cruisers-weather-guru
- https://www.popsci.com/eat-pigeons-squab
- https://news.northwestern.edu/stories/2023/01/caribbean-breadfruit-traced-back-to-capt-blighs-1791-93-journey/#:~:text=Breadfruit%20on%20the%20'Bounty'&text=Aboard%20a%20British%20Royal%20Navy,plantations%20in%20the%20Caribbean%20islands
- https://www.thechocolatejournalist.com/blog/questioning-terroir-in-chocolate

agiftofbluewater.com

About the Illustrator

Deb Sigel is an illustrator, mechanical and aerospace engineer, and STEM educator. When she's not designing complex things for space or cool medical implants, you can find Deb drawing, doing creative woodworking, sewing, building a sculpture, or designing fun interactive toys for kids. She loves making curly and curvy art like sea monsters. She lives with her family in Vermont.

About the Author

Danica grew up on the coast of Maine, sailed from Maine to the Caribbean and back when she was 16, and again at 28. During the first voyage she wrote for her local newspaper about her family's adventures. During the second voyage she collected water samples for a microplastics research project. She now lives in Berkeley, CA with her husband Isaac, son Everett, and cat Cornelius.

They are planning their next family adventure...

www.ingramcontent.com/pod-product-compliance
Lightning Source LLC
Chambersburg PA
CBHW050858160426
43194CB00011B/2207